Performance
Measurement

Harry P. Hatry

with a chapter by
Joseph S. Wholey

Performance Measurement

Getting Results

2nd edition

Harry P. Hatry

THE URBAN INSTITUTE PRESS
Washington, D.C.

THE URBAN INSTITUTE PRESS
2100 M Street, N.W.
Washington, D.C. 20037

Library of Congress Cataloging-in-Publication Data

Hatry, Harry P.
  Performance measurement : getting results / Harry P. Hatry. — 2nd ed.
    p. cm.
  Includes bibliographical references and index.
  ISBN 0-87766-734-9 (alk. paper)
  1. Benchmarking (Management). 2. Performance--Evaluation. I. Title.
  HD62.15.H38 2006
  658.4'013—dc22

                                                              2006036093

Printed in the United States of America

10 09 08 07 06   1 2 3 4 5

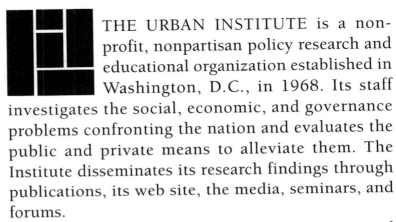 THE URBAN INSTITUTE is a nonprofit, nonpartisan policy research and educational organization established in Washington, D.C., in 1968. Its staff investigates the social, economic, and governance problems confronting the nation and evaluates the public and private means to alleviate them. The Institute disseminates its research findings through publications, its web site, the media, seminars, and forums.

Through work that ranges from broad conceptual studies to administrative and technical assistance, Institute researchers contribute to the stock of knowledge available to guide decisionmaking in the public interest.

Conclusions or opinions expressed in Institute publications are those of the authors and do not necessarily reflect the views of officers or trustees of the Institute, advisory groups, or any organizations that provide financial support to the Institute.

"Your Majesty, my voyage will not only forge a new route to the spices of the East but also create over three thousand new jobs."

Contents

Part I: Introduction

Part II: The Performance Measurement Process

Part III: Analysis and Use of Performance Information

Part IV: Other Performance Measurement Issues

Part V: Summary

Exhibits

Preface

In every enterprise, consider the outcome.
—found by the author in a fortune cookie.

Since the publication of the first edition of *Performance Measurement: Getting Results* in 1999, a veritable explosion in performance measurement has occurred. The federal government has fully implemented the 1993 Government Performance and Results Act. From GPRA has emerged such federal activities as annual Performance and Accountability Reports from each department and "PART" analyses of each major federal program. A number of federal governments, such as those in the United Kingdom, Canada, and Australia, have implemented forms of performance measurement.

Other levels of government have also started using performance measurement. Many, if not most, U.S. states have some form of state legislation calling for some form of performance measurement. In addition, numerous city and county governments have introduced some form of performance measurement. Efforts have begun at the state and local levels (led by the National Conference of State Legislatures and the National League of Cities, respectively) to encourage legislative bodies themselves to use outcome information in their deliberations.

The expansion of performance measurement goes beyond governments. Important national organizations such as the Governmental Standards and Accounting Board (with its encouragement for "Service Efforts and Accomplishments" reporting by state and local governments) and the Government Finance Officers

Association are encouraging such work. Nonprofit, nongovernmental organizations have made considerable efforts to introduce outcome measurement, initially to satisfy funders such as governments and foundations. This movement was led originally by United Way of America and a number of private foundations.

Many multilateral and bilateral donors—including the World Bank, Inter-American Development Bank, Asian Development Bank, and African Development Bank—have placed considerable pressure on developing countries to implement performance monitoring and evaluation systems. This edition draws on efforts undertaken in a few of these countries.

Most of the basic concepts from the first edition are still very much present. A number of developments, however, have affected at least the way and extent to which performance measurement is conducted. We have tried to introduce these changes into this new edition. Four are listed here:

- **Measurement-related technology has developed considerably**, including handheld calculators for trained observer ratings, which are becoming more widely used at various levels of government. Basic computer technology is accessible to most managers and professionals. This means that breaking out aggregate data into demographic and service characteristics has become much more practical. Any citizen in any country can visit a great many web sites and pull much information on the outcome indicators and data for a wide variety of sectors and services. This includes the PART reports mentioned earlier from individual federal agencies and the U.S. Office of Management and Budget, and individual state and local government web sites. Geographic Information System technology has enabled organizations to map performance indicators by smaller and smaller geographical areas within communities and to cover the indicators for many services.

  One of the remaining major areas that still needs to progress technically is following up with clients after they have left services. Many, if not most, programs provided by social and health services agencies are intended not to merely improve clients' immediate condition but also to enable the clients to sustain the improvements over a reasonable amount of time after the completion of service. We need better tools for tracking former clients effectively and inexpensively.

- Through modern computer technology, **presentation and reporting of performance information has become much fancier**, though not always more informative. Many performance indicators still are not identified as outputs, or outcomes, or something else. On the whole, the presentation of outcome information is still dubious. The use of color and graphics has greatly improved the appearance of performance information. But the problem is garbage in, garbage out: often the graphics are of a much higher quality than the data the graphics display. Or the graphics have become overly crowded and difficult to read, even though they leave an attractive visual impression.

- Increasingly in very recent years, the field is becoming concerned with **using outcome data to make things better,** not merely to satisfy requirements from upstairs. This edition reflects additional emphasis on ways to make outcome information useful. It is clearly very important that people within governmental and nongovernmental organizations know how to use outcome information to help them improve their services and better the lives of the citizens they are serving. The concern remains as to how deeply outcome-focused information is penetrating into individual organizations and how it is used at lower levels to help shape services.

- Also, users of the information are becoming increasingly concerned about the **quality of the outcome data.** As the data begin to be used and for more high-stake purposes (such as to support budget proposals or as the basis for monetary rewards), this issue becomes more important. This is a difficult area. Because of the large amount of data that can be generated from even a small agency, developing a quality control process is not easy. This problem is faced in chapter 14 on data quality in this volume, but data quality control needs considerably more attention.

In preparing this second edition, we have further developed the chapter on basic, first-order analysis of outcome data (chapter 10) and on reporting the information to improve its content and clarity. Because of its major importance, reporting is now discussed separately, in chapter 11.

We hope this second edition will be a resource for ideas on performance measurement and performance management, and that it will encourage readers to consider how they can improve the use of outcome data to enhance the quality of life in communities throughout the world.

Part

I

Introduction

The Scope of Performance Measurement

In New York City, a priest and a taxicab driver died and went to heaven. Saint Peter showed the priest his eternal dwelling place—a shack. Saint Peter then showed the driver his eternal dwelling place—a mansion. The priest was angry and asked Saint Peter, "Why the difference?" Saint Peter said, "When you preach, people sleep. When riders get into his cab, they pray!"

For this book, RESULTS are what count!

What Is Performance Measurement? Why Do It?

Managers of any sports team need to know the running score so they can assess whether changes are needed for the team to win. Managers of public agencies and private, nonprofit organizations need similar information. For businesses, the running score is data on profits and market share. Costs alone mean little. Measuring that running score and using it for better performance are the subject of this book—a subject popularly called performance measurement.

Performance measurement has many meanings, but it is defined here as *regular measurement of the results (outcomes) and efficiency of services or programs*. The new element in this definition is the regular measurement of results or outcomes. Regular measurement of progress toward specified outcomes is a vital component of any effort at managing-for-results, a customer-oriented process that focuses on maximizing benefits and minimizing negative consequences for customers of services and programs.[1] The customers may be citizens receiving services directly or citizens or businesses affected indirectly.

If the right things are not measured, or are measured inaccurately, those using the data will be misled and bad decisions will likely follow. As the old saying puts it: garbage in, garbage out.

A major use of performance information is to establish accountability, so citizens and elected officials can assess what programs have achieved with the funds provided. Another major use is to help programs develop and then justify budget proposals. But performance information is at least as important to help managers throughout the year. Public and private managers often say that performance information will not help them because their problem is too few resources to do what needs to be done. Yet managers need performance information to help them decide how to *increase their ability to get the job done with whatever resources they have*—and to provide evidence to the budget decisionmakers that they are indeed getting the biggest bang for their buck.

Programs have been tracking expenditures and physical outputs for decades. Tracking these elements is important but says little about what resulted—how customers and the public benefited. Regular tracking of outcomes is intended to fill this gap.

Outcome tracking is the new kid on the block for most public and private services and programs, although ample precedents exist. Police and other law enforcement agencies for many years have regularly tracked and reported such data as crime and clearance rates. Transportation agencies have tracked accidents, injuries, and deaths. Health officials have tracked the incidence of serious diseases and mortality. Fire agencies have tracked the number of fires and the resulting injuries and deaths. Environmental protection agencies have tracked the pollutant content of air and water. School districts have tracked dropouts and test scores. However, *such tracking focused on jurisdiction-wide data, not specific program outcomes that are essential information.*

Regular tracking is a key characteristic of performance measurement. For budget purposes, annual data are usually sufficient, but agencies and their managers need more frequent outcome information to assess the success of their program activities, identify where significant problems exist, and motivate personnel to strive for continuous service improvement.[2]

A particularly crucial outcome characteristic for public programs— often neglected in discussions of performance measurement—is equity. A well-designed measurement system enables agency managers to assess the fairness of a program and adjust it appropriately. A good performance measurement system will help officials demonstrate to the public and to policymakers that services are delivered fairly—thus building trust in the program. As chapter 8 discusses, disaggregating outcome data by the characteristics of the citizens affected is a major way to help assess equity.

All those using performance measurement information, whether inside or outside government or in a private agency, should understand what it can and cannot do and keep their expectations realistic. Performance measurement has three primary limitations.

Performance Data Do Not, by Themselves, Tell Why *the Outcomes Occurred*

In other words, performance data do not reveal the extent to which the program caused the measured results. This point is an important one. The analogy to managers of sports teams helps here. The manager needs to know the running score. If the team is losing, whether an individual game or over the whole season, the manager and other team officials may need to change the game plan. But the score does not tell the officials why the score is the way it is. Nor does the running score tell what specifically needs to be changed to improve the score. For that information, the managers, coaches, and other team officials need to seek explanations before they act.

It is the same for service delivery. Managers and other officials need to track results and use that information to help guide them about what, if any, future actions to take. Performance measurement is designed primarily to provide data on outcomes (the score). But to be most helpful (as discussed in chapters 9 and 10), performance measurement systems also need to have built into them opportunities to analyze the details of program performance and steps to seek explanations for the outcome data such systems produce.

This limitation raises a major issue in performance measurement that generates controversy: *accountability*. What should managers be held accountable for? In the past, the government of New Zealand had taken the view that responsibility for program outcomes rested solely with officials at the policymaking level, thus removing all accountability for outcomes from the operating departments. *Important outcomes are seldom, if ever, fully under the control of a particular agency (public or private). Nevertheless, the agency and its personnel do share responsibility for producing those outcomes.* As long as a program has any role in delivering a service intended to help produce particular outcomes, the managers of that program—and its personnel—have a responsibility to track the relevant outcomes and use that information to help improve results.

Agency personnel and other officials are often too ready to believe they lack responsibility over outcomes—in part out of fear that they will be blamed unfairly for poorer-than-desired outcomes. This fear is reasonable. However, recognizing shared responsibility helps agencies create innovative solutions that can improve service outcomes, even in the face of highly limited resources. And this understanding can lead to more use of performance partnerships among programs, agencies, levels of government, and between the private and public sectors.

Some Outcomes Cannot Be Measured Directly

The classic example is success in preventing undesirable events, such as prevention of crime or reduction of illicit drug use. In such cases, surrogates can usually be used, such as indicators that reflect trends over time in the number of incidents that were not prevented. This is not ideal, but this is the real world.

Performance Measurement Provides Just Part of the Information Managers and Elected Officials Need to Make Decisions

Performance measurement does not replace the need for expenditure data or political judgments, nor does it replace the need for common sense, good management, leadership, and creativity. *A major purpose of performance measurement is to raise questions. It seldom, if ever, provides answers by itself about what should be done.*

Exhibit 1-1 presents common objections from agencies and programs required to implement an outcome-based performance measurement process. Each objection is an element for concern. Subsequent chapters will address most of these concerns and hopefully will at least allay them.

EXHIBIT 1-1

Common Complaints about Performance Measurement

- You can't measure what I do.
- The measures aren't fair because I don't have total control over the outcome or the impact.
- It will invite unfair comparisons.
- Performance data will be used against our program.
- It is just a passing fad.
- We don't have the data/we can't get the data.
- We don't have the staff resources to collect the data.
- We can't measure prevention.
- It's not our responsibility.

Source: Minor adaptation from Budget Office, "Performance Measurement Manual for FY 2007" (Multnomah County, OR: Budget Office, 2005), V1.2, 26–27.

In performance measurement, efficiency is usually defined as the ratio of the amount of input (usually monetary expenditures or amount of employee time) to the amount of product created by that input. Unit-cost ratios that relate expenditures to physical outputs have been common in public agencies for years. *The trouble with input-to-output ratios is they can be improved by reducing the quality of the output.* If outcomes are tracked, a considerably more accurate indicator of true efficiency becomes possible. For example, "cost per client served" is an output-based efficiency indicator. Efficiency appears to increase when a program spends less per client, even if the condition of the typical client deteriorates. "Cost per client whose condition improved after services" is an outcome-focused efficiency indicator. It gives a much more meaningful picture of a program's real accomplishments.

Take the example of a program that holds regular sessions to help customers stop smoking. "Cost per session held" is considerably under the control of the program. "Cost per customer who quits smoking" is not, because whether someone quits probably also depends on a host of other factors besides the stop-smoking sessions. But is "cost per session held" a true measure of efficiency? Officials and citizens are considerably more likely concerned with efficiency in producing the desired outcome. *Even if a causal link cannot be firmly drawn, the program still has some responsibility for affecting the desired outcome. An outcome-based indicator provides more insight into how much the program is helping accomplish that objective.*

Which Organizations Are Suitable for Performance Measurement?

Managing-for-results applies to all agencies that provide services to the public, whether the agency has ample or highly limited resources, is small or large, is public or private, or is in a developing or developed country.[3] As long as the agency is delivering services to the public, its management and elected officials should be intensely concerned with the quality, outcomes, and efficiency of those services and should measure performance.

Even small agencies with very limited resources should be able to track some aspects of service quality and outcomes (probably more than seems possible at first glance) and improve operations with their existing resources. Poorer agencies with fewer resources will have to rely on less sophisticated procedures and, perhaps, more volunteers.

The same principles apply to all agencies. Officials and managers need to recognize and support the need for outcome information and be willing to use it to improve services, however tight their budgets.

Which Services Are Suitable for Performance Measurement?

The procedures and issues of performance measurement are applicable to most public and private services—ranging from public safety programs, to public works programs, to human service programs, to environmental protection programs, to regulatory programs, and to defense programs. Performance measurement is even applicable to internal support services, such as building maintenance, fleet maintenance, information systems, personnel activities, and purchasing. However, outcomes of support services occur primarily within an organization, and it is usually difficult, if not impossible, to estimate the effect of these internal services on the outcomes of external services. This book focuses on external services, but the same principles apply to support services.

The regular tracking of performance measurement may not be readily applicable to activities whose important outcomes do not occur for years, if not decades. Long-range planning and basic research are primary examples. The federal government's Government Performance and Results Act of 1993 has been applied broadly to every type of federal program. Nevertheless, basic research programs have had only slight success at fitting tracking systems into the annual outcome-oriented performance measurement process. Regular tracking can be used to assess whether timelines have been met, expenditures have been kept within budget, and the quality of any interim product is acceptable (such as by using expert panels to rate the quality and progress of ongoing research). For assessing the major outcomes of research, analytical resources are better spent on later, in-depth evaluations.

Performance Measurement in Relation to Other Evaluation Activities

Program Evaluations and Other In-Depth Studies

Performance measurement can be considered a field of program evaluation. However, program evaluation usually refers to in-depth, special studies that not only examine a program's outcomes but also identify the "whys," including the extent to which the program actually caused the outcomes. Such in-depth program evaluations are not the subject of this book.[4]

In practice, many of the so-called program evaluations undertaken by governments (federal, state, or local) provide information on outcomes but little evidence on the causal link between activities and results. Even so, in-depth studies can provide many insights about what happened and why. Performance measurement cannot generally provide this information.

Because of the time and cost involved, in-depth evaluations are usually done much less frequently and only for selected programs. Performance measurement and in-depth program evaluations are complementary activities that can nourish and enhance each other. Findings from a program evaluation completed during a given year can add to or supersede that year's performance measurement data. Data from an agency's performance measurement system can offer program evaluators data, useful indications of trends, and questions that encourage more in-depth evaluation. Sometimes evaluators can use the existing performance measurement procedures to collect data.

Performance Auditing

Performance audits, which are becoming more frequent, are typically conducted by auditors or inspectors general. They are ad hoc studies, often closely resembling in-depth program evaluations, that are applied to a selection of public programs each year. Performance auditors should have considerable interest in performance measurement systems as ways to provide data on outcomes for use in audits. In addition, these offices are likely to be given the responsibility for periodically assessing agencies' performance measurement systems, the indicators used, and the data provided. (This quality control responsibility is discussed in chapter 14.)

Budgeting, Strategic Planning, and Policy Analysis

Performance measurement provides information primarily about the past. Budgeting, strategic planning, and policy analysis are primarily about the future. As discussed in later chapters, performance data provide a baseline for decisions and give clues about what might happen in the future. The future-oriented processes require estimation and judgment skills that performance measurement systems cannot provide by themselves. Subsequent chapters (especially 12 and 13) introduce these issues but do not attempt comprehensive coverage of budgeting, strategic planning, or policy analysis. Rather, these topics are discussed only in the context of the (important) role that outcome-focused performance measurement systems play in these activities.

Role of Agency Employees

The employees of agencies undertaking performance measurement clearly have a stake in the process. Later chapters address the roles of this important stakeholder group in helping identify appropriate performance indicators and in using performance information to help improve services. The performance measurement work described here does not address the measurement of employee job satisfaction, however, because employees are considered suppliers of services, not customers.

Moving Performance Measurement into Performance Management

Performance measurement focuses on measuring outcomes and efficiency. If the measurement information generated is not used, the effort and cost of the performance measurement process will be wasted. Use of the performance information—whether by program managers, agency officials, officials in the central government, elected officials, members of boards of private nonprofit organizations, or citizens—transforms performance measurement into performance management. The purely measurement chapters of this book are chapters 1 through 7, 14, and 15. Chapters 8 through 11 discuss key components that can greatly enhance usefulness and that reflect the transition from measurement into usefulness. Chapters 12 and 13 discuss the various uses of performance information.

Thus, this book is about both performance measurement and performance management.

A Guide to This Volume

Chapter 2 completes Part I by providing definitions that are the basic background for the material in the rest of the book.

Part II addresses the performance measurement process. Chapter 3 discusses organizational start-up. Chapters 4 through 6 address determining what the program's objectives are and who its customers are (chapter 4), what outcomes should be tracked (chapter 5), and what the specific outcome indicators should be (chapter 6). Chapter 7 addresses how the data can be obtained.

Part III covers the critical issues of how to analyze, report, and use the performance measurement data. Chapters 8 and 9 focus on ways to make performance data useful to program personnel and others. Chapter 8 discusses the importance of procedures for providing more detailed breakouts of outcome data. Chapter 9 discusses benchmarking—that is, what comparisons should be made to help interpret outcome levels. Chapter 10 discusses analyses that can make the outcome information fully useful. Chapter 11 provides suggestions on an all too frequently neglected key element: reporting the findings. Chapters 12 and 13 identify major uses of performance information, with special attention to results-based budgeting.

Part IV (chapters 14 and 15) addresses various other important performance measurement concerns, including the long-term problem of controlling the quality of the information performance measurement produces (chapter 14), political considerations, and the need for personnel training (chapter 15).

Part V (chapter 16) summarizes the principal points about performance measurement that are important in producing a practical process with real-world utility.

References and Notes

1. "Governing-for-results" and "results-oriented government" refer to the same process. We have used "managing-for-results" here to indicate that the process is not restricted to government (executive or legislative) but is equally applicable to private service agencies. Other phrases have been used, such as "results-based management," "managing by results," and the like. Recent work on legislatures has used the phrase "legislating for results."

2. A distinction is often made between the way in which a service is delivered (such as its timeliness, accessibility, and courteousness to customers) and the results the service is intended to achieve (such as actual improvements in the condition of customers). As will be discussed in chapter 4, aspects of service delivery quality are important to customers (and, thus, we have categorized them "intermediate outcomes"), but they usually do not indicate how much progress has been made toward service objectives.

3. Numerous publications have been written on this subject. A few recent ones are John Kamensky and Albert Morales, eds., *Managing for Results 2005* (Lanham, MD: Rowman & Littlefield Publishers, 2005); Barry White and Kathryn Newcomer, eds., "Getting Results: A Guide for Federal Leaders and Managers" (Vienna, VA: Management Concepts, 2005); and Dall W. Forsythe, ed., *Quicker, Better, Cheaper? Managing Performance in American Government* (Albany, NY: Rockefeller Institute Press, 2001).

   For those interested in performance measurement in the international scene, some publications are Jody Zall Kusek and Ray Rist, *Ten Steps to a Results-Based Monitoring and Evaluation System* (Washington, DC: The World Bank, 2004); Anwar Shah, ed., *Public Services Delivery* (Washington, DC: The World Bank, 2005); Korean

Development Institute, "Reforming the Public Expenditure System: Medium-Term Expenditure Framework, Performance Management, and Fiscal Transparency" (Seoul and Washington, DC: Korean Development Institute and The World Bank, Conference Proceedings, March 2004); Hans de Bruijn, *Managing Performance in the Public Sector* (London: Routledge, 2002); and Burt Perrin, "Moving from Outputs to Outcomes: Practical Advice from Governments around the World" (Washington, DC: The World Bank and IBM Center for The Business of Government, 2006).

4. Considerable literature exists describing in-depth program evaluations and how they might be done.

What Types of Performance Information Should Be Tracked?

The central function of any performance measurement process is to provide regular, valid data on indicators of performance outcomes. But performance measurement should not be limited to data on outcome and efficiency indicators.[1] It should also include information that helps managers measure the incoming workload and gain insight into the causes of outcomes. And, performance measurement should relate the costs of the service to what the service produces.

A consistent set of definitions categorizing various types of performance information—to be used across all programs—is the cornerstone of any performance measurement system. All too often, confusion among programs within an agency results from unclear, inconsistent use of terms.

Definitions—or labels—enable users of performance information to distinguish reliably among data categories with different implications and uses. Numerous labels have been used over the years to categorize performance information. Which particular set of labels an agency or program chooses is not the primary issue. The primary issue is to determine which items should be tracked. Appropriate labels help with that.

No two people will categorize every element in a data set in exactly the same way. Gray areas inevitably exist because it is not always clear where a particular piece of information falls. In addition, for some performance information, the category may depend on the perspective of the agency. For example, to the state agency that develops an educational reform strategic plan, the completion of that plan is an output. However, to the U.S. Department of Education that encourages such plans, their completion by states is an intermediate outcome, as discussed later.

Exhibit 2-1 presents the categories of performance information used throughout this volume. Data on the amount of resources expended for particular programs (inputs) differ from internal information that indicates the amount of activity a program is undertaking (process). These data, in turn, differ from the products and services a program has completed (outputs), which should be distinguished from results-based information (outcomes). These distinctions are important in order to avoid misleading those who use the information.

Each of these categories is discussed briefly in turn. Exhibit 2-2 provides summary definitions of key performance measurement terms.

Categories of Performance Information

Inputs

Input information is the amount of resources used, usually expressed as the amount of funds, the number of employee-years, or both.

This category, when related to figures on the amount of output or outcome (see further below), produces indicators of efficiency or productivity.

For performance measurement purposes, the amounts that were actually used, not the amounts budgeted, are the relevant numbers. Agencies occasionally call the work that comes into any agency an input. In this volume, work-

---

EXHIBIT 2-1

Categories of Information Used in Performance Measurement Systems

- Inputs[a]
- Process (workload or activities)
- Outputs[a]
- Outcomes[a]
    - Intermediate outcomes
    - End outcomes
- Efficiency and productivity[a]
- Demographic and other workload characteristics
- Explanatory information
- Impacts

[a] These categories are usually labeled "performance indicators" in performance measurement systems.

EXHIBIT 2-2

Performance Measurement Definitions

- **Inputs:** Resources (i.e., expenditures or employee time) used to produce outputs and outcomes.
- **Outputs:** Products and services delivered. Output refers to the completed products of internal activity: the amount of work done by the organization or by its contractors (such as number of miles of road repaired or number of calls answered).
- **Outcomes:** Events, occurrences, or conditions that are outside the activity or program itself and that are of direct importance to customers and the public generally. An outcome indicator is a measure of the amount and/or frequency of such occurrences. Service quality is also included under this category. While outputs are what work the organization does, outcomes are what these outputs accomplish.
- **Intermediate outcomes:** Outcomes that are expected to lead to a desired end but are not ends in themselves (such as service response time, which is of concern to the customer making a call but does not tell anything directly about the success of the call). A service may have multiple intermediate outcomes.
- **End outcomes:** The end results sought (such as the community having clean streets or reduced incidence of crimes or fires). A service may, and usually does, have more than one end outcome.
- **Efficiency, or unit-cost ratio:** The relationship between the amount of input (usually dollars or employee-years) and the amount of output or outcome of an activity or program. If the indicator uses outputs without considering outcomes, a jurisdiction that lowers unit cost may achieve a measured increase in efficiency at the expense of the outcomes of the service.
- **Performance indicator:** A specific numerical measurement for each aspect of performance (e.g., output, efficiency, or outcome) under consideration.

Source: Adapted from *Comparative Performance Measurement: FY 1996 Data Report* (Washington, DC: International City/County Management Association, 1997), 1–4.

load data are *not included* under this category, because the amount of incoming work is quite different from the amount of cost or staff time expended.

Process (Workload or Activities)

This category includes the amount of work that comes into a program or is in process but not yet completed. For some agencies, such as human service agencies, the workload is usually expressed as the number of customers that come in for service (individual clients, households, or businesses). For others, the number of customers is not appropriate. Road maintenance programs, for example, might express their workload as number of lane-miles of road needing repair.

Amounts of work are not considered performance indicators because they do not indicate how much product the program generated. Workload information is very important, however, when program managers want to track the flow of work into and through their programs. (For example, the amount of work pending from the previous reporting period plus the amount of new work coming in indicates a program's workload during the current reporting period.)

While amounts of work by themselves are not outputs or outcomes, workload data can be used to produce outcome data. In some programs, the amount of work not completed at the end of a reporting period can be considered a proxy for delays of service to customers (an intermediate outcome). Examples include the size of the backlog of eligibility determinations for loan applications and the size of customer waiting lists. But more direct, and probably more meaningful, indicators of delays and backlogs would be indicators of the extent of delays, such as the "percent of cases in which the time between a service request and when the service was provided exceeded X days," where X is a service standard established by the program; and the "percent of customers who reported excessive waiting times to obtain service."

Outputs

Output information indicates the amount of products and services delivered (completed) during the reporting period. Reporting of output information is common in agencies throughout the world. Keeping track of the amount of output accomplished is good management. Common examples of outputs include miles of roads paved, reports issued, training programs held, and students served by the program. Outputs do not by themselves tell anything about the *results* achieved, although they are expected to lead to desired outcomes. (Program personnel should ask what results are expected from each output. Those results should be included under the next category, *outcomes.*)

As defined here, *outputs are things that the program's personnel have done,* not changes to outside people or changes that outside organizations have made.

Outcomes

In some contexts the word *output* refers to any product of work, whether a program's completed physical product or the outcomes (results) of that work. Performance measurement of public services, however, makes an important distinction between *outputs* and *outcomes.*

Outcomes are the events, occurrences, or changes in conditions, behavior, or attitudes that indicate progress toward a program's mission and objectives. Thus, outcomes are linked to the program's (and its agency's) overall mission—its reason for existing.[2]

Outcomes are not what the program itself did but the consequences of what the program did. An excellent example illustrating the difference between outcome and output comes from the state of Texas:

> The number of patients treated or discharged from a state mental hospital (*output* indicator) is not the same as the percentage of discharged patients who are capable of living independently (*outcome* indicator).[3]

As another example, City of San Jose sewer cleaning crews were being rated on how many miles of streets they cleaned. Crews focused their operations on cleaning sewers they had already cleaned because cleaning dirty sewers slowed them down. They were very proud of the high number of miles they cleaned each year. When the director of the operation learned of this behavior, he pointed out that the purpose of cleaning sewers was to keep sewage from backing up into people's homes and businesses, not to rack up cleaning mileage.[4]

Outcomes should be something the program wants either to *maximize,* such as evidence of increased learning by students, or to *minimize,* such as crime rates. Some outcomes are financial. For example, for public assistance programs, reducing the dollar amount of incorrect payments (whether overpayments or underpayments) is likely an appropriate outcome. The amount of owed child support payments recovered from absent parents is an appropriate outcome for child support offices. In such cases, outcomes can be expressed in monetary terms.

Outcomes include side effects, whether intended or not and whether beneficial or detrimental. If the program recognizes in advance that important side effects can occur, it should design the performance measurement process to regularly measure them.

As long as outcomes are important and can be tracked, they should be included in the performance measurement system, even if they are not explicitly identified in the program's mission and objective statements (and even if they are only partly under the control of the program or agency, as will be discussed later). Formal program mission and objective statements seldom include all the outcomes an agency needs to track. It is not the function of such statements to itemize all the outcomes that the program should seek, just the central, most vital ones. For example, complaints against police officers should be tracked as well as crime clearance rates, even if the mission statement of the police agency does not include statements about providing law enforcement fairly and honestly.

It is important to distinguish *intermediate* outcomes from *end* outcomes. This will help programs differentiate between the ends ultimately desired from a program and interim accomplishments, which are expected to lead to those end results (but may or may not).

It is helpful to distinguish two key dimensions of outcomes: their importance and when they occur. The primary criterion for distinguishing intermediate from end outcomes should be their importance, not when they occur. While intermediate outcomes usually occur before the end outcomes to which they are linked, an end outcome can occur very early. Agencies whose personnel save lives during emergency situations are producing end outcomes.

The following discussion highlights the difference with definitions and examples.

Intermediate outcomes. These outcomes are expected to lead to the ends desired but are not themselves ends. Examples of intermediate outcomes include the following:

- People completing employment training programs where program participation is *voluntary*. This reveals how successful the program has been in convincing customers not only to participate in, but also to complete, the sponsored training sessions. However, completion is only one step toward the ultimate end of improving the condition of people in the program.
- Citizens exercising more or switching to a better diet, as recommended in an agency-sponsored health program (perhaps as measured by surveying clients 12 months after completing the agency's program). Such changed behavior is expected to lead the participants to better health, but since this connection is uncertain, the behavior is an intermediate outcome.
- A state or local agency developing a comprehensive plan of action encouraged and supported by a federal program (where acceptance of the assistance is voluntary). For the federal government, states or local governments actually completing a reasonable plan can be considered an initial step toward improving services, although completing the plan says little about the end outcome of service improvement.[5]

For most agencies and products, deciding whether something is an output or an intermediate outcome is clear. One exception is the number of arrests for a law enforcement program. Many people argue that arrests are an output because they are actions taken by agency employees. But arrests involve citizens outside the agency, the people arrested, and their families. In that sense, arrests might be better be counted as intermediate outcomes.

Other exceptions include qualities of the service provided to customers, such as response times to requests for service.

Service quality characteristics: A special type of intermediate outcome. This category of performance indicator refers to the quality of the service customers received; how well a program delivered a service, based on characteristics important to customers. Although such characteristics do not measure a final result, they are important to program customers and thus can be considered intermediate outcomes an agency should track. Exhibit 2-3 lists quality characteristics that an agency might consider when developing a list of program outcomes to track.

Some agencies label quality characteristics (such as response times to requests for services) outputs because they characterize the outputs. But if a characteristic is expected to be important to customers, it is better to consider it an intermediate outcome, not an output. Labeling quality characteristics outcomes helps ensure that they are given proper attention by agencies.

For some customers and under some circumstances, one or more of these quality characteristics might be extremely important—and can even be considered end outcomes. For example, low-income families consider it vital that assistance checks (whether Social Security or any public assistance

---

EXHIBIT 2-3

Typical Service Quality Characteristics to Track

- Timeliness of service provision
- Accessibility and convenience of the service
  —Convenience of location
  —Convenience of hours of operation
  —Staff availability when the customer needs the service (whether by phone or in person)
- Accuracy of the assistance, such as in processing customer requests for service
- Courteousness with which the service is delivered
- Adequacy of information disseminated to potential users about what the service is and how to obtain it
- Condition and safety of agency facilities used by customers
- Customer satisfaction with a particular characteristic of service delivery
- Customer satisfaction with the service overall

payment) arrive on time and be accurate. Otherwise, these families will be unable to pay their bills and may be evicted or go hungry.

End outcomes. These outcomes are the desired results of the program—conditions of importance to program customers and citizens more generally. End outcomes might, for example, be aspects of health, safety, educational achievement, employment and earnings, or decent housing and neighborhoods, such as

- reduced incidence of specific diseases,
- improved student test scores,
- lower crime rates,
- less violence in schools,[6]
- reduced number of households living in substandard housing,
- increased real household earnings, and
- reduced household dependency on welfare.

For some programs, customer satisfaction with the *results* of a service can be considered an end outcome. For example, customers' satisfaction ratings of parks, recreational activities, libraries, and cultural programs or children's satisfaction ratings of the homes in which they are placed by child welfare agencies can be considered end outcomes—even though those programs have aims that go beyond satisfaction, such as a library's mission to increase public awareness of literature.

Many programs produce both *short-term* and *long-term end outcomes*. Education is a classic example. Educational programs produce early improvements in student learning and self-esteem, but they also help students obtain employment (and higher salaries) later on. Employment, self-sufficiency, and reductions in welfare dependency are basic long-term outcomes of education programs. Information on these long-term end outcomes, however, will not be available early enough to guide program personnel on the success of most of their current activities. Short-term end outcomes, such as improved learning and skill development, need to be tracked to encourage ongoing program improvement. Short-term outcomes also have value in themselves. Intellectual development and dropout rates, for example, are outcomes of key concern to education managers, staff, and parents—and can be considered end outcomes for this reason.

Issues in the relationship between intermediate and end outcomes. Intermediate outcomes, by definition, occur before—and are expected to help lead to—end outcomes. Thus, intermediate outcomes usually provide more timely information than end outcomes. For example, customers complete employment counseling programs (intermediate outcome) before they obtain employment (end outcome), which is expected to occur after completion of the program. When a program has long-term end outcomes for which data may not be available for many years (such as reduction in adverse health effects due to smoking and achieving rewarding employment careers), the program can usefully focus on short-term ends (such as reduced smoking and improved learning and skills). Much evidence exists that both reduced smoking and improved learning and skills directly affect long-term end outcomes and intermediate outcomes.

Another important advantage of intermediate outcomes is that *programs almost always have more influence over intermediate outcomes than they do over end outcomes.* For example, many federal programs (such as education, health and human services, housing and community development, and employment programs) provide assistance to states, local agencies, and/or nongovernmental organizations rather than providing help directly to citizens. Changes sought by federal programs and made by these other organizations can be considered intermediate outcomes. The federal programs have more direct influence on these outcomes than on the end outcomes, which are also affected by many other factors (such as family circumstances and motivation). The same is true of state programs that work through local governments and of local government programs that work through the business or private nonprofit community.

Early occurrence of an outcome does not necessarily mean it is not an end outcome. For example, family counseling programs hope to produce more stable and happier families in the short run as well as in the long run. Some treatment actions produce quick ends (purification of drinking water), while others require many years before water quality improves significantly (cleanup of rivers).

Intermediate outcomes usually are related to the particular way the program delivers the service, whereas end outcomes typically do not vary with the delivery approach. For example, a government attempting to improve the quality of rivers and lakes can achieve this goal in many ways, such as by providing funding for wastewater treatment, providing technical assistance to certain classes of businesses, and encouraging lower levels of government to pass stricter laws and ordinances. Each such approach would have its own intermediate outcomes. But regardless of the approach, the same end outcomes, such as the quality of rivers and lakes, apply.

Efficiency and Productivity

The ratio of the amount of input to the amount of output (or outcome) is typically labeled *efficiency.* Flipping the ratio to the amount of output (or outcome) to the amount of input is typically labeled *productivity*. These numbers are equivalent.

Efficiency and productivity have traditionally related costs to outputs (labeled *technical efficiency* by economists). However, to the extent that the performance measurement system provides data on *outcomes* (sometimes called *allocative efficiency* by economists), it provides a much truer picture of efficiency and productivity. Focusing on output-to-input ratios carries with it the temptation for managers to increase output at the expense of results and service quality.

Following are some examples of outcome-based productivity indicators:

- Number of people gaining employment after completing an agency's training program per dollar of program cost (or per program employee-hour)
- Number of customers who reported that the service received had significantly helped them per dollar cost of that service (or per service employee-hour)
- Number of clients who 12 months after completing the service had stopped the risk behaviors targeted by the program per dollar cost of that service (or per service employee-hour)

Flip these ratios over and they become efficiency indicators.

For example, if 160 customers reported being significantly helped and the program cost $96,000,

- efficiency = $96,000/160 = $600 per customer helped.
- productivity = 160/$96,000 = 1.67 customers helped per $1,000.

Efficiency and productivity ratios can be calculated for any *output* indicator. For *outcome* indicators to be incorporated into these ratios, however, the outcomes need to be expressed as something to be maximized. Let us take crime as an example. "Cost per reported crime," though easy to calculate, makes little sense as an efficiency indicator (although it does make sense in the context of measuring the total costs of crime to a community). The outcome to be maximized here is *crimes prevented.* "Cost per crime prevented" would be a highly desirable indicator. Unfortunately, valid data on the crimes a program prevented are virtually never available. (Estimation of number of crimes prevented, if it is to yield reliable information, requires ad hoc studies that are usually quite costly. Even then, the estimates are likely to be highly uncertain. This measurement problem applies to most prevention programs.) For police apprehension services, an outcome efficiency indicator might be the cost per crime cleared (preferably adjusted for clearances that were later dropped).

Efficiency ratios using outputs are common. Efficiency ratios using outcomes are rare. This is partly because few public or private agencies have developed outcome data. With the growth of more outcome-based performance measurement systems at all levels of government and in the private nonprofit sector, increased use of outcome-based efficiency ratios has become possible.

Demographic and Other Workload Characteristics

If agencies are to make full use of their performance data, they need to collect information on the amount of work coming into a program (sometimes called *demand*) and key characteristics of that work (such as those relating to its difficulty) and to link that information to outcome information. (This is discussed at length in chapters 8 and 10). Thus, a program that processes applications wants information on the complexity of the incoming workload. A program working with business customers wants information about each business's industry classification, size, and location. A road maintenance program needs to be concerned with the soil conditions and the amount and type of traffic for specific road segments. A hospital needs information on the type and severity of its patients' illnesses to help it interpret changes in patient outcomes.

Similarly, programs that use different service delivery approaches need to have information on the particular approach used to produce certain outputs and outcomes. The amount and types of assistance provided to customers with similar problems may vary. Programs may use private contractors for some of their work and their own employees for other, similar work. Programs need to know which work was done using which service approach and then link the outcomes to each approach (see chapter 8).

Explanatory Information

Programs should be encouraged to provide explanatory information, qualitative or quantitative, to help readers of performance reports properly interpret the data—especially for outcomes that were worse or much better than expected. In some instances, this will be information about internal factors (e.g., the program unexpectedly lost funds or key personnel during the reporting period). In other cases, the explanations will identify external factors over which the program had little or no control (e.g., a major change in economic conditions or highly unusual weather conditions). This information is discussed further in chapters 10 and 11.

Impacts

A number of analysts have begun to use the term *impact* to refer to data that estimate the extent to which the program actually *caused* particular outcomes.[7] For example, an indicator of impact would be labeled something like "number of expectant teenage mothers who, *because of the program,* had healthy babies." (Without the program, they would have lost their babies or had babies with substantial health problems.)

The outcome data from ongoing performance measurement systems will seldom, if ever, reveal the extent to which the program has caused the outcome. Other factors—over which the program has only partial control—will inevitably be present. For example, some people who stopped smoking after completing a stop-smoking program may have stopped because of pressure from family and/or a health care professional, not because of the program. In-depth studies, such as formal program evaluations, may at times be able to estimate the program's impact on some outcomes reasonably well. When available, those data should also be included in the program's performance report.

Because of the time and cost required to obtain impact data, such information is seldom likely to be available for any given program (or groups of programs).

Indicators That Are Particularly Difficult to Categorize

Many service attributes are easy to classify, but some are not. Here are three typical indictors that have caused healthy debates.

Customer Participation

The number of customers participating in a program is an ambiguous indicator because it depends on the particular situation in which it is used. Often, such indicators can be considered intermediate outcomes.

- If participation is mandatory, the number participating would be, at best, output information.
- If participation is voluntary and the program includes activities aimed at attracting customers (such as employment training programs and health risk-reduction activities), participation can be categorized as an intermediate outcome. Success on indicators of participation level depends on the program's ability to attract citizens. Similarly, the program's ability to retain participants until the activities are completed is an inter-

mediate outcome. Completion is more important than participation, because it indicates that customers found the activity sufficiently attractive to stick with it until the training program's end.

- For such public programs as parks, recreational facilities, libraries, and public transit and for such private programs as boys' and girls' clubs (all activities in which participation is voluntary), the number of participants can be considered an intermediate outcome. (Examples of outputs are the number of programs or classes held, number of bus miles, and amount of reading materials purchased.)

Many professionals and agencies tend to think of such performance indicators as outputs. An indicator expressed as the "number of people served by the program" can be considered a classic case of an output. However, an indicator worded "the number of people who came in for service," can be considered an intermediate outcome. The first indicator focuses on the program's work. The second indicator focuses on what customers did. Both indicators might have the same value. The advantage of the second indicator to managers is that they can take credit for having been able to attract customers ("people vote with their feet"). Thus, managers who want to track their "marketing" success will likely prefer the second indicator.

Customer Satisfaction

As stressed earlier, a guiding principle in the search for outcomes is to identify features of a service of direct concern and value to the public—particularly those who have used the service (they may be called customers, clients, patients, or another term). Customer "satisfaction," whether with the service overall or with specific characteristics of the service (such as timeliness and accessibility), fits this description and is usually considered an outcome.[8] Customer satisfaction is usually of concern to elected officials, as well as service users.

What kind of outcomes are these? They are usually *intermediate* outcomes because they do not take the place of measuring the actual condition of customers after receiving the service. For example, customer satisfaction with the employment and training services received is not ultimately as important as whether these customers find employment. Satisfaction with the jobs they obtain with the program's help is also likely to be valuable to these customers and might be categorized as an *end* outcome.

For certain services—recreational activities and libraries, for example—customer satisfaction can be an end outcome. Even here, though, satisfaction is seldom the only outcome sought. In virtually all cases where customer satisfaction is important, other outcomes must also be included to obtain a comprehensive picture of a service's performance.

Response Times for Service Requests

Some people label response time an output and others label it an intermediate outcome. Because response time is usually of direct concern to customers, this book includes it in the intermediate-outcome category. By the same logic, the level of satisfaction customers have with the response times to their requests is also an intermediate outcome.

Relationships among Types of Performance Information

A logic model (or outcome-sequence chart) that diagrams the continuum of relevant factors for a performance measurement system is a highly useful way to summarize the flow across the information categories just discussed. Exhibit 2-4, based on material developed by United Way of America, displays such a system. Chapters 5 (on identifying outcomes) and 6 (on iden-

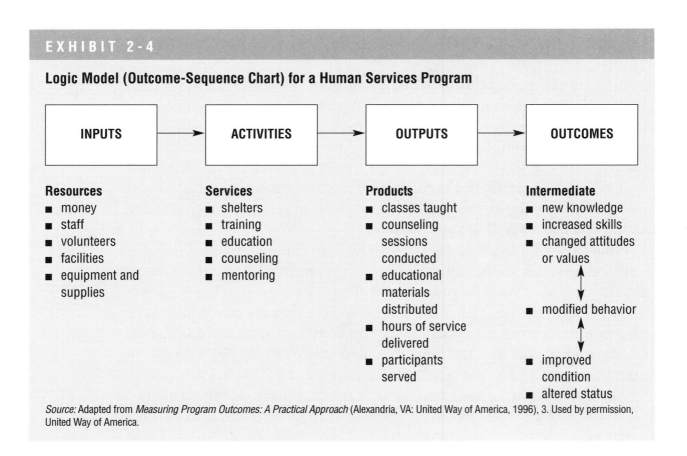

EXHIBIT 2-4

Logic Model (Outcome-Sequence Chart) for a Human Services Program

| INPUTS | → | ACTIVITIES | → | OUTPUTS | → | OUTCOMES |

Resources
- money
- staff
- volunteers
- facilities
- equipment and supplies

Services
- shelters
- training
- education
- counseling
- mentoring

Products
- classes taught
- counseling sessions conducted
- educational materials distributed
- hours of service delivered
- participants served

Intermediate
- new knowledge
- increased skills
- changed attitudes or values

↕

- modified behavior

↕

- improved condition
- altered status

Source: Adapted from *Measuring Program Outcomes: A Practical Approach* (Alexandria, VA: United Way of America, 1996), 3. Used by permission, United Way of America.

tifying indicators that should be used to measure the outcomes) further discuss such diagrams and include a number of additional examples.

References and Notes

1. The words *indicator* and *measure* are essentially interchangeable, but *indicator* seems preferable. The noun *measure* is ambiguous. It can mean an action taken to improve a situation as well as something to be measured, thus causing confusion in such sentences as "Several *measures* were used."
2. The word *effectiveness* has been used by some governments in place of *outcomes*. However, *effectiveness* implies a stronger causal link than the data usually warrant, so the word *outcome* seems preferable and is more often used (such as in the federal Government Performance and Results Act of 1993).
3. Texas Governor's Office of Budget and Planning, Legislative Budget Board, *Instructions for Preparing and Submitting Agency Strategic Plans: Fiscal Years 1999–2003* (Austin, January 1998), 39.
4. Paul Epstein, Paul M. Coates, and Lyle D. Wray, with David Swain, *Results that Matter: Improving Communities by Engaging Citizens, Measuring Performance, and Getting Things Done* (San Francisco: Jossey-Bass, 2006), 110.
5. From the perspective of an individual state or local government, completion of its own plan is an output.
6. Some may prefer to consider this aspect an intermediate outcome needed to achieve improved learning.
7. Some organizations have used the word *impact* to refer to societal outcomes, as distinguished from outcomes to individuals. Such societal outcomes are better considered broad end outcomes.
8. Some analysts view customer satisfaction as an output, which demeans its importance. Fortunately, even these analysts often agree that such service characteristics should be measured and tracked.

The Performance Measurement Process

Chapter 3

What Are the First Steps?

The rivers were rising after days of rain. A friend came by in a pickup truck and stopped at Joe's house. "Joe, Joe, come in and you will be saved." Joe responded, "No, no, the Lord will save me." The rains kept coming. Joe went to the roof of his house. A friend came by in a rowboat. "Joe, Joe, get into the boat and you will be saved." "No, no, the Lord will save me." Joe found himself floating on top of a sofa in the middle of a raging sea. A friend came by with a helicopter and lowered a rope. "Joe, Joe, come up the rope and you will be saved." "No, no, the Lord will save me." Joe drowned. At the gates of heaven, he said to Saint Peter, "What happened? I kept praying to the Lord to save me and He failed me." Said Saint Peter, "Who do you think sent you the truck, the boat, and the helicopter?"

Joe expected too much. Excessive expectations about how easy performance measurement is to implement and what it is capable of doing can also dash the hopes of would-be managers-for-results. This chapter suggests prerequisites and initial efforts that maximize the chances of success.

This chapter is primarily directed to organizations that are just introducing a performance measurement process. The suggestions provided, however, may also be useful to organizations or agencies with ongoing performance measurement that want to introduce it into another part of the organization or to substantially overhaul their existing performance measurement system.

Desirable Prerequisites for Performance Measurement

Results-based performance measurement is a valuable management tool that is widely applicable to public service programs, including those in developing countries. Three prerequisites are highly desirable before proceeding.

1. High-level support for the performance measurement effort. High-level support is a familiar requirement for almost any significant new agency activity. Performance measurement is no exception. Obviously, explicit, strong support from the top of the organization is the ideal—but it is not a must. Strong support from the head of an individual department, or even the head of a particular division in a department, can be sufficient to sustain a good performance measurement process within the department or division.

High-level support is needed for two crucial purposes. The first is to secure a commitment of adequate time and resources to develop, implement, and operate the performance measurement process. The second is to help ensure official interest in the performance management work and increase the likelihood that the resulting performance information will be used.

Program staff typically perform the primary work in developing the performance measurement process, but some outcome measurement elements may require outside support, particularly for ongoing data collection, tabulation, and analysis. The program's own resources, such as contract funds, will probably finance such activities, but such expenditures inevitably depend on upper-level agreement. Certain tasks will require special help from other parts of the agency's operation—such as computer services for data processing or central expertise for customer surveys. The encouragement and support of high-level officials are essential to ensure that such help will be forthcoming.

2. Reasonable program stability. Programs undergoing major change in mission or personnel are poor candidates for a new performance measurement process. Managers should wait until the situation has settled down.

3. At least some basic data-processing capability. For very small programs and those in very poor countries, basic performance data collection and processing can be done manually—if necessary, by volunteers. But most programs have such demanding data requirements that manual data handling can be a highly time-consuming, error-prone nightmare. In the 1970s, when manual data processing was still common, an Urban Institute project team had to perform manual tabulations with cross-tabulations on detailed outcome indicators for 150 social service clients. In developed countries, no project of that size should be handled manually in these days of the personal computer and standard spreadsheet software.

The first steps toward developing or expanding a performance measure process are to

- determine what program activities to include, and
- establish a working group to oversee development and implementation of the performance measurement process.

Determine What Program Activities to Include

Many programs, even small ones, have more than one major activity. If measurement resources are severely limited, the program manager may need to assess relative priorities for implementing performance measurement and to select certain activities to be covered by performance measurement.

A park or recreation program likely sponsors many types of activities (such as various individual support and recreation activities). Should all activities be covered, or only the major ones?

Programs aimed at helping children's development include a variety of activities, such as information dissemination, parental education, and early childhood programs. Should each activity have its own performance measurement system, or should all these activities be covered in one integrated performance measurement process?

If the *missions* of a program's various projects are *very similar,* even though the approaches may differ, it is probably feasible (and good practice) to fold them into one combined outcome measurement process. The end outcomes sought will be similar for all projects, even though the intermediate outcomes will differ depending on the projects' service delivery approaches. *If program missions differ significantly from one another, separate outcome measurement procedures will be needed* and the advantages of combining them into one measurement process shrink.

Establish a Working Group

Under this approach, each program manager would form a working group to oversee development and implementation of the outcome measurement process.[1] In addition to the program manager, who normally should act as the group's facilitator, the working group might consist of

- members of the program staff;
- representatives of related program areas within the agency;
- a representative of the agency's central office (to provide a broader perspective);[2]
- a measurement expert, either from the agency's technical staff (such as from an agency evaluation or analysis office) or an outside consultant or contractor (preferably, someone familiar with the agency's work);
- a representative of the budget office; and
- a person knowledgeable about information processing.

Working groups of 8 to 12 people are typically effective. For very small programs, working groups can be smaller. For particularly complex programs, groups may need to be larger.

Initially, the working group should meet frequently and regularly. It should plan on existing for at least two years in order to work through development and initial implementation, which should include quality-checking the first products of the performance measurement process. The group needs to undertake a number of steps. Exhibit 3-1 lists these steps and notes which chapter provides further information about them. Exhibit 3-2 organizes the

EXHIBIT 3-1

Key Steps for Performance Measurement Working Groups

1. Establish the purpose and scope of the working group (chapters 1–3).
2. Identify the mission, objectives, and clients of the program (chapter 4).
3. Identify the results (outcomes) that the program seeks to measure (chapter 5).
4. Hold meetings with interest groups, such as customer groups (in individual interviews or in focus groups), to identify outcomes desired from a variety of viewpoints (chapter 5).
5. Select specific indicators for measuring each outcome and efficiency indicator (chapter 6).
6. Identify appropriate data sources for each indicator and the specific procedures needed to obtain the data. Develop data collection instruments, such as survey questionnaires (chapter 7).
7. Identify the specific breakouts needed for each indicator, such as breakouts by customer demographic characteristics, organizational unit, geographical location, type of approach used, and the like. Breakout information is extremely useful in determining the conditions under which successful, or unsuccessful, outcomes are occurring (chapter 8).
8. Identify appropriate benchmarks against which to compare program results (chapter 9).
9. Develop an analysis plan—ways the performance data will be examined to make the findings useful for program officials and others (chapter 10).
10. Select formats for presenting the performance information that are informative and user-friendly (chapter 11).
11. Determine the roles that any program partners (such as project grantees and contractors) with substantial responsibility for service delivery should play in developing and implementing the performance measurement process. For example, many federal and state programs support a number of projects operated by local government agencies (which, in turn, provide services to customers). They are likely to have important roles in both data collection and use.
12. Establish a schedule for undertaking the above steps, pilot-testing the procedures, and making subsequent modifications based on the pilot results. (A sample project schedule is shown in exhibit 3-3.)
13. Plan, undertake, and review a pilot test of any new or substantially modified data collection procedures (chapter 7).
14. Prepare a long-term schedule (typically about three years) for implementation, indicating the timing of data collection and analysis relevant to each year's budgeting cycle and the people responsible for each step in the process.
15. Identify the uses of the performance information by agency personnel, such as helping improve programs and budgeting (chapters 12 and 13).

EXHIBIT 3-2

Sample Agendas for Working Group Meetings

Meeting One

1. Identify the purposes and uses of outcome and efficiency data.
2. Discuss working group mission, objectives, and overall schedule.
3. Begin defining program mission, objectives, and customers.
4. Plan focus groups to obtain input from customers.

Meeting Two

5. Complete defining the program mission, objectives, and customers.
6. Begin identifying outcomes and efficiency aspects to be tracked.
7. Role-play as customers.
8. Prepare outcome sequence charts.
9. Work out details of customer focus groups, which should be held before meeting three.

Meeting Three

10. Review findings from focus groups.
11. Finalize list of outcomes to track.
12. Begin selecting outcome and efficiency indicators.
13. Discuss possible data sources and data collection procedures.

Meeting Four

14. Work on identifying outcome and efficiency indicators, data sources, and basic data collection procedures.
15. Identify desirable breakouts of indicator data.
16. Plan for development of detailed data collection procedures, such as customer survey questionnaires.

Meeting Five

17. Finalize outcome and efficiency indicators and data sources.

18. Review initial drafts of detailed data collection procedures, such as customer survey questionnaires, and develop a plan for analyzing the performance data (including specifying comparison benchmarks).
19. Begin planning for pilot-testing of new data collection procedures.

Meeting Six

20. Complete plan for the pilot test and initiate the test.

Meetings Seven, Eight, and Nine

21. Review progress of pilot test.
22. Make needed modifications.
23. Identify needed tabulations for the performance data and select performance report formats.

Meeting Ten

24. Review pilot test outcome data.
25. Review results of pilot test procedures.
26. Identify and make necessary modifications.

Meeting Eleven

27. Begin documenting outcome measurement procedures for the ongoing implementation process.
28. Identify specific ways to make the outcome and efficiency data most useful (this includes determining frequency of reporting, improving analysis and presentation of the performance information, deciding on report dissemination, and developing ways to follow up on findings).

Meeting Twelve

29. Review all aspects of the performance measurement process.
30. Finalize documentation.
31. Develop a multiyear schedule for full implementation.

EXHIBIT 3-3

Sample Performance Measurement System Development Schedule (30 Months)

Project steps (see exhibit 3-1)	Month															
	0	2	4	6	8	10	12	14	16	18	20	22	24	26	28	30
Step 1: Set overall scope, get top-level support, and establish working group	▬															
Step 2: Identify mission and customers		▬														
Steps 3–5: Identify what is to be measured		▬														
Step 6: Identify data sources and data collection procedures				▬												
Steps 7–9: Determine data breakouts, comparisons, and analysis plan					▬											
Steps 10–12: Prepare for pilot test						▬										
Step 13: Pilot-test, make revisions							▬▬▬▬▬▬▬▬▬▬								
Steps 14–15: Plan for implementation															▬	

Note: At least six more months are likely to be needed to undertake the first round of performance measurement implementation.

How One Program Staffed Its Performance Measurement Working Group

For a U.S. Department of Education program aimed at improving student access to education through distance learning technology (the Star Schools program), the working group was chaired by the program manager. All seven members of the program staff participated. Representatives also included staff from the central office (of the division in which the program was located) and one representative each from another program in the same division, the Office of Planning and Evaluation Service in the department's central evaluation office, and the department's Office of Budget Services (this person was responsible for the program's budget).

steps into sample agendas for the initial working group meetings.

Before each meeting, the program manager should prepare and distribute an agenda, making the objectives of the meeting clear. In addition, the program manager should prepare a brief report on the key findings and results of the previous meeting and disseminate it for review *before* the next meeting (detailed minutes are seldom needed).

A sample tight 30-month schedule for developing a program outcome measurement process is presented in exhibit 3-3.[3] The program should also review the process regularly as it is developing—to make sure it is providing quality data *and* that the outcome information is being used beneficially.

Most programs require a minimum of three years from the start of the performance measurement development process to production of the first comprehensive performance data.[4] The program manager should negotiate with high-level officials for a reasonable overall time frame. Pressure on the program to have a *complete* performance measurement system in place can sometimes be reduced if, as is possible for some programs, early data are available on at least some major outcomes.

Notes

1. Alternative approaches include relying on contractors to design the process or using an in-house team of experts from other parts of the agency. However, the "not invented here" problem and the need for the program to have adequate tailoring for its special features make these approaches less attractive. A combination of approaches is, of course, another possible option.

2. Including stakeholders outside the agency, such as representatives of customer groups, is attractive in theory, but it complicates working group scheduling. Nevertheless, as described later, customer input can and should be sought through other means.

3. Seldom, however, are programs given 30 months; invariably, they are rushed to implement a process within a year or so. Unless the program has considerable background in collecting outcome information and already collects most of the needed information, this time span is likely too short to do an effective job.

4. This period can be shortened if the program is already producing some outcome information.

If you don't know where you are going, how can you know if you got there?

What Are the Program's Mission and Objectives? Who Are Its Customers?

Establishing a performance measurement process begins with identification of a program's, or agency's, mission and its basic objectives. What is the program intended to accomplish? Performance information should flow from, and be based on, the answer to this fundamental question.

Thus, a program's first technical step is to prepare a mission/objectives statement, including identification of its customers. Some mission statements are so general or vague that they provide little help in determining what outcomes or results the program seeks.

Other mission/objective statements can be quite specific but ultimately not very helpful because they indicate only *how* the mission is to be undertaken (the service delivery approach), not what results are sought from the specified strategies. Development of a mission/objectives statement provides an opportunity to step back and identify the program's fundamental purposes—the reasons it exists.

The Mission/Objectives Statement

A mission/objectives statement should identify the *major results* the program seeks. It is the starting point for identifying the outcomes to be measured and the performance indicators needed. The term *mission/ objectives* denotes both the overarching vision of the program (the mission) and the more specific—though still qualitative—program purposes (objectives) that flow from the mission.[1] These objectives normally should be stated in general, *not quantitative,* terms and should remain reasonably stable. Specific targets are likely to change, often annually, because of new circumstances.

The basic form of a mission/objectives statement is as follows:

To: [Identify the basic objectives (results) the program seeks and any major negative consequences the program should avoid.]

By: [Identify the basic way the service is provided.] WARNING: Do not constrain the options on ways to provide the service. The program is more likely to be stimulated to innovate and try different approaches if it allows managers to choose among specific methods.

An example from a U.S. Department of Education distance learning program (Star Schools) is shown in exhibit 4-1. Note that the **To** statement includes both end outcomes (improved student learning and employability) and intermediate outcomes (improved instruction and student access to a wide range of subjects). The general approach of the program is the use of distance-learning technologies. Specific technologies are not included, to avoid limiting the options of those delivering these program services.

Some programs use wording that implicitly places the **By** section first, as in this alternative wording of exhibit 4-1: "Use distance-learning technologies that improve student learning and employability, including providing access to, and improving instruction in, a wide range of subjects." This is *not* a good practice. Leading with the **To** statement keeps the focus more immediately and therefore more strongly on results.

A **By** statement may not be necessary for programs whose approach is expected to be clear to users of the performance information. Basic municipal services, such as waste collection and recreational programs, for example, are sufficiently clear in their approaches that even good **By** statements are not likely to be needed or helpful.

The following are suggestions for developing a mission/objectives statement:

1. Focus on how program activities are expected to affect both the program's specific customers and the public at large.
2. Identify all the major objectives that the program hopes to achieve. *Most programs have*

EXHIBIT 4-1

Mission/Objectives Statement for Distance-Learning Programs

To: Improve student learning and employability, including providing access to, and improving instruction in, a wide range of subjects.

By: The use of distance-learning technologies.

multiple objectives. It is better to include too many objectives in the statement than to run the risk of excluding objectives that may later be found important to one or more customer groups.

3. Call explicitly for *minimizing negative effects of the program.* Transportation is a good example of a program with negative effects that can be anticipated. Pollution is an inevitable by-product of transportation. Therefore, the mission statement of a transportation program might well include the words "and to minimize air, water, and soil pollution."

4. Include *conflicting objectives,* as appropriate, and *recognize in the statement the need to balance them.* Environmental and economic development programs, for example, have potentially conflicting effects on each other. Public land management programs may need to aim at a balance between promoting economic development and preserving green space, flora, and fauna.

5. Consider including objectives about *reducing the magnitude of unmet needs,* not just about helping customers who come in for service. For example, "reduce the number of households with incomes below the poverty level."

6. Include objectives related to the *quality of services delivered*—characteristics that are important to customers, such as timeliness and convenience of the help received. While these qualities are intermediate outcomes rather than end results, their importance to customers may warrant their explicit inclusion in a program's objectives, to help ensure that they receive ongoing attention.

7. Include the objective of *providing a service as efficiently as possible.* This is an objective of virtually all programs, even if only implicitly. Its explicit inclusion can serve to remind program personnel of its importance.

8. Include only qualitative, not quantitative, objectives to enhance the likelihood that the statement will remain stable over time. Numerical targets (such as "improve the outcome by 15 percent") should be avoided because they are unlikely to be valid for longer than one measurement period.[2] In some instances, public officials have chosen to include long-term numbers in their mission statements, such as "By 2015, the [outcome indicator] will double" or "by 2015, our [jurisdiction] will have the best [outcome indicator value] in the world." These are likely to be political statements aimed at securing public support. In general, they should be avoided.

9. Avoid vague or obscure wording that makes later measurement a guessing game about the statement's original intent. The strategic plan for one state's transportation department included "having all transportation systems and services work smoothly together." Such a statement makes it very difficult to determine how to track progress toward that objective.

EXHIBIT 4-2

Potential Sources of Information on Program Mission/Objectives

- Legislation, ordinances, and regulations
- Mission statements in budget documents
- Strategic plans
- Program descriptions and annual reports
- Discussions with upper-level officials and their staffs
- Discussions or meetings with customers and service providers

- Discussions with legislators and their staffs
- Input from program personnel
- Complaint information (what customers have complained about)
- Other jurisdictions with similar programs
- Program evaluations and performance audits

Sources of information to help identify the program's mission/objectives are listed in exhibit 4-2.

Identifying Categories of Customers

Look again at exhibit 4-1. The **To** part of the statement identifies the program's primary customers: students. This is good practice. Mission/objectives statements should identify who the program's customers are, unless it is already obvious to users.[3]

Almost always, programs have multiple categories of customers. Questions such as the following are helpful in identifying customer information from each source, such as those listed in exhibit 4-2:

- Who benefits from the program? Who are direct recipients? Who are indirect recipients?
- Who might be hurt by program activities? (This question may also help identify potential negative effects of the program that should be identified in the mission/objectives statement.)
- What other people not directly targeted by the program can be significantly affected by it?
- Which demographic or interest groups are particularly affected by the program? (For example, is its primary focus low-income households?)
- Is the public at large likely to have a major interest in what the program accomplishes (rather than just what it costs)? For programs that help businesses reduce hazardous waste and pollution generated by their activities, for example, the general public clearly is a major customer. But the assisted (and perhaps regulated) businesses are also customers, and the performance measurement process should include outcome indicators that address their concerns as well, such as higher costs.

Examples of key customer (stakeholder) groups for various programs include the following:

- For school-to-work opportunity programs: students, recent dropouts, parents, and prospective employers
- For programs aimed at combating teenage pregnancy: teenagers (But should boys as well as girls be targeted by such programs? Are parents also customers?)
- For school violence prevention programs: the student body as a whole, school staff, and the families of the students
- For economic development programs assisting U.S. businesses to increase their exports (and profits): businesses and persons seeking employment
- For local sanitation, crime control, parking and traffic, water services, and code enforcement programs: businesses and individual members of the public

Both *end customers* and *intermediate customers* need to be considered. Intermediate customers can be important. State and local government agencies, for example, are the intermediate customers of many federal agency programs. The federal programs work through these lower levels of government to produce favorable outcomes to the end customers. The U.S. departments of Education, Health and Human Services, Housing and Urban Development, and Labor are particularly dependent on lower levels of government to deliver programs that provide support to citizens.

As with defining mission and objectives, determining the program's or agency's customers is often more complicated than it appears at first glance. These complications, as well as difficulties in identifying missions and objectives, are not caused by performance measurement. The complications are already there and should not be ignored in a comprehensive performance measurement system. Here are some examples:

Are the inmates of prisons and jails customers? The public who are protected from these inmates are the central customers of correctional programs. However, society also is concerned that inmates have some protection in terms of *their* health and safety. Thus, indicators of correctional activities should include counts of inmate sicknesses, hospitalizations, deaths, suicides, and injuries. Minimizing the frequency of such incidents in correctional facilities is desirable, making such minimization at least an intermediate but probably an end outcome.

Are the organizations or persons that government regulatory agencies regulate customers? The effects on those regulated—such as the amount of time, money, and effort required to obtain permits or licenses—should be of concern to regulatory programs. The agencies running regulatory programs should seek to minimize such problems, even though the ultimate and more vital outcomes are to protect the health and safety of those whom the regulation is intended to protect. Environmental protection agencies, offices of consumer protection, and boards that regulate doctors, nurses, hospitals, nursing homes, and other health care organizations are among those that can reasonably view the subjects of their regulation as intermediate customers.

Whether or not an agency labels such groups explicitly as customers, its mission statement would do well to articulate the need to reduce undesirable negative effects for them—if only to minimize efficiency-reducing protests from these groups.

Sort Objectives into a Hierarchy

Many mission/objectives statements include a mix of end objectives, intermediate objectives, and means. Agencies need to determine and delineate which is which.

Working through an example is useful here. The federal government's drug policy office strategic plan has identified three primary objectives: stopping use before it starts, healing America's drug users, and disrupting the drug trade market.[4] The first two objectives can be considered ends. Is the last objective an end outcome? Probably, it is primarily an intermediate result. It is a major way to keep potential drug users from being tempted by drugs.

Chapters 5 and 6 explain ways, such as the use of logic models, to help sort through objectives and develop an appropriate hierarchy.

A Special Problem for Pass-Through Programs

A special problem arises with federal or state programs that dispense funds (grants) to lower levels of government. Is their sole mission to provide funds accurately and efficiently? Such outcomes should, of course, be tracked—they are indicators of the quality of the program's service. But would elected officials and the public agree that the purpose of the program is merely to dole out funds accurately and expeditiously? Or should the program's mission statement also include the end purpose for which those funds are to be used: helping improve citizens' health, education, welfare, or whatever the program needs to ultimately achieve? Clearly, the program and its personnel have only partial—perhaps a very small degree of—influence over the ultimate purpose. But program personnel *are* part of the overall service delivery process. *If personnel feel part of the process, they have an incentive to make innovative recommendations that can lead to significant improvements in the service's effectiveness.* Even if those recommendations require legislation, identifying them is a valuable first step in improving program results.

This dilemma frequently confronts agencies in both public and private service delivery. The philosophy in this book is to encourage use of a broad and more proactive outlook for agencies and their programs—to foster innovation. This includes efforts by programs to seek (explicit or implicit) *performance partnerships* with other agencies, other governments, and other private-sector organizations that can help produce the ultimately desired end.

References and Notes

1. This book avoids the term "goals." Although the term is sometimes used to refer to what are here called objectives, it is also often used to refer to specific numerical targets, which generally should not be included in a mission/objectives statement.
2. Numerical targets should be developed separately, as discussed in later chapters, for each performance indicator that flows from the mission/objectives statement.
3. This book uses the word "customers" to refer to any category of people that a program serves or affects (other than those involved in delivering the service). Some people object to considering direct service customers the primary customers. They believe that the public, the taxpayers, are the real customers and point out that the latter two groups are often ignored when staff are developing objectives. While taxpayers and citizens at large should not be left out, it does not seem necessary to explicitly include them in all mission/objectives statements.
4. See the U.S. Office of National Drug Control Policy, *National Drug Control Strategy* (Washington, DC: The White House, 2005).

If you don't know where you
have been, how can you know
where you are going?

What Outcomes
Should Be Tracked?

A performance measurement system is only as good as the outcomes it tracks. Each program needs to develop a specific list of outcomes important to it. (The next chapter discusses transforming each outcome into specific, measurable outcome indicators.) Exhibit 5-1 presents a checklist of broad, basic categories to consider when identifying outcomes.

Selecting the outcomes that should be tracked is essentially a judgment call (as is the identification of a program's mission and objectives, described in chapter 4). Public service agencies almost always have multiple objectives and multiple categories of customers. Thus, those selecting outcomes should attempt to include all these perspectives, at least to the extent practical.

Outcome selection will be affected by the agency's scope of responsibility and influence and by its circumstances. An example is an impoverished country with weak infrastructure. It will likely focus initially on getting citizens access to such basic needs as health services with adequate staffing and medical supplies and water that meets drinking standards. Measurements of these outcomes become extremely important. In more developed countries, these outcomes will take on somewhat different forms, such as focus on the percent of children with adequate immunizations and with health insurance coverage.

A problem arises when managers feel they have very limited influence over particular program outcomes.

EXHIBIT 5-1

Categories of Outcomes to Consider

Consider for inclusion outcomes that

- *reflect the results sought by the specific program* (by either preventing unwanted incidents or remedying existing problems).
- *minimize undesirable or negative effects* that are likely to occur (such as complaints about the service, excessive harassment by public officers to increase traffic tickets or arrest counts, environmental problems from transportation or economic development programs, and adverse economic effects from environmental protection programs).
- *improve the quality of service delivery.*[a]
- *reduce the amount of unmet need.* Many programs focus on customers who come in for assistance. Customers may represent only a portion of the citizens eligible for the assistance.
- *produce benefits for the general population by providing effective services to specific customer groups* (such as reduction in crime from programs aimed at keeping youths in school).
- *provide equitable outcomes to customer groups.* As noted in chapter 4, this outcome is not often explicitly stated in program mission/objectives statements, except for programs that directly address equity issues, such as equal opportunity programs.

[a] See exhibit 2-3 for a list of potentially applicable service quality attributes.

This problem can arise, for example, in many federal grant programs where lower levels of government deliver services to the ultimate beneficiaries. As long as the public agency has some influence, however small, the outcome should be included and measured. To be fair, however, the program should always have an explicit opportunity to provide its view of the reasons for the results—and not be blamed for outcomes beyond its control.

The sources listed in chapter 4 for identifying a program's mission/ objectives can also be useful in the search for a program's outcomes. They are listed again in exhibit 5-2 for the reader's convenience. This chapter discusses four promising approaches to identifying outcomes and then briefly discusses how the candidate outcomes obtained from all sources might be combined.

This chapter describes four approaches:

- Focus groups
    —of customers
    —of program staff (especially field personnel and including contractors or grantees that help deliver services)
- Input from meetings with other partners (such as federal, state, and local personnel)

EXHIBIT 5-2

Potential Information Sources for Outcomes

- Legislation and regulations
- Mission statements from budget documents
- Strategic plans
- Program descriptions and annual reports
- Discussions with
    — upper-level officials (and staff)
    — legislators (and staff)
    — customers and service providers
- Input from program personnel
- Complaints reported by customers
- Other jurisdictions with similar programs
- Program evaluations and performance audits

- Role-playing by program staff acting as customers
- Outcome-sequence charts (logic models)

Focus Groups

Focus groups of customers are an excellent way to obtain input on a program's outcomes and service delivery quality. But be prepared to hear groups gripe about the program. Gripes—including such matters as delays in providing services—can identify program characteristics that represent important outcomes for tracking.[1] Focus groups of program or project personnel, especially those who frequently work in the field with customers, are another useful way to obtain customers' perspectives on outcomes.

Exhibit 5-3 identifies typical steps for planning and implementing a focus group.

The direct costs of focus groups are not high. Participants do not usually need to be paid, and the meetings, which could be held in various locations within the program's service area, do not need to be in luxurious surroundings. Considerable staff preparation and administrative effort are needed, however, to ensure that the process goes smoothly and produces the information sought.

Meetings and Related Input from Other "Partners"

Many federal, state, and local programs involve participation by other agencies or organizations. These partners are usually public or private

Steps for Running a Focus Group

- Plan the sessions. Determine the information needed, the categories of participants, and the timing, location, and other administrative details.
- Select an experienced facilitator to manage the meeting and a person to take notes on the information provided by the participants.
- Invite 8 to 12 customers to participate in each focus group meeting.

  Members can be chosen from lists of customers without regard to the statistical representativeness of the selection. The information obtained from focus group participants does not provide statistical data, so statistical sampling, though an optional selection method, is not necessary. The main selection criteria are that the participants have experience with the program and be at least somewhat varied in their characteristics.
- Set a maximum of two hours. Hold the meeting in a pleasant and comfortable location. Soft drinks and snacks help provide a relaxed atmosphere.
- Begin with introductions and an overview of the purpose of the meeting.
- Have the facilitator ask the participants two questions. For customer focus groups, the questions should be
  — what do you like about the service?
  — what don't you like about the service?

  The facilitator can ask these questions in many different ways. The fundamental requirement is to establish an open, nonthreatening environment and to obtain input from each participant. *Facilitators should not debate or argue with the participants.*
- The recorder and the facilitator should work together to provide a meeting report. The report should identify outcome-related characteristics raised explicitly or implicitly by one or more participants. The program should consider tracking these characteristics.

---

nonprofit agencies but can also be the business community (such as with school-to-work, community development, and economic development programs). When identifying outcomes for tracking, seeking the input of these other agencies and organizations is usually advisable.

The program can obtain such input through meetings, telephone and conference calls, mail, faxes, the Internet, or any other form of communication, as well as focus groups.

Preferably, programs would work with other organizations as partners in designing and implementing the whole performance measurement process. For example, service agencies at various levels of government, private non-profit organizations, business organizations, and churches might all be delivering services aimed at the same objective. Partnerships are warranted when the program believes that desired outcomes would be best achieved if organizations agree voluntarily on (a) the outcomes and outcome indicators to be tracked, (b) how the data should be collected, (c) the short- and long-term targets for each outcome indicator, and (d) the roles and responsibilities of each organization in providing the particular service.

The involvement of each partner from the outset can facilitate future data collection efforts and possibly reduce the costs of data collection to any one partner. Such a process is not easy, however, and takes considerably more effort than the traditional go-it-alone approach.

Such agreements are called performance partnerships. They are a relatively new concept and require significant time and effort to work out with other organizations.

Role-Playing by Program Staff

An easy—and sometimes fun—procedure for helping identify program outcomes is to have program staff role-play as customers, with each staff member playing a particular category of customer. For example, a state child welfare agency might ask its program staff to play the roles of local county and city office personnel, parents and other child care givers, and the children themselves. Staff who work directly with customers (including staff from field offices) are likely to be particularly valuable participants.

This procedure is especially useful for programs that are not able to hold customer focus groups.[2]

The sessions should last perhaps two hours. Each participant, in his or her customer role, should be asked the same questions posed to customer focus groups: "What do you like about the program? What don't you like about it?" Participants then draw on their own knowledge of the program and what their experiences have indicated are the likely reactions of customers.

As with focus groups, someone should act as the recorder to take down the findings of the role-playing, especially the potential outcome characteristics identified during the session. The recorder should then draft a report listing all outcomes explicitly or implicitly identified by the role players as either intermediate (including service quality) or end outcomes.

Outcome-Sequence Charts (Logic Models)

Programs are likely to find outcome-sequence charts (often called logic models) helpful in identifying outcomes.[3] Such charts depict visually what a program is expected to produce. They allow staff to construct the anticipated progression of what is hoped to result from the work of the program through to the end outcomes.[4]

Every program has implicit hypotheses about what actions will produce what results. Outcome-sequence charts attempt to identify these hypotheses by showing the flow of intermediate and end outcomes expected to result from program activities and the outputs produced by those activities. (These charts are not *activity* flow charts.)

Exhibit 5-4 illustrates a sequence of expected events for a dropout prevention program focused on parental involvement. The program provides classes to help parents better support their children's learning efforts. Holding classes (block 1) is the program activity and is an output of that work. (The number of classes held is an associated output indicator.) The program then hopes that parents will enroll in, and attend, these classes (block 2), and then complete the program (block 3). The numbers of parents enrolling in and completing the program are intermediate outcomes. These outcomes indicate, respectively, the program's success in attracting parents into the program and retaining them through the end of the program.

It is hoped that as a result of the program, parents encourage their children to learn (block 4). This outcome indicates that the program actually affected those parents—a more advanced outcome, but still an intermediate outcome. While it is *expected* to lead to improved student learning, this encouragement does not guarantee that improved learning occurred. Increased attendance (block 5a), fewer behavioral problems in school (block 5b), and improved grades (block 5c) of students whose parents completed the program activities are likely to be the specific desired short-term end outcomes. Fewer students dropping out of high school (block 6) is also hoped for, but this outcome cannot be completely determined until all current students are through their final year of high school. It is, therefore, a longer-term end outcome. The logic goes even further. School learning and completion are hoped to lead to better employment and earning histories of the students—very long-term end outcomes (block 7).

Each outcome on the chart is important and should be included in the program's performance measurement process, along with the outputs. (However, regular measurement of outcomes expected to occur far into the future, such as post-high school work histories, block 7, is not likely to be appropriate.)

This example considers improved attendance (5a), fewer behavioral problems (5b), and improved grades (5c) end outcomes. Others might consider them intermediate outcomes. People can legitimately disagree over outcome categories.

This example also considers parents entering and completing the program short-term intermediate outcomes. Others may prefer labeling these

EXHIBIT 5-4

Outcome-Sequence Chart: Parental Involvement in Dropout Prevention Program

Activity/Output ← → **Intermediate Outcomes** ← → **End Outcomes**

School holds parenting classes (1)	Parents attend program (2)	Parents complete program (3)	Parents provide more school encouragement to their children (4)	Children have better attendance (5a)	Fewer children drop out (6)
				Children have fewer behavioral problems in school (5b)	Long-term economic well-being is increased (7)
				Children have improved grades (5c)	

Source: Adapted from Harry P. Hatry and Mary Kopczynski, *Guide to Program Outcome Measurement for the U.S. Department of Education* (Washington, DC: Planning and Evaluation Service, U.S. Department of Education, February 1997).

actions outputs. However, because these programs are voluntary and involve customers themselves taking steps, we consider these items outcomes, as defined in chapter 2.

Whether something is classified as an output, intermediate outcome, or end outcome rarely affects the measurement process itself. The label, however, can affect the importance the organization attaches to the outcome. Therefore, management should consider carefully the categories assigned to its measurements: whether particular measurements are outputs or outcomes and whether outcomes are intermediate or end outcomes.

Exhibit 5-5 depicts a community policing program. Getting residents to attend the program's meetings is the first intermediate outcome sought. Attendance, it is hoped, will encourage residents to protect their own homes better and provide leads to police—both intermediate outcomes because they still do not indicate whether fewer crimes were committed or more crimes solved. Reduced crime and increased feelings of safety are the end outcomes intended for the program.

Exhibit 5-6 is an outcome-sequence chart for programs offering assistance to businesses to reduce hazardous waste pollution. The program's objective is to reduce the amount of hazardous waste emitted by businesses, whether into the water, air, or soil. This, in turn, is expected to improve the quality of the air, water, and soil, producing fewer health problems among people and other living animals and vegetation.

Developing such charts is extremely useful in helping people recognize the progression from outputs to end outcomes. Program personnel should first individually, and then collectively, construct sequence charts for their program. *The various intermediate and end outcomes identified then become candidates for regular outcome measurement.* For example, people often consider access to health care and reduction in the number of families without health insurance to be end outcomes. Seeing them in a logic model helps people classify them as intermediate outcomes on the way to the end outcomes of maintaining and, as necessary, improving citizens' health.

The earlier steps in the process—the blocks showing program activities and outputs—are the items over which the program has fullest control. The closer the products are to end outcomes, particular the longer-run end outcomes, the less influence the program is likely to have over them because more non-program factors can influence these outcomes.

Outcome-sequence charts have weaknesses. For large programs, the charts can become quite complex, beyond what is useful. It is then helpful to break the charts out into components. Another weakness is that users almost always start from *existing* activities and identify outcomes that flow from those activities. Limiting a chart's focus to existing service delivery

Outcome-Sequence Chart: Community Policing Program

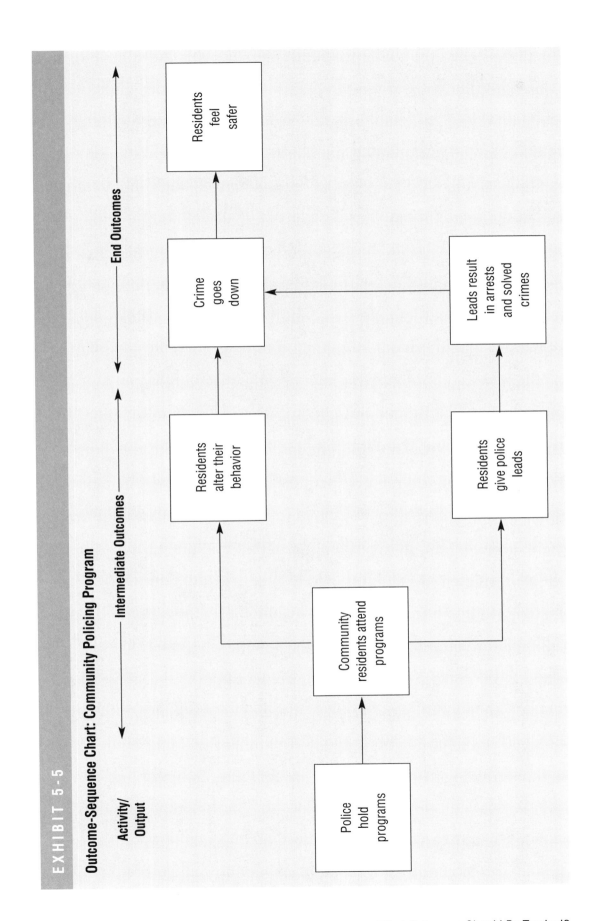

Activity/Output ◄—————► Intermediate Outcomes ◄—————► End Outcomes

Police hold programs → Community residents attend programs → Residents alter their behavior → Crime goes down → Residents feel safer

Community residents attend programs → Residents give police leads → Leads result in arrests and solved crimes → Crime goes down

EXHIBIT 5-6

Outcome-Sequence Chart: Technical Assistance to Businesses to Reduce Hazardous Waste Pollution

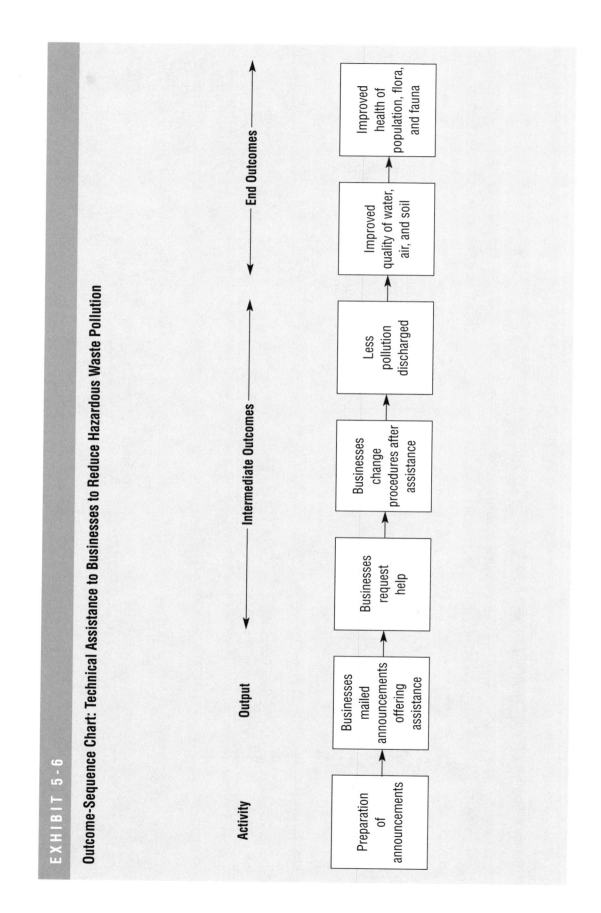

approaches can restrict innovative thinking. Users can also start these charts from the other end, that is, with the program's mission and objectives, and work back. This is more difficult but is likely worth the extra effort. *In any case, outcome-sequence charts should be used in combination with other outcome-identifying procedures,* such as those described in this chapter.

For some programs it will be helpful to attach to the chart the approximate times the individual outcomes are expected to occur. This particularly applies to programs for which at least some end outcomes are not expected until years into the future. Times will help identify outcomes that are too far out to be considered part of the outcome measurement process (and should better be examined as part of special studies).

Combining Candidate Outcomes from All Sources

Before completing the list of candidate outcomes, program staff should ask the following questions:

1. Do the outcomes assembled cover all the needed objectives, all those identified in the mission/objectives statement?
2. What bad things would happen to customers if the program's budget and resources were substantially cut or deleted? What would the consequences be? What benefits would customers receive if the program's budget and resources were increased? Thinking through the answers to these questions may help identify outcomes that have not yet been included and should be added to the list.
3. Are there any potentially bad consequences or effects associated with the program that should also be monitored? If these can be tracked regularly, they should be included as outcomes. (Some of these may have been identified in the mission/objectives statement as something the program should be minimize, or at least contain.)

When these additional questions have been answered satisfactorily, the outcomes obtained from all sources described in this chapter should be assembled into one list. At this stage, outcomes should be categorized as intermediate or end, and overlaps and duplications should be identified.

The resulting list of outcomes is likely to be very long. Even so, it is best not to screen out any outcomes at this stage, except for those that appear truly trivial or duplicative. *Outcomes should not be deleted simply because no feasible way to measure them is currently known.*

For Each Outcome, One or More Outcome Indicators Needs to Be Identified

It is important to distinguish between outcomes and outcome indicators. The outcomes discussed in this chapter do not identify which measurements are needed to adequately track the outcomes. The next chapter discusses the selection of outcome indicators.

References and Notes

1. These gripes might also be summarized by the focus group facilitator (retaining the anonymity of the complainers) and presented to the program manager and staff for possible action—a side benefit of focus groups.
2. Role-playing has the additional advantage of increasing the sensitivity of program staff to customer concerns.
3. The first publication of which the authors are aware that used the term "logic model" and provided examples was published nearly three decades ago: see Joseph S. Wholey, *Evaluation: Promise and Performance* (Washington, DC: The Urban Institute, 1979).
4. This process is also an excellent component in training on performance measurement— for any and all levels of personnel. Plus, the process itself can stimulate program personnel to consider alternative ways to achieve outcomes.

Chapter 6

A policeman making his rounds on a dark night came upon a drunk on his hands and knees under a streetlight searching for his house key. "Where did you lose it?" asked the policeman. "Over there," said the drunk, pointing to a pitch-black alley. "Then why are you looking over here?" asked the policeman. "This is where I can see," said the drunk.

What Outcome Indicators Should Be Tracked?

Selecting the specific indicators to measure is a key part of developing a performance measurement system. *Too often, agencies base their selection of indicators on how readily available the data are, not how important the indicators are for measuring the achievement of outcomes.*

What Gets Measured and Reported Gets Attention!

This chapter focuses primarily on outcome indicators—a major focus of results-based performance measurement systems.

What Outcome Indicators Are

Outcome indicators are not the same as outcomes. Each outcome to be tracked needs to be translated into one or more outcome indicators. An outcome indicator identifies a specific *numerical measurement* that indicates progress toward an outcome. Performance indicators usually begin with the words *number of, percent of, ratio of, incidence of, proportion of,* or similar phrases.

Some people argue that, since change between reporting periods is the fundamental objective, indicators should directly measure this change. In such a case, indicators would start with such words as *the change in.* . . . If the change version is used, the indicator needs to be calculated as the *difference* between the values for different reporting periods. The outcome indicator would be, for example, "the percentage by which the number increased this reporting period compared with the previous period," rather than "number of cases correctly resolved during the period." Indicators that show the value for particular reporting periods, not the change between periods, are probably preferable. They provide added information by showing the level of performance rather than merely the change. Changes over time can be readily calculated for any two (or more) periods for which values are available.

Translating outcomes into outcome indicators sounds relatively straightforward, but numerous measurement issues can arise to complicate the task.

A fundamental guide to developing successful indicators is to ask about each: *Is the wording sufficiently specific?* Addressing this question often reveals terms in the indicator that need to be defined in more depth, perhaps with the help of experts. Often it reveals problems that need to be hammered out with experienced program personnel. For example, a program might seek to track "the percent of clients completing the program in this reporting period who were helped to a significant extent." To be measurable, at least four wording elements need to be defined more specifically:

- What exactly is meant by "a significant extent"?
- What exactly is the period covered? (See box.)
- How much service is required before a person is counted as a client (in order to determine the correct number for the denominator of the percents)?
- What constitutes completion?

Data sources and data collection procedures (discussed in more detail in the next chapter) often dictate the specific wording of an indicator. For example, if service timeliness is being assessed by customer surveys, the indicator will be something like "percent of customers giving satisfactory ratings to service timeliness." But if program records are the data source, the indicator will be something like "percent of service requests for which the program exceeded the standard time for responding."

If a transportation system outcome is "roads will be in good rideable condition," the outcome indicator might be "percent of roads in good condition." However, this needs to be defined more precisely. Should roads be expressed as lane-miles? Should unpaved roads be included? And what determines whether a lane-mile is in "good" condition? Numerous road rating procedures exist; technical personnel need to use them to work out the detailed definition. Another approach is to measure "ride-able condition" from the viewpoint of customers, transforming the outcome indicator into "percent of sampled respondents who rated the ride-ability of roads as either good or excellent." In this situation, the program will need to decide which of these two basic indicators, or both, it wants to track. Data collection procedures, their reliability, and their costs often affect which specific indicator is used (as described in chapter 7).

Exhibit 6-1 lists a set of criteria for selecting outcome indicators. A program might rate each candidate indicator on each of these. Exhibit 6-2 shows a specific example: indicators recommended for solid waste collection services.

A major potential criticism of performance measurement is that *it focuses attention on the indicators being measured to the neglect of outcomes that cannot yet be measured.* If important outcome characteristics are neglected, then a program's resources and efforts can be misallocated. The system needs to include a comprehensive set of indicators.

Comprehensiveness means *including indicators that track undesirable outcomes.* For example, a law enforcement agency that focuses solely on number of police arrests will tempt staff to harass individual citizens (and businesses) to increase these values. This can also be true of a tax collection agency that focuses solely on the amount of dollars collected (by auditing federal, state, or local tax returns). Including other indicators, such as the number of validated complaints, considerably reduces such problems and alters the incentives facing staff.

Usually, more than one indicator will be appropriate for measuring an outcome. For example, "improvement in the quality of life of senior citizens" might be measured by such indicators as (a) "the percent of served senior citizens reporting that their life situation has improved since service receipt" and (b) "the percent of key family members who reported find-

The Need to Be Clear about Time Covered by an Indicator

Each outcome indicator needs to be clear about the time covered:

- Some indicators report on the number of incidents that occurred during a specified reporting period, such as *number of traffic accident deaths occurring in the past 12 months.*
- Some indicators apply to a particular point in time, such as *number of cases of tuberculosis on record as of December 31, 20xx.*
- Some indicators track clients over a period of time. The period needs to be carefully specified, *such as percent of clients whose condition had improved substantially 12 months after the client began service AND whose condition was assessed during the current 12-month reporting period.*

This last indicator is particularly complex (but can be particularly important for health and human service programs). To calculate the required indicator, the program needs to (a) have assessed the clients' condition at the time they started service (i.e., sometime during the previous 12 months) AND (b) assess each client 12 months after that date (i.e., during the following 12-month period).

Criteria for Selecting Outcome Indicators

- *Relevance* to the mission/objectives of the program and to the outcome the indicator is intended to help measure.
- *Importance* to the outcome. Does the indicator measure an important aspect of the outcome?
- *Understandability* to users of what is measured and reported.
- *Program influence or control over the outcome.* Do not use this criterion as a way to avoid measuring important outcomes. A program will almost always have less than full influence over most outcomes, especially end outcomes. As long as the program is expected to have some tangible, measurable effect on a specific outcome, an indicator of that outcome should be a candidate for inclusion—whether the effects are direct or indirect. (As suggested elsewhere, however, the program should in its performance reviews consider how much the program can influence the outcome.)
- *Feasibility* of collecting reasonably valid data on the indicator.
- *Uniqueness.* If an indicator is duplicated by, or overlaps with, other indicators, it becomes less important.
- *Manipulability.* Do not select indicators that program personnel can easily manipulate to their advantage.[a]
- *Comprehensiveness.* The set of indicators should include outcomes that identify possible negative or detrimental effects. Classic examples are harassing citizens to achieve large numbers of arrests, indictments, or tax collections. Where negative effects are a danger, indicators such as the number of valid complaints should be tracked as a counterbalance. Other questions about comprehensiveness include the following: Does the list of indicators cover all the quality characteristics of concern to customers, such as service timeliness? Does the list of indicators include relevant feedback from customers?
- *Cost of collecting the indicator data.* This criterion should be used with caution. Sometimes the most costly indicators are the most important.

[a] Manipulability depends considerably on the particular data collection procedure used, as discussed in chapter 7.

ing their senior family members more pleased with life since service receipt." An agency could decide to use only one of these indicators but would probably obtain a more comprehensive perspective on the outcome by using both.

Seeking comprehensiveness will be constrained by available measurement resources and inherent data problems. For some outcomes that cannot be measured directly, reasonable surrogates can be found (see discussion later in this chapter). For some outcomes, it may not even be possible to find a reasonable surrogate. In such a case, *the performance measurement system should explicitly identify the omissions.*

The aim is to provide valid, useful data on which managers and other officials can rely—and to recognize explicitly the limitations of those indicators.

EXHIBIT 6-2

Objectives, Outcomes, and Outcome Indicators for Solid Waste Collection

Overall objective: To promote the aesthetics of the community and the health and safety of the citizens by providing an environment free from the hazards and unpleasantness of uncollected refuse with the least possible citizen inconvenience.

Objective	Outcome	Specific indicator
Pleasing aesthetics	Street, alley, and neighborhood cleanliness	1. Percentage of (a) streets, (b) alleys the appearance of which is rated satisfactory (or unsatisfactory)
		2. Percentage of (a) households, (b) businesses rating their neighborhood cleanliness as satisfactory (or unsatisfactory)
	Offensive odors	3. Percentage of (a) households, (b) businesses reporting offensive odors from solid wastes
	Objectionable noises	4. Percentage of (a) households, (b) businesses reporting objectionable noise from solid waste collection operations
Health and safety	Health	5. Number and percentage of blocks with one or more health hazards
	Fire hazards	6. Number and percentage of blocks with one or more fire hazards
	Fires involving uncollected waste	7. Number of fires involving uncollected solid waste
	Health hazards and unsightly appearance	8. Number of abandoned automobiles
	Rodent hazard	9. Percentage of (a) households, (b) businesses reporting having seen rats on their blocks in the past three months
		10. Number of rodent bites reported per 1,000 persons
Minimum citizen inconvenience	Missed or late collections	11. Number and percentage of collection routes not completed on schedule
		12. Percentage of (a) households, (b) businesses reporting missed collections
	Spillage of trash and garbage during collections	13. Percentage of (a) households, (b) businesses reporting spillage by collection crews
	Damage to private property by collection crews	14. Percentage of (a) households, (b) businesses reporting property damage caused by collection crews
	Citizen complaints	15. Number of verified citizen complaints, by type, per 1,000 households served
General citizen satisfaction	Perceived satisfaction	16. Percent of (a) households, (b) businesses reporting overall satisfaction with the solid waste collection service they receive

Source: Adapted from Harry P. Hatry et al., *How Effective Are Your Community Services? Procedures for Measuring Their Quality,* 3rd ed. (Washington, DC: International City/County Management Association and the Urban Institute, 2006).

Using Outcome-Sequence Charts to Help Identify Outcomes and Indicators

The previous chapter discussed the usefulness of logic models to identify outcomes. Exhibits 6-3 and 6-4 repeat the outcome-sequence charts for parental involvement and community policing presented in chapter 5, adding illustrative outcome indicators. Exhibit 6-5 displays an outcome sequence chart for a stop-smoking program.

These charts can also be used to help identify outcome-based efficiency indicators. As noted in chapter 2, dividing outcome indicator values by inputs (funds expended or employee hours) yields outcome-based efficiency ratios. For example, in exhibit 6-5, the number of persons reporting that they had stopped smoking 12 months after program completion, when divided by the cost of the program, yields "program cost per person who stopped smoking," the end outcome–based efficiency indicator. Number of persons who completed the program, when divided by the cost of the program, yields "cost per person completing the program," the intermediate outcome–based efficiency indicator.

The latter is a less meaningful indicator of program efficiency, because program completion has a less direct relationship to the ultimate goal of the program. But it is based on data that are available more quickly and is still a more meaningful indicator of program efficiency than the output-based efficiency indicators commonly used by government, such as cost per program held.

Reminder from chapter 2: Outcome values expressed as something to be minimized, or as a percent, make no sense when used in efficiency indicators. For example, number of children dropping out of school (exhibit 6-3) and number of reported crimes (exhibit 6-4) cannot be used to provide indicators of efficiency (but the number *prevented* can be used, if measurable).

"Community Impact Indicators"

In recent years, private nonprofit organizations, such as United Ways and foundations, have begun funding community-level efforts as a complement to funding many small individual activities. This strategy focuses on one or a few community needs and supports work aimed at reducing the overall need in the community. The strategy often includes efforts to bring in other partners (other nonprofit organizations, government, and businesses) to help with funding and implementation. Traditional funding is spread out among multiple small organizations. The improvement in

EXHIBIT 6-3

Outcome-Sequence Chart with Indicators: Parental Involvement in Dropout Prevention Program

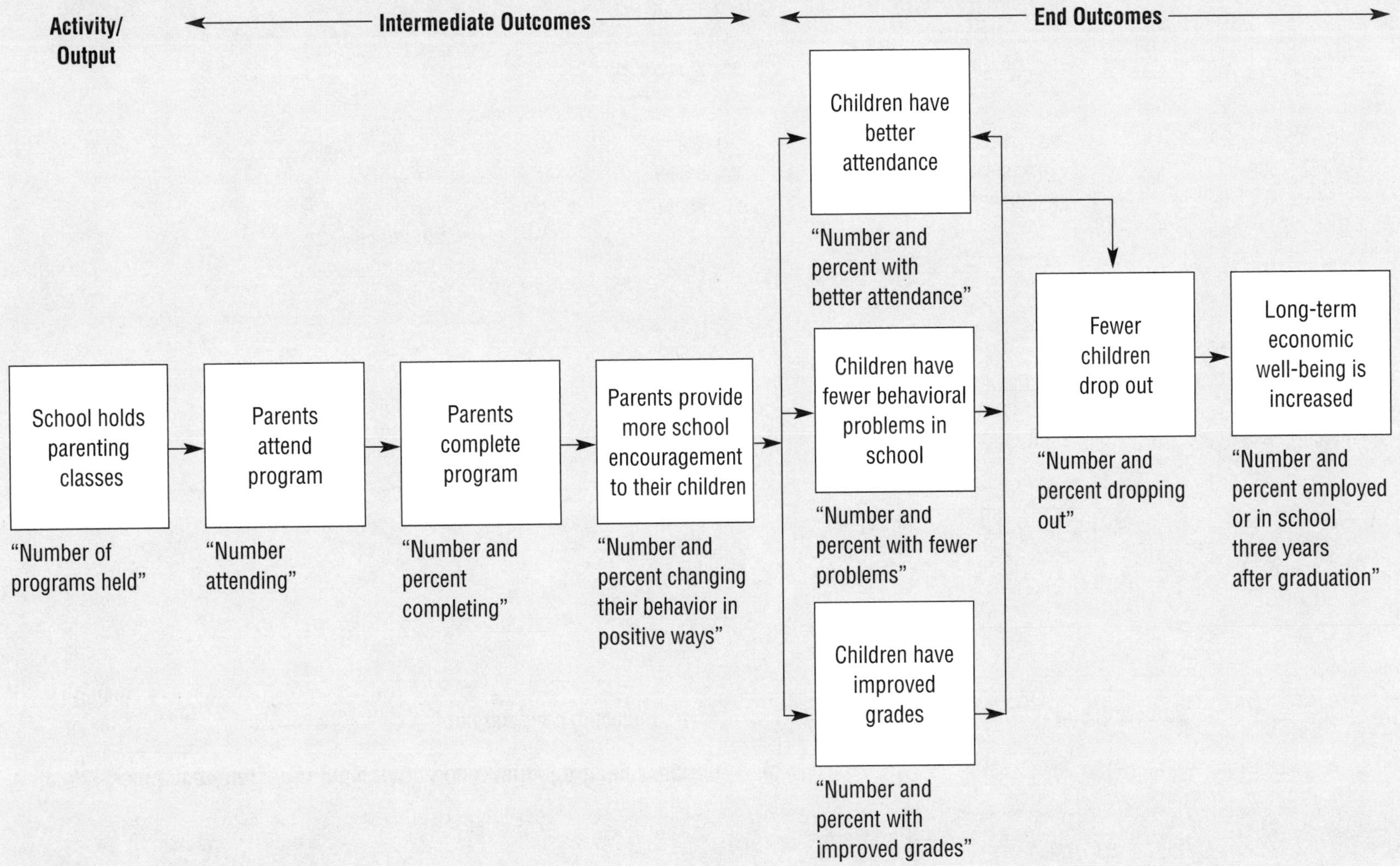

Source: Harry P. Hatry and Mary Kopczynski. *Guide to Program Outcome Measurement for the U.S. Department of Education* (Washington, DC: Planning and Evaluation Service, U.S. Department of Education, February 1997).

EXHIBIT 6-4

Outcome-Sequence Chart with Indicators: Community Policing Program

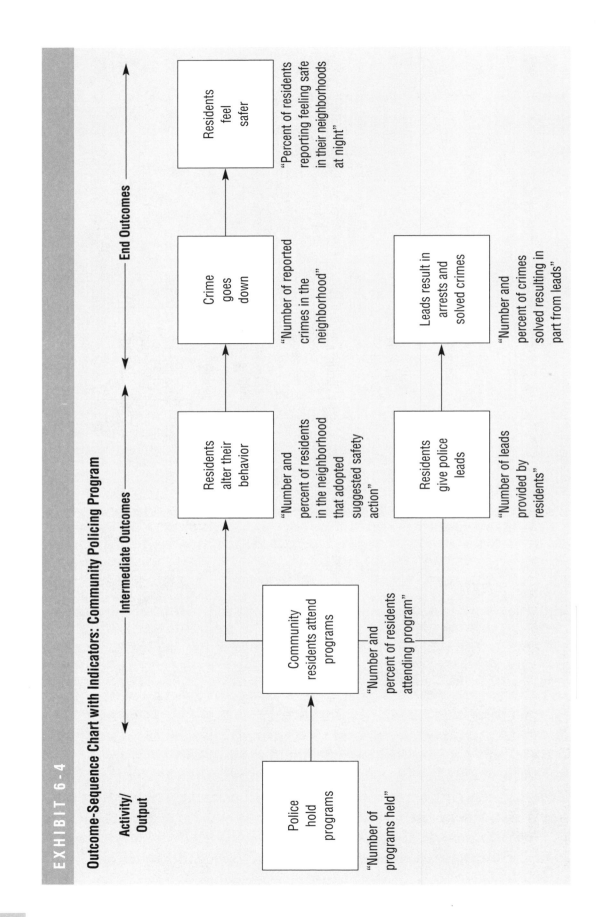

Activity/
Output

←——— Intermediate Outcomes ———→

←——— End Outcomes ———→

Police
hold
programs

"Number of
programs held"

Community
residents attend
programs

"Number and
percent of residents
attending program"

Residents
alter their
behavior

"Number and
percent of residents
in the neighborhood
that adopted
suggested safety
action"

Crime
goes
down

"Number of reported
crimes in the
neighborhood"

Residents
feel
safer

"Percent of residents
reporting feeling safe
in their neighborhoods
at night"

Residents
give police
leads

"Number of leads
provided by
residents"

Leads result in
arrests and
solved crimes

"Number and
percent of crimes
solved resulting in
part from leads"

EXHIBIT 6-5

Outcome-Sequence Chart with Indicators: A Stop-Smoking Program

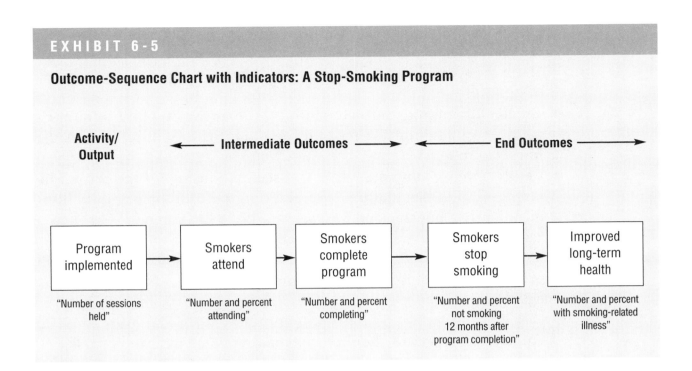

outcomes for any one need is usually too small to affect appreciably the community-wide value of the outcome indicator—even if more than one program has received funds to tackle that need.

Some outcomes and outcome indicators, particularly the *end* outcomes and outcome indicators, are likely to be the same for either strategy, such as lowered infant mortality, improved school readiness, reduced drug use, and the like. However, two differences in the indicators will likely arise.

First, the program-oriented strategy generally tracks help to each funded program's clients only. The community-wide strategy is primarily interested in tracking the community-wide value of the indicator. Thus, *the coverage of the performance indicator is considerably greater.*

Second, the community-wide strategy will need to *include citizens who have not been clients of individual programs.* For example, added outcome indicators may be needed to assess how well intended clients know about, and can access, the services available to them in the community. The outcome indicators (intermediate outcome indicators) needed to make these assessments are usually not ones needed by individual service programs, except for their own clients.

Typically, community-wide efforts focus on only a few outcome indicators. But obtaining data for them may be expensive, since such procedures as community-wide surveys may be necessary. Data on some indicators, however, may be available from government sources, such as local health departments providing community infant mortality rates.

Here are some examples from United Ways:[1]

- Greater Richmond and Petersburg, VA, focused on child immunizations. It substantially increased the immunization rate for children in community.
- Central Ohio (Columbus), OH, focused on housing for the chronically homeless. It substantially increased the number of homeless who lived in supportive housing and had not returned to an emergency shelter.
- Thomas Jefferson Area (Charlottesville), VA, focused on children in low-income families without health insurance. It substantially increased the proportion of eligible children enrolled in Virginia's free or low-cost health insurance programs.

Individual programs should focus their outcome indicators on aspects over which they have responsibility. A maternal and child health program may seek to help children jurisdiction-wide, but its limited resources preclude it from making much of a dent in the outcome values for the whole jurisdiction. Such a program will need to focus on outcome data pertaining to its own customers, such as the percent of low-birth-weight babies *among the program's clients.* Clearly, the program can be expected to help those particular women.

Public agencies whose missions cover the entire population may have a responsibility for the whole population in need, even if they do not have sufficient resources to meet that need. In this case, the program should track both the outcomes of the customers served (over which it has considerable influence) and the outcomes reflecting jurisdiction-wide low-weight births (over which it has much less influence). At least the program can identify for political officials that it lacks sufficient resources to handle the problem.

The individual nonprofit organization's performance measurement effort should continue to track outcomes for the client population to whom it tried to provide service. For example, a program that attempts to reduce a jurisdiction's teenage pregnancy rate but that only has resources to work with in-school youth at a few schools would track the intermediate and end outcomes for youth *attending those schools.*

To make a real dent in the overall community value for those indicators (such as the community's overall teenage pregnancy rate), the funding organization (such as a community foundation, a local United Way, or a government) needs to

- select specific community needs and the key outcome indicators needed to track progress,
- concentrate significant resources on those needs, and
- find partners with which it can make a substantial improvement in the overall community on those indicators.

An organization that chooses to focus on a community-wide need would track and attempt to improve the condition for the whole community (e.g., the overall community teenage pregnancy rate).

An example is the "Community Impact Operational Plan" of the United Way of Tucson and Southern Arizona.[2] The United Way selected three major focuses: kids, strengthening families, and supporting seniors. For each, it selected one or two key outcome indicators ("impact targets"). The United Way uses its discretionary funds primarily as a basis for requests for proposals from local nonprofits. Those proposals that the United Way's reviewers believe have "the best chance of achieving measurable outcomes in support of one or more of the impact targets" are funded. Contracts may be for up to two years with a possible extension for an additional two years, depending on the funds available and the results achieved. Exhibit 6-6 is an example of the United Way's tracking sheets. It is for one of the two targets the United Way selected for its focus on kids: "More children enter school ready to learn and succeed." At the bottom of the exhibit, the United Way identifies its partners in the effort.

Numerical Forms for the Indicators

Outcome indicators are often expressed as either the number or the percent (proportion or rate) of something. Programs should generally report *both* forms. The number of successes (or failures) in itself does not indicate the rate of success (or failure)—what was not achieved. The percent by itself does not indicate the size of the success. Assessing the significance of an outcome typically requires data on both number and percent.

Numbers can be expressed in a variety of ways, including these three:

- *Number,* such as the total number of customers that had a particular condition, that improved, or that reported satisfaction with a service.
- *Mean,* the arithmetic average of a set of numerical values. A typical example is the average time between a call or request for a service and the response. Arithmetic averages have the advantage of being widely

Tracking Sheet for a Community Impact Operational Plan

Impact target: More children enter school ready to learn and succeed

Long-Term Community Outcomes

- At least 4,000 more children each year receive quality child care and education by 2006
- Tucson 1st grade achievement scores in targeted neighborhoods rise 20 percent in reading, language, and math by 2009
- Ten percent more mothers receive prenatal care in the first trimester by 2009

Current Statistics

Number of children under 6 in Pima County	65,621
Number of children under 6 below the poverty level	14,488 (22%)
Percent of Arizona's children enter kindergarten without essential skills for learning	33%

2005–2006 Projected Results

People Served

Over **3,500** children, with a special emphasis on those from racially and ethnically diverse backgrounds, receive substantially higher quality child care than they did in 2003.

1,000 women receive care and support for a healthy pregnancy and learn about raising and nurturing their baby.

Results/Outcomes

18,000 families receive age-appropriate books when they visit their medical clinic and learn tips for reading to their child.

50 child care centers in Tucson request or maintain national accreditation and significantly improve the quality of care for young children.

500 families learn new parenting skills through interactive parent education, training, and group activities.

Changing Community Conditions

The Center for Early Child Education at Pima Community College opens and creates strategies to increase the number of early childhood specialist that graduate.

Community Impact Partners

Blake Foundation	La Frontera
Pio Decimo Center	Child & Family Resources
Make Way for Books	The Parent Connection
Jewish Family and Children's Services, Inc.	Reach Out and Read
Tucson Nursery Schools and Child Care Centers	St. Elizabeth of Hungry Clinic, Healthy Babies Clinic
United Community Health	Tucson Jewish Community

Source: United Way of Tucson and Southern Arizona. Used with permission.

understood. Their disadvantage is that they can be greatly affected by extreme values.

- *Median,* the middle value of a set of numerical values. (If the set includes an even number of values, the median is usually determined by taking the arithmetic average of the two middle values.) Medians have the advantage of not being influenced by extreme values, as arithmetic averages are.

Percents can also be expressed in a variety of ways, including these three:

- Percent that fell into a particular outcome category, such as the percent that rated some service characteristic as good
- Percent that fell above (or below) some targeted value, such as the percent of persons with blood pressure above an identified danger level
- Percent that fell into particular outcome intervals, such as the percent between two specified values representing high and low blood pressure, respectively

In addition, sometimes it will be useful to calculate some form of combined score or index. For example, customer service percentages for ratings of "excellent" and "good" can be added to produce a summary value for an indicator. (Of course, the percentages of the ratings "fair" and "good" might be used instead to focus on less than fully satisfactory ratings.)

Customer ratings and similar measurements might assign numerical values to each grade on the scale that can be used to calculate overall averages. For example, numerical values often have been assigned to grades on trained observer scales used to rate street cleanliness. (If used alone, however, averages hide the actual distribution of the ratings, information that often is of considerably more use.)

Some indicators are expressed as something the program wants to *maximize*. Others are expressed as something the program wants to *minimize*. Often there is a choice: do you want to report the glass as half full or half empty? The percent (or number) not improved after services or the percent (or number) improved? The percent (or number) of citizens who were victims of crimes or the percent (or number) not victimized? The percent of customers satisfied with a service or the percent not satisfied? The percent (or number) of persons who reported not using illegal drugs during the past month or the percent (and number) who reported using illegal drugs during that period?

Agency officials typically prefer to report the positives. However, reporting problems is more likely to lead to attention to those problems. In situations where the number or percent of negative events is likely to be very low, but the negative events are very important, agencies should use the negative form. Many health and safety programs, for example, commonly report the number of negative incidents, such as numbers of deaths, murders, and cases of infectious diseases. Environmental protection programs probably should use "number of days that the effluent from water treatment plants exceeded pollution level standards" rather than "number of days in full compliance."

Key Factors Affecting the Choice of Outcome Indicators

For any given outcome, a program is likely to be faced with many indicator choices. These choices will depend on such factors as the following:

- *The data collection procedure needed to provide the data for the indicator—and its practicality, validity, and cost.* The specific indicator will be determined in part by the data collection procedure. Procedures are discussed at length in chapter 7.
- *The particular data source.* For example, in an educational program, customer surveys might be used to track perceptions of school safety. Three groups—children, teachers, and parents—might be surveyed. If so, each group would provide its own perspective and require its own outcome indicator.
- *Different aspects of, or perspectives on, the outcome.* For example, the outcome *improved water quality* might be measured by a variety of pollutant-count indicators, by fish-kill counts, or by some combination of these. Multiple indicators are likely needed. Often a condition, such as whether a road is too bumpy or a park too dirty, can depend on whether the condition is measured by a customer survey or by something more objective, such as equipment or trained observers. If feasible, both procedures would be used, resulting in two different perspectives and indicators.
- *Different points in time at which the measurement is taken relative to when the service was provided.* For many outcome indicators, programs can choose when the measurements will be made and at what intervals. For example, changes in a customer's condition for many human services programs (such as health, social service, and employment programs) might be measured at the time the service was last provided, at specified periods from the time the customer entered the service, or at different lengths of time after the service ended.

Cautions

Programs will be tempted to confine their measurements to the *customers' condition while still receiving services or at their last official visit.* This approach is relative easy for measurement and has lower measurement cost. For programs that are meant to have lasting effects after customers finish receiving services, however, this restriction will prevent tracking considerably more important outcomes.

Some organizations have required that their programs *limit the number of indicators to some pre-selected number.* Officials who receive performance data from many different programs often prefer to see only those indicators the program believes most important. However, for *internal* tracking, program management should use *as many indicators as it believes will be useful and for which it has sufficient resources for regular data collection.* Even for reporting to upper levels, programs should be given some leeway in the number they report. The program manager may believe that data on some of these other indicators may be valuable to upper-level officials.

Do not exclude an outcome indicator merely because the program has been doing very well on it for a period of time. Include *any* outcome indicator that is important for the program. Continue to take credit for good accomplishments and continue to monitor for possible change. Suppose, for example, that the number of pollution incidents in a particular body of water drops to virtually zero. This does not mean there will never be new cases in the future. Excluding the indicator will tend to reduce considerably the attention that the body of water should get.

Aggregate Outcome Indicators, Including Indices

In some instances, it is desirable to combine data from one or more basic outcome indicators into an aggregate indicator or index. This is usually done to provide a more useful and summarized perspective on the outcome. Examples are air and water quality indices that combine data from individual pollutant levels into one summary of water and air quality. In these cases, the aggregate indicators are considerably easier for laypersons to grasp and use than data on numerous esoteric pollutant values.

In most cases, the relative weights given each outcome indicator are based on value judgments, as when programs attempt to combine outcome indicators based on the "judges'" perceptions of each indicator's relative importance. Different judges can, and are likely to, disagree.

In addition, the importance of an outcome indicator can depend on the recent levels for the indicator. An indicator perceived as relatively unimportant, such as the courteousness of public employees to requests for information, could become considerably more important if officials receive many complaints about lack of courteousness.

Another application of aggregating indicators is combining the results from a number of projects, or programs, whose outcome indicators are measured differently. For example, a useful indicator might be "Number, or percent, of school districts whose standardized test scores improved by at least 5 percent from the previous year." Such indicators are particular useful in situations where an upper level of government does not control the data collection procedure and different units (school districts in the example) use somewhat different procedures (different standardized tests in the example). The lower units of government might also use somewhat different reporting periods.

Another example are aggregations of environmental cleanup efforts in various areas in a country, state, or local government. For example, a government might be supporting efforts to improve the quality of water in a number of jurisdictions that used their own procedures to assess changes in water quality. The government might use an overall aggregate outcome indicator, such as "number, or percent, of designated jurisdictions (or bodies of water) whose water quality improved at least 10 percent over the most recent 12-month reporting period."

Such aggregations can be helpful, but they need to be used with considerable care. These indicators implicitly or explicitly *apply a weight to each "project."* Are these weights reasonably valid? For example, for water and air quality indices, the public depends on the technical expertise of scientists to determine how the values of the individual pollutants should be combined. In the above school district example, test score changes are combined from different school districts that might have used different tests, or testing procedures, and the school districts may have varied considerably in size. Is each school district using satisfactory testing to make the combination meaningful? Is the fact that the school districts varied considerably in size important for interpreting the results of the aggregate indicator? Should the aggregate value be weighted by school sizes?

A common practice is to weight all indicators equally (after each indicator has been expressed in common units). This is easy and on the surface avoids controversy. This practice, however, assumes that each indicator is as important as the others.

A somewhat similar but more subtle problem arises when *criteria that should not be combined are combined,* such as combining output (or process) indicators and outcome indicators into one aggregate score. Unfortunate major occurrences of this problem are the summary scores used by the National Institute of Standards and Technology's Baldrige National Quality Program and the U.S. Office of Management and Budget's PART (Performance Assessment Rating Tool) program. In both programs, the organization rates several management process criteria (based on judgments of the raters) along with criteria on results. The findings on individual criteria can be quite useful. However, Baldrige and OMB assign points to each criterion and then add all criteria up to provide a total score. Such totals tend to overshadow the scores on the individual criteria. Baldrige assigns 45 percent of its total score to "results." OMB assigns 50 percent. (In both instances, the percentages given to actual organization results is considerably less. The results score itself comprises both process and actual results criteria.) If an organization is concerned with actual results, it should not use process criteria when determining the bottom line.

Another example of the potential *misuse* of aggregate indictors is the indicator "number, or percent, of outcome indicators for which targets were met for the year." This type of index (which some federal agencies have used in their annual accountability reports) typically does not distinguish target achievement for more important indicators from less important ones. It also is subject to easy manipulation by including easier-to-meet (and probably considerably less important) targets.

A way to alleviate aggregation problems is to *allow users access to the individual indicator values that make up the aggregate figure.* This access enables users to use the information without relying on an index and lets them create their own index.

Difficult-to-Measure Outcomes

"Not everything that counts can be counted." Some outcomes may require indicators that are extremely difficult or expensive to track directly, in which case surrogate indicators or in-depth evaluations (or both) are likely needed. The following activities are particularly difficult to measure:

- *Prevention programs.* These include programs such as crime and fire prevention, child abuse prevention, and disease prevention. Regulatory programs such as environmental protection and state licensing boards face the same dilemma: They also are ultimately intended to prevent a variety of public health and safety problems. But how can one measure the number of incidents that were prevented? Such a direct determination typically requires highly sophisticated and expensive program evaluation designs that attempt to provide some way to measure what would have happened in the absence of the program.

  For regular performance measurement, less sophisticated and less expensive alternatives are needed. The traditional approach is to use the number of incidents that were *not prevented* as a surrogate for cases prevented. In addition, sometimes surrogates can be found that track reduction in major factors known to lead to undesirable incidents, such as *risk factors*—factors that, if reduced, are expected to help prevent the unwanted incidents. These indicators are important, however; reducing risk factors is an intermediate outcome. For example, the U.S. Department of Health and Human Services regularly surveys behaviors presumed to lead to health and safety problems among young people. These risk factors include poor diet, inadequate physical activity, alcohol and other drug abuse, tobacco use, and unsafe sexual behavior.[3] Surrogates used for prevention of communicable diseases include age-appropriate vaccination rates (or non-vaccination rates). The survey data provide indicators of the presence of each risk factor among youth in the United States.

For regulatory programs, useful indicators of intermediate outcomes track the detection and correction of violations and complaints.

- *Basic research and long-range planning activities.* These programs can take many years to produce outcomes. As the period until major outcomes can be expected lengthens, the usefulness of regular measurement declines and more factors likely have intervened—making the task of relating outcomes to these activities extremely difficult. What can be done in such cases? Agencies can track early intermediate outcomes—such as the percent of time that reports and plans were provided on schedule; the results of peer reviews; or, for research programs, the number of citations in the technical literature. This information, however, tells little about results. End outcomes for these programs are better assessed, if they can be assessed at all, by in-depth special studies.

- *Programs in which the customers are anonymous, such as hotlines.* How can programs tell if their customers have been helped? Some hotlines have asked callers if they would permit a call-back in a few days and have asked for a telephone number for a later survey to find out what happened.[4] Or programs might ask customers to call back, giving a code name to preserve customers' anonymity.

- *Programs in which major outcomes apply to a very small number of events.* For some programs, the results of a small number of particularly important events may have significance far beyond their statistical incidence. For example, the results of a very small number of major federal or state litigation programs may be extremely important, even though the program has also litigated a large number of other cases that individually and collectively are much less important. Tabulations of overall litigation success rates, though useful, do not adequately consider the impact of the few very important cases. Another example is that of emergency response programs if only a few major emergencies occur during a reporting period.

In these instances, *quantitative data are insufficient.* A pragmatic option is to provide qualitative information separately for these few but very important cases. This procedure will not be very satisfactory to people who only like numbers. However, the procedure is reasonable and can provide important performance information to users of the data.

For emergency response programs, indicators might include response times and the number of people provided food and shelter. For periods in which no emergencies occurred, surrogates that measure the degree of preparedness would need to be used—such as response times that occur in simulated or test events—as is typically done by the Department of Defense (using war games and simulations).

Internal Support Services

Should performance measurement systems be used for internal support services, such as facility maintenance, fleet maintenance, purchasing, information technology, personnel, and accounting?

The relationships of these activities to the end outcomes of operating programs are typically extremely difficult to assess. Nevertheless, most organizations, particularly those applying substantial resources to these activities, would find performance measurement a useful planning and management tool.

Even though support activities do not produce external outcomes, their quality should be tracked. They have their own customers—the personnel in the agency's operating programs. Tracking "outcomes" such as the timeliness and accuracy of their work and internal customer satisfaction is feasible and an important aspect of good management.

Constructing Outcome Indicators to Help Identify Causes

Outcomes do not necessarily reveal anything about what caused them. In almost all cases, a program will have only partial influence over the values of its outcome indicators. External factors beyond the control of the program will affect indicator values. This applies to most intermediate outcomes and even more strongly to end outcomes. But sometimes outcome indicators can shed light on how much the service affected outcomes.

Two major approaches are the following:

1. *Ask customers to rate the extent to which the program contributed to the outcomes they reported.* For example, for a health (or any social service) program, customer surveys can ask customers whether their condition has improved since the service began. This provides the indicator "number, and percent, of customers whose condition improved since the service began." But surveys can go further. They can also ask customers to rate how strongly they believe the service contributed to the improvement. The outcome indicator then might be: "Percent of customers who reported both having improved *and* that the service had contributed significantly to the improvement."

2. *Ask data sources, where possible, to also identify and record the reasons for any problems identified.* For example, surveys of households can provide measurements of the percentage of households not using a park or a library. Also include in the questionnaire the follow-up question to those respondents who indicate nonuse, "WHY have you not used the facility?" Respondents might be given pre-identified possible reasons, such as "locations not convenient," "hours not convenient," "cost too high," "too crowded," "used service and didn't like it," or "not interested." An "other" response should also be included. The number and percent of citizens giving each reason can be tabulated.

   It will be even more helpful if the data on reasons are grouped by the program's influence over them, to distinguish reasons over which it has little control.

   The program can then use the information on nonuse and reasons for it to help identify appropriate actions. For example, as part of measuring the frequency of traffic accidents, an agency can group the accidents by cause, producing such indicators as the number of traffic accidents in which specific problems (such as faulty traffic signs or signals) played a role.

Providing for Qualitative Outcomes

A program manager may believe that one or more important outcomes are not covered by the performance data. Many, if not most, program managers will believe that quantitative measurement cannot capture all the benefits of their programs—and, indeed, a good case can be made for this belief. To help allay this concern, *a performance measurement system should include explicit provision for programs to report such outcomes* even though they have only qualitative evidence. Not everything that is important is measurable!

For example, a program aimed at encouraging students with disabilities to consider science or math careers might believe that improving students' confidence in their ability to do well in academic courses is an important intermediate outcome. The program may not have reliable quantitative data on improved confidence. (However, questionnaires can help detect respondent confidence, self esteem, and similar "subjective" information.)

Programs should provide as much evidence as possible to back up qualitative statements. In the above example, the program should provide any evidence that student confidence has improved, even though only qualitative information is available. Qualitative evidence is, in general, considerably less convincing than quantitative evidence of progress.

An Option: Identify a Program's Influence on Individual Outcomes

As long as a program can have some effect on the value of an outcome indicator, it should be a candidate for inclusion. But agencies can alert users to a more accurate and fairer picture of performance by also *identifying and reporting the approximate degree of influence they have over each outcome indicator.*

Agencies should consider this step in their efforts to provide a fair picture of their performance. The program might, for example, assign categories to each indicator, such as whether the program has little, some, or considerable influence. Such categories should be defined as specifically as possible, and staff should categorize cases soon after they come in. Agencies will also want to ensure that similar category definitions are used by all their programs—so agency performance reports will offer comparable judgments on degree of influence.

Ratings would likely be made by the program manager, but with review by higher-level managers to ensure comparable ratings across programs.

The New Mexico Department of Health has rated each indicator in its quarterly performance reports by whether the department had "substantial influence," "some influence," or "little influence" over the indicator. Exhibit 6-7 is an example from one report. As is typical with intermediate outcomes, the agency believes it has "substantial influence" over the indicator's value. For most end outcomes, agencies are more likely to report that they have only some or little influence over the outcome.

EXHIBIT 6-7

Sample Presentation of an Agency's Degree of Influence over Outcomes

Strategic Direction: Increase access and choice for behavioral health services

The Department of Health is dedicated to maintaining the "safety net" of behavioral health services for the uninsured adult population and will work with 16 other state agencies to increase capacity for behavioral health services.

Source of data: Behavioral Health Information System files based on the registration file submitted on each new client.

Percent of newly registered adults with urgent behavioral health treatment needs who have first face-to-face meeting with a community-based behavioral health professional within 24 hours of request for services

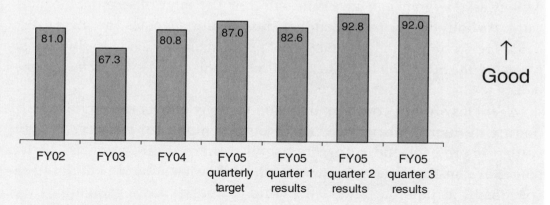

Because of the ongoing self-correcting data warehouse, discrete quarterly data are not possible. Data are reported for July 2004 through January 2005.

DOH influence over measure

● Substantial influence (75%–100%)   ○ Some influence (30%–75%)   ○ Little influence (< 30%)

The program manager and staff should normally select performance indicators. They are the persons that can make most use of the information and usually are responsible for data collection. However, upper levels should review the selection to assure that the set of performance indicators covers the primary mission and objectives of the program. Program managers will tend to select performance indicators over which they have most control, tending to neglect the more important end outcomes.

Note that while program customers are a major source of input in identifying the outcomes that should be tracked (as discussed in the previous chapter), the selection of the specific measurement, the indicator, is a more technical matter.

Specific indicators cannot really be selected until the program has also considered the specific data collection procedure that will be used. The data collection procedure will affect the particular indicator wording. For example, an indicator used to track response timeliness will be worded differently depending on whether the data will come from agency records to calculate actual response times or will be obtained by asking citizens what they thought about the timelines of the response to their service requests.

Data collection procedures are the subject of the next chapter.

References and Notes

1. Summary sheets for each of these three projects are available from the United Way of America. For more discussion of community initiatives and outcome measurement, see United Way of America, "Community Initiatives: Tracking Progress and Results" (Alexandria, VA: United Way of America, 2005).
2. See United Way of Tucson and Southern Arizona, "The United Way Community Impact Operational Plan," updated February 15, 2005.
3. See the U.S. Department of Health and Human Services Centers for Disease Control and Prevention's biennial Youth Risk Behavior Surveillance surveys.
4. A call-back is potentially available if the hotline has caller ID, though its use is probably unethical. Caller ID has been used in cases of obvious danger—primarily to provide help if the caller sounds dangerously suicidal. But even caller ID will not reach people who have used a pay phone.

What Methods of Data Gathering Should Be Used?

The choice of collection procedures is key to getting valid, useful data. As the old saying goes: "Garbage in, garbage out." You cannot finalize performance indicators before deciding on data collection methods.

This chapter discusses five major alternatives for collecting quantitative performance indicator data:[1]

- Administrative data from program and/or agency records
- Customer surveys
- Trained observer ratings
- Role-playing ("testing")
- Special technical equipment

Program and Agency Records

Most agencies and programs routinely record data on customers and/or transactions for administrative purposes.[2] This data collection procedure has been by far the most widely used for producing performance data. Agency records can be used to calculate performance indicators. Records may come from the program itself, from other programs within the agency, or from other agencies (including other levels of government). The relevant information needs to be extracted from those records and tabulated (if not already tabulated) in order to yield the desired outcome indicators.

Agency records are also the main data source on amounts of input (both dollars and employee time) and amounts of output produced by the program. This information is needed for output-based efficiency indicators. Records can also contain demographic characteristics of customers and other characteristics of the workload for breaking out outcome indicators (see chapter 8).

Examples of outcome indicators for which agency records will be a source include the following:

- Data on timeliness and response times for police, fire, and emergency service calls or for any other customer requests for services or information.
- Number of complaints received, preferably broken out by the subject of the complaint and the severity of the problem. If the data are not already in the database, staff will have to develop a reliable procedure for producing the information. Number of *legitimate* complaints is the preferred indicator. Staff will also have to develop a way to assess which complaints are legitimate.
- Number of people who participated in services, such as for particular recreation, library, or social service programs. This information is needed in calculating customer success rates.
- Number of traffic accidents, injuries, and deaths.
- Number of reported crimes and fires.
- Clearance rates for each crime category.
- Incidence of various illnesses and deaths and their rates among program customers.
- Number of people receiving public assistance payments.
- Number and rates of low-weight births.
- Percent of clients employed and earnings levels after receiving employment and training assistance (from state unemployment insurance records).
- Recidivism rates.

Agency record data may be based in part on other procedures, such as trained observer ratings. For example, child welfare agency data on the number of children removed from unsafe homes may be based on staff members' observations of home conditions routinely tracked in agency records.

Advantages of Agency Records

- The data are readily available at low cost.
- Most program personnel are familiar with the procedures for transforming the data into indicators.

Disadvantages of Agency Records

- Agency records seldom contain enough service quality and outcome data to create an adequate set of performance indicators.
- Existing record collection processes often need modification to generate useful performance indicators. For example, though collecting data on program response times to requests is common for some types of services, others will need to modify their procedures to make sure that the following are provided:
  — Time of receipt of the service
  — Definition of what constitutes a completed response
  — Time of completion of response
  — Data-processing procedures to calculate and record the time between receipt of request and completion of response for individual requests
  — Data-processing procedures for combining the data on individual requests into aggregate response-time indicators
- Obtaining data from the records of other programs or agencies, which are sometimes needed to calculate an indicator, can be administratively difficult and can raise issues of confidentiality. For example,
  — indicators of the success rates of health and social service treatment programs may take the form of recidivism rates. Such data might need to be obtained from hospitals, police, courts, and other health and social service agencies where "failed" clients end up.
  — indicators on bringing criminals to justice need information from prosecutors and/or court systems on the dispositions of arrests (often difficult for other agencies to access).

Customer Surveys

Customers—whether citizens, clients, or businesses—are an important source of information about service quality and outcomes. A major way to obtain reliable feedback from customers is through professionally prepared surveys.[3] Exhibit 7-1 lists the variety of information obtainable from such surveys.

Statistically valid surveys of customers, properly designed and implemented, are an excellent way to obtain information on such outcomes as customer condition, behavior, experiences, and satisfaction—especially after customers have completed services. Complaint data, while useful, do not cover the full range of information on service performance, because complainers are not likely to be representative of the full population of

EXHIBIT 7-1

Information Obtainable from Customer Surveys

1. Customer condition and attitudes after receiving services, as well as the results of those services
2. Customer action or behavior after receiving program services
3. Overall satisfaction with a service
4. Ratings of specific service quality characteristics
5. Extent of service use
6. Extent of awareness of services
7. Reasons for dissatisfaction with, or for not using, services
8. Suggestions for improving services
9. Demographic information on customers

those served. (Only some people complain.) Focus groups are not designed to collect statistically representative data, though they are a very good way to help identify what outcomes should be measured and how to interpret data findings.

Advantages of Customer Surveys

- Surveys are often the most feasible, if not the only, way to obtain data for some outcomes. Much of the information listed in exhibit 7-1, for example, is unavailable from other sources.
- Surveys provide direct input from the program's customers, adding not only valuable information but also credibility.

Disadvantages of Customer Surveys

- Surveys require special expertise, especially for development of the questionnaire and sampling plan and for training of interviewers.
- Surveys can require more time and are more costly than other forms of data collection, especially if the work is contracted out.
- Evidence based on respondents' perceptions and memory may be less convincing than data obtained from agency records.
- Some customers may not respond or will not be honest in their responses. This potential problem can be alleviated by well-worded questions and good interviewing. It is also alleviated with regularly repeated performance measurement, assuming the proportion of disaffected customers is likely to be about the same in each instance, with no significant net effect on measured changes over time.

Content of Customer Surveys

The types of information listed in exhibit 7-1 fall into five major categories:

Questions providing data on outcomes (items 1–4). Responses to these questions provide the data for both end and intermediate outcome indicators. Questions can ask about *specific* service delivery characteristics (to help program personnel identify specific service problems) and *overall* service ratings.

Questions seeking information about the type and amount of the service used (item 5). For some programs, amount of service can be used as an outcome indicator (such as to calculate the number and percent of families who used a park, library, or public transit service at least once during the past month). These data can also be used to relate service outcomes to the types and amounts of services respondents received. (If the agency links the service information from its records to individual survey respondents, it can use data from agency records for this purpose. This option allows the survey questionnaire to be shorter and is presumably more accurate, since it does not rely on respondents' memories of services received.)

Diagnostic questions (items 6 and 7). These questions ask why respondents gave particular answers or ratings, especially unfavorable ones.[4] In addition to being used in the performance measurement process, an edited list of such responses should be provided to program personnel, anonymously of course, to help them identify needed improvements. The information can also be used to construct more detailed outcome indicators, such as percentages of people who did not use the service in the past year for particular reasons.

Requests for suggestions on improving the service (item 8). It is good practice to ask respondents at the end of the questionnaire for suggestions for improvement. These suggestions should also be provided, again anonymously, to program personnel.

Questions seeking demographic information (item 9). Demographic information allows the program to break responses out by specific customer characteristics. For a school program, for example, relevant characteristics could include grade level, age, gender, school lunch participation status, disability status, race or ethnicity, state, urban versus rural versus suburban school system, and so on. (Chapter 8 discusses uses for demographic breakouts.)

Survey All Potential Customers or Only Service Users?

A program needs to decide what kind of survey to use: a survey of the full population in its jurisdiction (called here "household surveys"), a survey of its own customers only (called here "user surveys"), or both.

Household surveys include representative samples of all potential customers in a jurisdiction, regardless of whether they have used the services about which they are being asked. *User surveys* are administered to customers who have actually used the particular service. (User surveys can seek responses from all customers or a representative sample.)

Advantages of Household Surveys over User Surveys

- Household surveys can obtain information about several services simultaneously.
- If surveys cover several services, their costs can be shared among agencies, reducing the costs to each.
- They can obtain information from and about nonusers, enabling programs to estimate *rates of participation* by different types of households.[5]
- They can obtain feedback from nonusers on reasons a service is not used.
- Since they are usually administered centrally, they are likely to have better quality control.
- They are less of a burden on individual agencies. In addition to being usually administered centrally, they do not require information on the addresses or telephone numbers of specific agency customers.

Advantages of User Surveys over Household Surveys

- User surveys usually can provide more in-depth information on a particular service because users are familiar with it and do not need to be asked about other services.
- Sample selection is easier because addresses and/or telephone numbers of users are usually available to the agency. For household surveys, the sample needs to be drawn from some census of households or businesses.
- They can sometimes be conducted at the facilities customers use (such as parks, libraries, public assistance offices, and schools).
- Higher response rates are likely because users have a personal interest in and knowledge of the service.
- They are likely to be less expensive because of the advantages cited above.
- The information is likely to be considerably more useful to program personnel because it is more extensive and detailed.

Examples of Customer Survey Questionnaires

- Exhibit 7-2 is a very simple user questionnaire. An on-site, written user survey that has been used by the Long Beach, California, Community

EXHIBIT 7-2

A Simple User Questionnaire

How Are We Doing?

Date _____

The quality of service I received today was:

HELPFULNESS				Please circle one
1	**2**	**3**	**4**	**5**
Unsatisfactory		Satisfactory		Excellent

WAIT TIME				Please circle one
1	**2**	**3**	**4**	**5**
Unsatisfactory		Satisfactory		Excellent

The primary reason for my visit was:

_____

Comments _____

_____

_____

_____

(Use reverse side for additional comments)

Optional _____

Name   Date

FOR STAFF USE ONLY

Action taken _____

_____

_____

_____

Name   Date

Development Agency, this questionnaire is about as short as one can be. It asks service users to provide comments and suggestions for improvement, but it does not ask about any end outcomes. Note that the questionnaire also calls for identification by the agency of any action taken.

- Exhibit 7-3 is an extract from a questionnaire for users of specific public facilities. Originally designed to obtain feedback on park and recreation facilities in Saint Petersburg, Florida, it asks about particular aspects of services, as well as an overall satisfaction rating. Such questions can be readily adapted to most types of services and facilities.

EXHIBIT 7-3

Survey of Facility Users

How Would You Rate the Following?	Excellent	Good	Fair	Poor
1. Hours of operation	☐	☐	☐	☐
2. Cleanliness	☐	☐	☐	☐
3. Condition of equipment	☐	☐	☐	☐
4. Crowdedness	☐	☐	☐	☐
5. Safety conditions	☐	☐	☐	☐
6. Physical attractiveness	☐	☐	☐	☐
7. Variety of programs	☐	☐	☐	☐
8. Helpfulness of personnel	☐	☐	☐	☐
9. Overall	☐	☐	☐	☐

- For internal support activities, other government staff and departments are customers. Exhibit 7-4 is a written survey that Seattle, Washington's Fleet Services Division used for its motor pool. Seattle has also undertaken surveys for other internal services, such as its copy center, janitorial services, and personnel. All customers were given a copy of the survey when they obtained a vehicle and were asked to complete it and send it back. This survey was printed on heavy paper with the return address printed on the outside. To return it, the user had only to fold the form and put it in the interoffice mail. Similar fold-over forms can be used for brief mail surveys to citizens.
- Exhibit 7-5 shows three questions from a mail survey of customers of family counseling services, used by what was then called the Family Services Association of America.

These questions illustrate the multiple types of information that can be obtained from surveys:

— The first question focuses only on satisfaction with the client's counselor. It does not ask about the results of the service, so it provides only information on an *intermediate outcome.*

— The second question asks for information about customer improvement, an *end outcome* indicator.

— The third question asks respondents to identify the extent to which the agency's service *contributed* to the improvement (as the respondents saw it). This is also an end outcome indicator, but it has the additional value of providing information on the extent to which the

EXHIBIT 7-4

**Department of Administrative Services Fleet Division
Motor Pool Customer Service Checklist**

1. How often do you use the pool?
   ☐ Daily   ☐ Weekly   ☐ Monthly   ☐ Other

2. For this trip, did you call to make a reservation?   ☐ Yes   ☐ No

3. Was a car available when you needed it?   ☐ Yes   ☐ No

4. If not, how long did you have to wait? _____

5. Have you ever been turned down when you wanted to use a car?   ☐ Yes   ☐ No
   If yes, what did you do?

   ☐ Waited until a car was available   ☐ Used a private car

   ☐ Other: _____

   _____

6. Was the car clean?   ☐ Yes   ☐ No

7. Was the car in good mechanical condition?   ☐ Yes   ☐ No

8. Were you treated courteously by motor pool staff?   ☐ Yes   ☐ No

9. Please rate our quality of service:
   ☐ Excellent   ☐ Good   ☐ Fair   ☐ Poor

Comments or suggestions: _____

_____

_____

_____

_____

_____

Name: _____ Department: _____ Phone: _____

Please fold in half and send back to DAS in interoffice mail. This form is preaddressed. If you have any questions or need additional information, please call 684-0137. Thank you.

Source: City of Seattle.

program has caused the outcome. The responses from questions 2 and 3 can be combined into the following end outcome indicator: "Percent of clients reporting [a particular level] of improvement AND reporting that agency services contributed to the changes reported."

By now, survey questionnaires have been prepared and administered on almost every public service. As a starting point for developing their own questionnaire, readers can search the Internet and various literature for questionnaires on the service in which they are interested.

EXHIBIT 7-5

Mail Survey Questions on Family Counseling

1. How satisfied were you with the way you and your counselor got along with each other?
   - Very satisfied
   - Satisfied
   - No particular feelings one way or the other
   - Somewhat dissatisfied
   - Very dissatisfied

2. Since you started at the agency, has there been any change for better or worse in the way the members of your family get along with each other? Would you say you now get along:
   - Much better
   - Somewhat better
   - Same
   - Somewhat worse
   - Much worse

3. How do you feel the service provided by the agency influenced the changes you have reported?
   - Helped a great deal
   - Helped some
   - Made no difference
   - Made things somewhat worse
   - Made things much worse

Survey Administration Methods and Their Trade-Offs

Mail surveys. This is a low-cost method, including second and third mailings and/or telephone follow-ups to secure response rates high enough to yield reliable information. Mail questionnaires are not, of course, useful for respondents who cannot read them. (For people who do not speak English, the questionnaire would need to be translated into their native language.) To obtain satisfactory completion rates, mail questionnaires generally need to be short and simple. Cluttered, complex questionnaires and questionnaires that are longer than four to five pages are likely to yield excessively low response rates. Response rates are likely to be much higher among people who have used the particular service than among a general sample of households in the area. (See exhibit 7-6 for ways to increase response rates to mail surveys.)

Telephone surveys. Telephone surveys can achieve good response rates from households at lower cost than the in-person alternative. They are more expensive than mail surveys because they require considerable interviewer time and training. They cannot cover populations without telephone access or people who do not speak English (but foreign language

EXHIBIT 7-6

Suggestions for Increasing Response Rates to Mail Surveys

- Include a transmittal letter signed by a respected, high-level official. Guarantee complete confidentiality of responses. Address the letter to a specific individual whenever feasible.
- Emphasize the need for information *from customers* to *improve future services.*
- Mail an advance postcard notifying recipients that they will soon receive a questionnaire and asking explicitly for their help.
- Keep the questionnaire short and easy to use. Make sure each question has a clear purpose and stick primarily to response categories that only require a check mark. Open-ended questions (requiring an answer in the respondent's own words), though rich in information, should be limited to a very small number.
- Keep skip patterns (instructions to respondents to skip certain questions depending on their response to a previous question) to *an absolute minimum,* and when unavoidable *be sure skip patterns are crystal clear.*
- Go for a professional, polished look. Even if the questionnaire is prepared in-house, it should look typeset and be printed on high-quality, preferably colored paper. *Cutting corners by using low-quality copiers and so forth risks unacceptable response rates.*
- Enclose a stamped, self-addressed envelope in each questionnaire mailing.
- Use two or three mailings. One mailing is seldom enough. Postcard and telephone reminders can also be used, especially for small samples.

interviewers can be used if resources are available to translate the questionnaire and for foreign-language interviewers).

Phone surveys have faced considerably lower response rates in recent years, due to such factors as increasing use of answering machines, people's greater resistance to phone surveys, and greater use of cell phones. Cell phones pose particular problems because their phone numbers may be unavailable for sampling, and cell phone providers often charge users for each call. These factors are less of a problem for user surveys, where the agency sponsoring the survey has contact information on those to be surveyed and has gained the trust and cooperation of its customers.

In-person surveys administered at the respondent's home or business. These surveys tend to yield high response rates and can provide detailed information since they can be longer and more complicated than mail questionnaires. Except in developing countries, where labor is inexpensive, they are the most costly to administer and are usually too expensive for repeatedly collecting the data needed for performance measurement.

In-person surveys administered at a service facility. In-person survey administration at a facility—such as a park, library, school, or social service agency—has the advantages of obtaining high response rates without the high cost of finding respondents at their homes or businesses.[6] This option is a good one if the primary purpose of the survey is to capture the quality of the person's immediate experience at the site. It cannot, by definition, be used for outcomes that occur after the customer leaves the facility. However, respondents can also be asked about previous experiences with the service.

The survey might ask respondents only about the services provided by the facility or about other services. For example, the Centers for Disease Control and Prevention of the U.S. Department of Health and Human Services have used the method effectively in surveying school-age children in school facilities on a number of health risk factors (such as tobacco and drug use, physical inactivity, and unhealthful dietary behaviors). These surveys yield intermediate outcome indicators on important health and safety programs.

Internet surveys. An emerging option is to tap the increasing access of organizations and families to personal computers. These surveys are increasingly being used for surveys of *organizations* (such as of government agencies and in surveys by government agencies of businesses) and for populations expected to have ready access to a computer. For example, the University of North Carolina has used Internet surveys to survey its students about several university services. The Corporation for National and Community Service has used the Internet to survey its AmeriCorps members about the quality of their experiences in AmeriCorps.

When applicable, Internet surveys often can be done at low cost. They require effort to obtain adequate response rates, however, perhaps including advance or follow-up mailed postcards to encourage completion of the questionnaire.

The primary obstacles to widespread use of Internet surveys are many households' lack of ready access to computers and interest in using their computers, even if available. But access and interest are both growing, so Internet surveys are likely to become more widely used.

Combination of survey methods. A good option often is to use combinations of methods. For example, mailings can be supplemented with telephone calls to people who failed to respond to follow-up mailings, mail or telephone might be used to supplement online surveys, and so on.

Mixing survey methods raises the question of the accuracy of combining responses from more than one method. The studies to date are far from conclusive about whether this significantly distorts the findings. Given the other issues, such as potential sampling errors and nonresponse biases, combining methods appears to be less of a concern.

Choosing among methods. In choosing which method is best, an agency needs to weigh the trade-offs between higher response rates (providing greater confidence that the findings represent the views of the population surveyed), larger sample sizes (providing greater precision), and cost of administration. *Whichever method is used, agencies should seek at least a 50 percent response rate.* (Techniques such as enclosing questionnaires with all utility bills will seldom yield high enough returns to make the data credible.)

How Many People to Survey

Surprisingly, for user surveys, it may be much less of a hassle, and involve less total effort, if a program surveys all its customers. For some programs, it may be feasible to survey all customers, such as by routinely mailing questionnaires to each customer. This will apply, for example, when a federal agency is surveying a small number of state agencies or when a small nonprofit organization seeks feedback on the outcomes of its services from its former clients. (If all a program's customers are surveyed, the program will not have to worry about possible sampling errors. The major remaining source of survey error comes from the possibility that if a large proportion of customers does not respond to the survey then the findings will not be sufficiently representative of all customers.)

When very large numbers of citizens, businesses, or clients are the population of interest, a sampling of the population is likely needed. The program will then have to decide on the sample size. Larger samples are needed if the program wants higher rates of precision, but high rates of precision are seldom needed in a customer survey. Larger samples will be needed if the program wants separate outcome information on a number of population subgroups. If, for example, the program wants outcome data for each of the 50 states, it will need to have large enough samples of respondents from each state to provide information at the desired level of precision. Materials such as those listed in the appendix have information on selecting sample sizes.

Whom to Survey

In general, *any single individual should be surveyed only once a year to avoid over-burdening citizens.* For household surveys this should not be a problem because those interviewed will make up only a very small percentage of those in the total population. For most household and user surveys, any one citizen or household typically need not be surveyed more than once a year.

Human services present some special issues. Should someone who came in only once be surveyed at all? The agency should probably establish *a minimum amount of service before the customer becomes part of those eligible to be surveyed.*

Even more of a problem is whether *former* customers should be surveyed. Many human services have as a major objective the improvement of an individual's or family's condition for a period well beyond when the customer receives services. To assess the outcomes, it is important to follow up with those customers at least once, such as 6 or 12 months later. This applies to such programs as employment, vocational rehabilitation, and mental health programs, as well as to programs that work with individual clients to get them to alter their risk behaviors, such as drug and alcohol abuse and smoking.[7]

For human services, the lack of follow-ups is a major gap, if not the most important gap, in current performance measurement in the United States, and probably the world. Obtaining feedback from former customers can be difficult. Agency records usually cannot help. Some programs have used recidivism indicators obtained from records or readmittances. The U.S. Department of Labor's Employment and Training Administration (ETA) has one of the few programs that follows up with customers after departure from the service. For many years, telephone interviews were required (13 weeks after exit) and were used to obtain data on earnings and success in retaining employment. However, ETA switched to using agency records: it currently asks each state government to use its unemployment insurance records for data on client employment and earnings after service exit (e.g., six months after exit).

Problems in surveying former clients include not having up-to-date contact information; even after contacting clients, not being able to obtain information from them; and the cost and effort of following up. Most human service programs resist doing follow-ups for these reasons, some because they believe it is not their responsibility. However, without such information, the real value of these programs can only be guessed at, and the program will have very limited information as to what works and what does not.

Much more can be done by individual human service programs, even small programs, than is realized. The above problems are considerably alleviated if programs include some form of "after care" activity. This is true even if the activity is only to undertake occasional contacts with former clients to find out how they are doing. Such activity will considerably improve the contact information and can also encourage those former clients to participate in the follow-up. Exhibit 7-7 provides a number of suggestions for increasing the likelihood that reasonable response rates can be obtained in a follow-up effort by a human service agency—and without much cost.[8]

For regular performance measurement, however, it is not likely to be practical for a program to keep track of former customers much beyond 12 months after they have left the service. For longer periods or in-depth studies, program evaluations are more likely to be appropriate.

EXHIBIT 7-7

Tips for Obtaining Follow-up Information from Former Clients

- Keep questionnaires short, attractive, and easy to complete.
- Notify clients in service of the need for follow-up information.
- Before clients depart service, obtain post-service contact information. Also obtain contact information for people (close friends, for example) who are likely to know the clients' contact information for six months to a year after their exit.
- Establish a rapport with clients to help gain their cooperation. At exit, give a choice of follow-up by phone, mail, or in person. Make sure that clients are comfortable with efforts to keep client information confidential. At exit, give clients a reminder card, indicating when, where, and how the questionnaire or interviews will be administered. Include the incentive for providing a completed questionnaire.
- Give clients who want to remain anonymous a code name so they can still complete the survey and receive the incentive.
- Maintain contact with clients after discharge. Mail them greeting cards with a reminder that they will be contacted within a specific time frame to schedule the follow-up.
- During any after-service contacts, obtain updated contact information, remind former clients of the need for the follow-up information, and encourage them to complete and deliver the questionnaire by the due date.
- Provide modest incentives for returning completed questionnaires. Try multiple mailings or phone calls in administering the follow-up. Also, provide multiple reminders (two to three) to complete the survey. Don't give up too soon.

Source: Ritu Nayyar-Stone and Harry Hatry, *Finding Out What Happens to Former Clients* (Washington, DC: The Urban Institute, 2003).

Tips on Customer Survey Design and Administration

- *Establish a working group to help develop content.* This group should include key service agency representatives, perhaps a representative of the chief administrative officer, a survey expert, and a spokesperson for program customers.
- *Beware of biased or muddled wording.* Always have a professional survey expert review final question wording and sequencing.
- *Always test a questionnaire on a small number of customers* before full implementation to catch (a) awkward, ambiguous, or redundant questions; (b) confusing or incorrect instructions; and (c) wording that sounds offensive or just plain foolish.
- *Translate questionnaires* if substantial numbers of the desired respondents are unlikely to speak English.
- *Use outside contractors for the administration of regular surveys if resources are available.* Contracting out is usually easier than in-house administration, even for a mail questionnaire. Suggestions about what to include in a survey contract are provided in exhibit 7-8.

EXHIBIT 7-8

Elements to Include in Contracts for Customer Surveys

- Number of *completed* questionnaires, including minimum sizes for each major category of customer for whom data are sought, and minimum acceptable response rates.
- Survey administration details, such as (a) whether mail, telephone, or both are to be used; (b) the number of mailings or number of follow-up telephone calls; and (c) the time between mailings and telephone follow-ups.
- Contractor's role in questionnaire development.
- The amount of testing of the questionnaire that the contractor will do.
- Provisions for maintaining respondent confidentiality.
- Any special coding to be done by the contractor (e.g., transforming location data provided by respondents into a more compact grouping of geographical areas).
- Specification of how tabulations are to be handled, such as whether "not applicables" and "don't knows" should be included in the denominators for the percents calculated.
- Products, and their formats, that will be provided to the agency. Products should include, at a minimum, (a) a detailed description of survey procedures used and response rates achieved, (b) frequency counts for each question, and (c) a fully legible printout of the responses for each returned questionnaire (with confidentiality preserved) in case the agency wants to do any of its own tabulations.
- Time frame for the work.
- Any restriction on release of the data to the media.
- Overall cost.

- *Keep to a minimum changes in questions and question wording from year to year.* Changes compromise the year-to-year comparability of the findings.

Ways to Reduce Survey Costs

Survey costs depend on the number of people surveyed, the frequency of the survey, the mode of administration, and efforts to increase response (and completion rates). Here are suggested ways to cut survey costs:

- *If the population represented is large, sample it rather than surveying everyone.* When a program has only a small number of customers (perhaps no more than one or two hundred each year), it is likely easier to survey all of them. But when very large numbers of citizens, businesses, or clients are the customers, selecting a representative sample is an efficient way to go.
- *Reduce required sample size by avoiding excessive precision.* For most programs, 95 or 99 percent confidence limits are overkill. While 95 percent limits are the standard in the academic community, they are likely excessive for most performance measurement work. Ninety percent lim-

its are likely sufficient. The required sample size will increase as precision requirements increase.

- *Do not seek higher response rates than you really need.* Statisticians often recommend achieving response rates of around 75 percent. A 50 percent response rate is likely adequate for most outcome measurement work. Survey administration costs rise steeply as response rate requirements increase.

- *Use agency personnel when appropriate and possible.* However, do *not* use as interviewers staff who are delivering the service. This undermines survey credibility.

- *Use the mail to administer the survey if you have mailing addresses for most customers. If the sample size is small, administer the mail survey in house.*

- *Use or adapt questionnaires that are already available.* Surveys might, for example, be available through the Internet, from other agencies in other locations, or from universities. After a questionnaire has been developed, keep it reasonably stable from year to year. It should be used to obtain the same data on the same performance indicators in future reporting periods. This practice avoids the need to invest in major new questionnaire development efforts.

- *Shorten the questionnaire.* Agencies are tempted, once they have decided to survey citizens, to add more and more subject matter and details. Be firm and consider the potential usefulness of each question. Another procedure is to identify some questions not likely to change much between questionnaire administrations. Rotate such questions, including them perhaps in every other administration.

- *Look for expert help within the agency* or other low-cost sources.

- *Use commercially available software for tabulations.*

- *Use volunteers to administer surveys whenever possible.* This is particularly practical for private, nonprofit agencies. Be warned, however, that volunteers need extensive training and may not be dependable. They also need to be carefully monitored.

- *Do not attempt to cover every category of customer in the sample.* Consider dropping groups that (a) are extremely costly to survey, (b) are only a very small proportion of the population of interest, and (c) are not vital to the survey objectives. Be sure that all such omissions are clearly identified in survey reports.

- *Add questions to already scheduled surveys, such as those of other agencies or universities.* For example, city (or county) governments might collect questions from a number of their agencies into one community household survey. Programs with related functions (such as various public or private child development programs) might develop a joint questionnaire and questionnaire administration process. State agencies might be able to add questions at low cost to existing statewide surveys administered by universities.

Trained Observer Ratings

Trained observers are used to rate outcome conditions that can be perceived by the eyes or other physical senses of an observer.[9] The physical observation can be through any of the five senses (sight, hearing, smell, taste, touch). Since most public-sector applications use sight, the text discussion focuses primarily on visual ratings.

The key element for performance measurement is that the rating scales and procedures provide values that are reliable enough to withstand challenge. The goal is to ensure that different observers at different times give the same or similar ratings to similar conditions.

The following elements are needed to ensure a high degree of reliability:

- Systematic rating scales that provide well-defined yardsticks against which the observers can assess conditions
- Adequate training and supervision of the observers and the process
- Periodic checking of the quality of the ratings

For trained observer ratings to be a suitable performance measurement procedure, the outcome needs to be measurable by physical observation and reliable on a scale that identifies several variations of the condition to be measured.

Inspections have traditionally been used to assess health, fire, and food safety at various facilities. For the most part, however, these findings were not aggregated to provide regular condition assessment ratings. In recent years, trained observer procedures have been used to track systematically these and other conditions. Trained observer ratings have been used for assessing the cleanliness of streets, condition of roads, condition of parks and playgrounds, condition of facilities (such as schools, hospitals, and prisons), condition of traffic signals and signs, and quality of food served to customers.

New York City has what is probably the longest running trained observer operation in the world. Since 1974, it has undertaken regular (currently daily) cleanliness ratings of a large sample of city streets. Its "service inspectors" use a seven-point photographic rating scale and enter the data into handheld computers. The data are uploaded into the computer at the end of the day to provide current reports for each of the city's sanitation districts.

The Fund for the City of New York, a nonprofit organization, has also been regularly providing trained observer ratings on a large number of New York City "street-level" conditions. These conditions include such items as rubbish collection, traffic and street light maintenance, tree plantings, graffiti, abandoned cars, rodent control, and potholes. The findings are reported to the government agencies and other organizations responsible for correcting the problems. Two examples of such reports are presented in chapter 11's discussion of operational uses of performance information.

New York City (for a number of years) and San Francisco (more recently) have both been using trained observer procedures to regularly assess the condition of their parks. In New York, the rating scales use detailed written descriptions. San Francisco's scale uses a combination of photographs and written descriptions.[10]

In Albania, as of 2005, seven local governments had used systematic ratings of the condition of their school buildings to set their budgets. Local government staff, teachers, and parents were trained in the technique and did the ratings.

Trained observer procedures are used for human services as well. For many years, agencies have rated the ability of clients with physical and mental problems to undertake basic activities of daily living. Another example are teachers' "readiness-to-learn" ratings of children in a number of states. These ratings are based on both physical observations and oral communications.

Kindergarten teachers in North Carolina have periodically assessed children on 40 characteristics based on their observations of each child in their classes. The data collection instrument uses a 1 to 5 scale (never, seldom, sometimes, often, or always) to rate physically observable items on each child's pre-academic and social skills—such as whether the child recognizes his or her own name in print, hurts other children or animals for no apparent reason, and speaks in sentences of more than three words. Averages and other statistics are calculated from the ratings, which are also used to measure time trends.[11]

In Georgia, children enrolled in kindergarten are assessed for first-grade readiness using an instrument that assesses literacy, mathematics, and social/emotional development in a variety of one-on-one, small group, and large group instructional settings throughout the school year. Each child is rated on about 32 skills by whether the skill is not evident, is in progress, or is accomplished.[12]

Advantages of Trained Observer Ratings

- Trained observer ratings can provide reliable, reasonably accurate ratings of conditions that are otherwise difficult to measure.
- Periodic ratings can be used to help allocate program resources throughout the year. *The findings can be used not only for periodic performance reporting but also to guide early fixes of problem conditions.* For example, the New York City Sanitation Department has for many years used trained observer ratings of street cleanliness to help allocate and reallocate its street-cleaning crews over time. The information provided by the ratings could be used to establish work orders aimed at correcting problems identified by the ratings.
- If handheld computers are used to record the ratings in the field, the data can be uploaded by the end of each day and reports made available to supervisors very quickly.
- The data can be presented in an easy-to-understand format, which is important in reaching officials and the public.

Disadvantages of Trained Observer Ratings

- They are labor-intensive procedures that require significant personnel time, including time for training observers.
- If the people doing the ratings are the same people delivering the service, the results will likely lack credibility. For example, some social service and mental health agencies have used caseworkers to rate their own clients' progress on selected condition scales. This rating does not require significant added expense and is appropriate for internal tracking of client progress. However, for external performance measurement purposes, using an agency's own caseworkers should be avoided because their potential self-interest in the ratings reduces the perceived, if not the actual, credibility of the results.
- Observers need to be checked periodically to ensure that they are adhering to the procedures adds costs.

Added Operational Use of Trained Observers: Identify Needed Early Corrective Action

As noted in the advantages, the trained observer process might be extended to provide corrective action information. Observers would be asked to suggest the needed corrective action and how soon action is needed. For example, observers rating streets, parks, or building conditions might be asked to rate each problem using a scale such as the following:

1. No action needed
2. Only minor improvement needed; no immediate action needed
3. Only minor, but immediate, action should be taken
4. Major, but not immediate, improvements are needed
5. Major action needed immediately (hazardous to health or safety)

To determine the priorities for action, program officials would also need to consider such information as the number of people affected and the cost of correcting the problem. Where the trained observers are expected to be sufficiently knowledgeable, they might also be asked to estimate the time and resources needed to correct the problem.

Types of Rating Systems

Trained observers use three major types of rating systems:

- Written descriptions
- Photographs
- Other visual scales, such as drawings or videos

Written descriptions. This type of system, the simplest and most familiar type, depends entirely on specific written descriptions of each grade used in the rating scale.

An abbreviated written scale for building or street cleanliness is the following:

- Rating 1: **Clean.** Building or street is completely or almost completely clean; a maximum of three pieces of litter per floor or block is present.
- Rating 2: **Moderately clean.** Building or street is largely clean; a few pieces of isolated litter or dirt are observable.
- Rating 3: **Moderately dirty.** Some scattered litter or dirt is present.
- Rating 4: **Dirty.** Heavy litter or dirt is present in several locations throughout the building or along the block.

The Metropolitan Transit Authority's New York City Transit and a citizen's group, the Straphangers Campaign, have been providing annual scorecards that provide information on each of the 22 New York City subway lines.[13] Each line is rated on the reliability of its train service, the chance of getting a seat, and the quality of subway car announcements. The data are obtained from agency records and trained observer ratings by travelers who come from departments not directly affected by the findings.[14] A scorecard for one subway line is presented in chapter 11.

Assessing the need for repairs is an additional, very important use for outcome information from observer ratings. The city of Toronto used the information obtained from the scale in exhibit 7-9 not only to help track road conditions but also to determine what repairs were needed in each location, as noted in the right-hand column comments. That is, the ratings were used for performance measurement and for determining needed actions.

EXHIBIT 7-9

Condition Rating

Rating	Condition	Description	Comments
9	Excellent	No fault whatsoever	
8	Good	No damage, normal wear, and small cracks	Recently constructed work
7	Fair	Slight damage, crackfill or minor leveling required	Average rating for City of Toronto pavements and sidewalks
6	Repair	10% of complete replacement cost	Pavement requires preventive overlay. Level of Tolerance for City of Toronto pavements
5	Repair	25% of complete replacement cost	
4	Repair	50% of complete replacement cost	Eligible for reconstruction programme. Condition Rating 4—Level of Tolerance for City of Toronto curbs and sidewalks
3	Repair	75% of complete replacement cost	Total reconstruction probably indicated
2	Repair	More than 75% of complete replacement cost	
1	Impossible to repair		Requires complete reconstruction

Performance Measurement: Getting Results

Photographs. Photographic scales can be more precise than written scales in clearly defining each rating grade. Generic photos are used to represent grades on the rating scale. Observers are given (and trained in the use of) a set of photos, with several representing *each grade* on the rating scale.

Exhibit 7-10 is an extract from a 16-photograph scale (four photographs for each grade) that was used in Dehradun, India. Such photographic rating scales have been used for many years by New York City's Sanitation Department to track street cleanliness.

Other visual scales. Visual rating scales can also use drawings or sketches that represent each grade on a rating scale. Exhibit 7-11 provides sketches representing conditions of school buildings—in this case, the condition of schoolroom walls. This rating scale was used by the New York City school system to track the physical condition of its schools and to help make decisions about building repairs.

Implementing a Trained Observer Process

Implementing a trained observer process requires the following steps:

- Decide what conditions should be rated.
- Develop a rating scale for each condition. If possible, adapt an existing scale. Use photographs and written guidelines as appropriate.
- Determine which facilities or areas should be rated, when, and how frequently. Ratings can be applied to all or selected facilities or areas. If resources are only available to rate a subset of locations, choose the subset by random sampling so the locations chosen will be representative.
- Select and train observers, who might be program personnel, college or graduate school students, or volunteers. Technical ratings, such as safety hazards, will require observers with the requisite professional training.
- Test the scale and observers on a small number of sites in the facility or area to make sure reasonably trained observers give consistent ratings.
- Establish procedures for supervising the observers and for recording, transcribing, and processing the data they collect.
- Conduct the ratings regularly.
- Establish procedures for systematically checking the ratings of trained observers to provide quality control. One way to do this is for the supervisor to check periodically a small sample of each observer's ratings.
- Develop and disseminate reports on the findings from each set of ratings for the current period and changes from previous periods. The reports

EXHIBIT 7-10

Photographic Scale of Street Litter Conditions

Condition 1 = Clean; 2 = Moderately clean; 3 = Moderately littered; 4 = Heavily littered

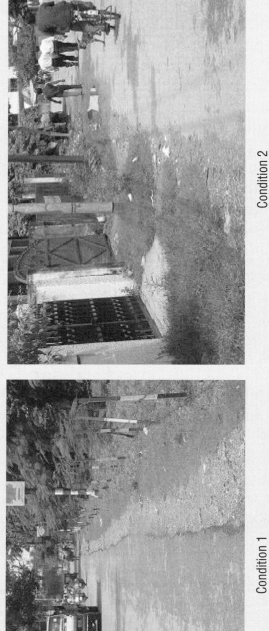

Condition 1

Condition 2

Condition 3

Condition 4

Source: City of Dehradun, India, 2005.

EXHIBIT 7-11

Trained Observer Rating Scale: Condition of School Classroom Walls

School Scorecard Rating Scale

Scale Value: 0

Scale Value: 1

Scale Value: 2

Scale Value: 3

Scale Value: 4

Scale Value: 5

Scale Value: 6

Source: New York City Department of Education.

should show the number and percent of locations that fell into particular rating categories. *Do not report only the average scores, which can hide very important distributional information.*

The following additional steps are needed for a photographic rating system:

- Take a large number of photographs in settings representative of the range of conditions to be rated. These photos should reflect the actual types of conditions the program wants to assess.
- Select a panel of judges made up of people with varied backgrounds who are not associated with the measurement activities. Select a set of familiar labels, each representing a condition that the program expects to find, such as clean, moderately clean, moderately dirty, and dirty. Ask the judges to sort the photographs into groups that represent each condition.
- For each condition, select the photographs (perhaps four or five) that the largest number of judges identified as representative. These photographs then become the rating scale.
- Develop written guidelines to accompany the photographs, if needed.
- Train observers in the use of the photographic scale and field-test it with those observers to determine the extent of agreement among them. Revise the ratings and procedures as needed.
- Develop the final scale. Package copies of the photographs selected for the final scale in a kit for each trained observer.

Automating Trained Observer Ratings

Handheld computers, available at surprisingly low prices, can be programmed to record observational data. This can considerably ease the amount of clerical work needed and reduce errors introduced by manual recording. New York City has been using such handheld computers to report on the condition of city buildings (including schools), as required to meet a legislative mandate. The Fund for the City of New York (a public interest organization) has also used handheld computers to collect data on several physically observable conditions in sample locations within the city. The conditions observed include, among others, defective street signs, abandoned cars, the presence of rodents or other pests, and defective street lights.[15] This information is used to identify both summary and specific conditions. Data entry, tabulations, and reports can be done quickly.

For some services, outcome information can be obtained by people acting as service customers. Using systematic guidelines, the role players assess the service organization's service delivery response. (This procedure can be considered a special form of trained observer procedures. However, it is sufficiently different to warrant its own discussion.)

This procedure is not widely used. It probably has been used more by performance audit agencies for ad hoc studies. But, role-playing also lends itself to regular performance measurement. Here are the two major types of applications for this procedure:[16]

- Assessing whether different citizen groups receive similar treatment or service from a public or private agency. For example, federal agencies, such as the departments of Labor, Housing and Urban Development, and Justice have used role-playing to assess the prevalence of discrimination, such as in employment, housing, and bank loans.
- Assessing the accuracy and quality of agency responses to requests for information, such as by the Internal Revenue Service, a state or local tourism agency, or any federal, state, or local agency.

For example, the District of Columbia's Office of Customer Service Operations hires external personnel to regularly test the quality of contacts with its agencies. The contacts may be face to face or by telephone, voice mail, or correspondence. The tester completes a rating form that assesses helpfulness, courtesy, knowledge, and etiquette (such as answering the call within three rings of the contact and checking back frequently with customer if the customer was put on hold). The tester rates most elements on a scale of 1 to 5, based on definitions developed by the Customer Service Office. An extract of the rating sheet is provided in exhibit 7-12. The Customer Service Office provides quarterly reports on the rating of each agency (and posts them on the Internet).

This procedure requires careful determination of what will be rated, instructions of what constitutes the various rating categories, and instructions on how the testers will do the ratings so similar circumstances will each be rated approximately the same by different testers.

For the more complex role playing, such as testing for discrimination, the role players need considerable training. (For discrimination applications, usually two players are paired. One plays the role of a minority, and one the majority, applicant. They would represent people with similar

EXHIBIT 7-12

Example of a Tester's Rating Scale

Explanation of Numerical Ratings for Agency Tester Calls

1. The service given is unacceptable
   — Courtesy: Operators use speakerphone, chew gum or food, carry on other conversations, or display brazen rudeness.
   — Knowledge: Operators demonstrate a complete lack of knowledge.
   — Etiquette: Operators do not answer calls in three rings, check with you after being on hold, transfer you more than once or without reference information, identify themselves, thank you for calling.
   — Overall Impression: Voice mail is reached or operators provide inferior service in all three criteria of courtesy, knowledge, and etiquette.
2. The service given is below average
   — Courtesy: Operators show minor irritation.
   — Knowledge: Operators have difficulty in finding basic information.
   — Etiquette: Operators do not answer calls in three rings, check with you after being on hold, transfer you more than once or without reference information, identify themselves, thank you for calling.
   — Overall Impression: Inferior service in courtesy, knowledge, and etiquette.
3. The service given is average and unremarkable
   — Courtesy: Operators are neither rude nor cheerful.
   — Knowledge: Basic knowledge is accurately provided.
   — Etiquette: Without enthusiasm or cheerfulness, operators make none of the mistakes outlined in the etiquette category in score 2.
   — Overall Impression: Operators answer questions, but the service is average.
4. The service given is above average
   — Courtesy: Operators are cheerful and friendly.
   — Knowledge: Operators provide useful information.
   — Etiquette: While maintaining a cheerful and friendly demeanor, operators make none of the mistakes outlined in the etiquette category in score 2.
   — Overall Impression: Superior service in courtesy, knowledge, and etiquette.
5. The service given is excellent
   — Courtesy: Operators show genuine concern and see calls through to resolution.
   — Knowledge: Operators know their respective agencies and resources very well.
   — Etiquette: Operators maintain a cheerful and friendly demeanor, put you at ease, and take care of your needs. Operators make none of the mistakes outlined in the etiquette category in score 2.
   — Overall Impression: Superior service in courtesy, knowledge, and etiquette; genuinely makes you feel good about your interaction.

Source: Government of the District of Columbia, Mayor's Office, "Telephone Tester Program," http://dc.gov/mayor/telephone_tester/rating.shtm.

qualifications and be as similar as possible other than in the discrimination characteristic being assessed.)

Special Technical Equipment

Special equipment is needed to collect data for outcome indicators that require scientific measurement, such as

- noise levels,
- air pollution levels,
- water pollution levels, or
- road conditions (using road meters).

Many state transportation agencies have been using road meters for years. The Fund for the City of New York used a special car outfitted with a "profilometer" to measure street roughness on a sample of 12 percent of the city's blocks. Exhibit 7-13 is a product of this initiative. Two outcome indicators were generated from these readings for each of the city's 59 community districts: a smoothness score (percent of blocks rated acceptable) and number of "significant jolts" encountered per mile.[17] (Acceptability was determined by correlating citizen ratings of sample blocks with the profilometer's readings.)

Advantages of Technical Equipment

- Appropriate technical equipment usually provides accurate, reliable data.
- It may be the only reasonable way to achieve fully credible information on important environmental outcomes such as those listed above. Programs can obtain subjective outcome data using trained observers or user surveys to assess the quality of roads, water, air, and so on, but such information is likely to lack the credibility, and validity, provided by technical measurement.

Disadvantages of Technical Equipment

- The equipment can be expensive to procure, operate, and maintain.
- The information obtained must be interpreted to be useful to program personnel and outsiders. For example, vertical displacement measurements need to be converted into an excellent, good, fair, or poor ride scale or similarly self-explanatory grouping, and air pollution measurements need

EXHIBIT 7-13

Use of Special Equipment to Measure Rideability
How Smooth Are New York City's Streets?

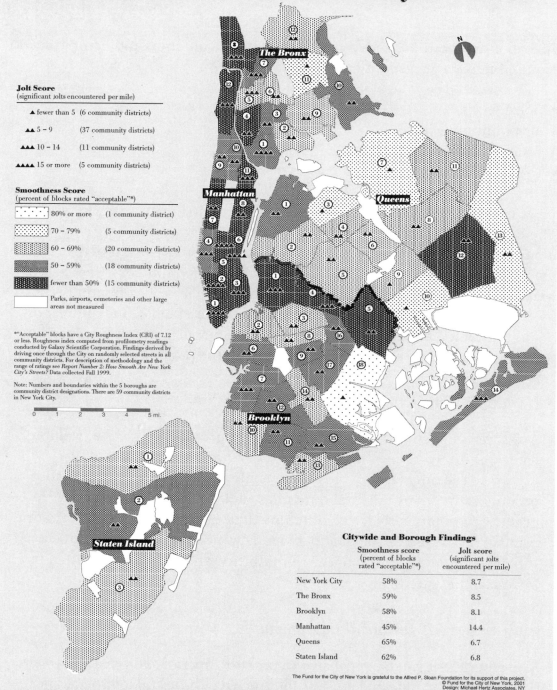

Jolt Score
(significant jolts encountered per mile)

▲ fewer than 5 (6 community districts)

▲▲ 5 – 9 (37 community districts)

▲▲▲ 10 – 14 (11 community districts)

▲▲▲▲ 15 or more (5 community districts)

Smoothness Score
(percent of blocks rated "acceptable"*)

80% or more (1 community district)

70 – 79% (5 community districts)

60 – 69% (20 community districts)

50 – 59% (18 community districts)

fewer than 50% (15 community districts)

Parks, airports, cemeteries and other large areas not measured

*"Acceptable" blocks have a City Roughness Index (CRI) of 7.12 or less. Roughness index computed from profilometry readings conducted by Galaxy Scientific Corporation. Findings derived by driving once through the City on randomly selected streets in all community districts. For description of methodology and the range of ratings see *Report Number 2: How Smooth Are New York City's Streets?* Data collected Fall 1999.

Note: Numbers and boundaries within the 5 boroughs are community district designations. There are 59 community districts in New York City.

0 1 2 3 4 5 mi.

Citywide and Borough Findings

	Smoothness score (percent of blocks rated "acceptable"*)	Jolt score (significant jolts encountered per mile)
New York City	58%	8.7
The Bronx	59%	8.5
Brooklyn	58%	8.1
Manhattan	45%	14.4
Queens	65%	6.7
Staten Island	62%	6.8

The Fund for the City of New York is grateful to the Alfred P. Sloan Foundation for its support of this project.
© Fund for the City of New York, 2001
Design: Michael Hertz Associates, NY

Source: Fund for the City of New York, Center on Municipal Government Performance, *How Smooth Are New York City's Streets?* (New York: Fund for the City of New York, 2001), 17.

to be converted into overall air quality levels understandable to the public, such as good, moderate, approaching unhealthful, and unhealthful.

Selecting Appropriate Data Sources and Data Collection Procedures

The following are criteria for selecting data collection procedures:

- *Cost.* This is always a primary concern. Sometimes bargain-basement procedures can be used effectively (such as mail rather than telephone surveys), depending on the response rates and types of data required. Also, some outcome indicators can ride the coattails of other procedures. For example, *data for several outcome indicators might be obtainable from a single customer survey; or, trained observers might be able to collect data simultaneously for a number of different outcome indicators,* such as street cleanliness, road bumpiness, and condition of traffic signs, with little added cost.
- *Feasibility.* This criterion covers identification of nonfinancial obstacles that are likely to make data collection very difficult or impossible. For example, if data are needed from other agencies, will they permit access to it?
- *Accuracy and reliability achievable with the procedure.*
- *Understandability.* The data should be understandable to program managers and people outside the program, including the public.
- *Credibility.* This includes the potential for data manipulation, especially by people with an interest in making the data look good (such as caseworkers assessing the results of their work with their own clients). Because of the potential for data manipulation, surveys by outside contractors are likely to be more credible than surveys administered by the agency itself. However, for cost reasons, many agencies will find it necessary to use their own resources to obtain outcome data, such as when surveying their clients or using trained observers. Such problems will be reduced if an agency uses agency personnel who are not delivering the service and has a data quality control process that is recognized as good. (See chapter 14 for further discussion of quality control issues.)

Pilot-Testing New Data Collection Procedures

All new or substantially modified data collection procedures should be pilot-tested to identify and eliminate bugs before full implementation. The pilot test should approximate the conditions that will exist during full implementation, but it will usually test the procedures only on some segments of the program. For example, a pilot test might cover

- only outcome indicators that are new or require substantial modifications to existing data collection procedures,
- only some activities,
- only some locations or customers, or
- only some part of a year.

The working group developing the performance measurement process should oversee this test if possible, working with program and project personnel to identify problems. Modifications should then be made to alleviate problems found in the pilot test—such as problems with the sampling plan, questionnaires and other data collection instruments, and individual outcome indicator definitions.

The program should keep track of the staff time and out-of-pocket costs required for the new procedures during the test and use this information to estimate the annual cost to the program. If this estimated cost is too high, the group should provide recommendations regarding possible elimination of particularly marginal outcome indicators, reduced sample sizes, shorter data collection instruments, and so on. The group should also be on the lookout for additional outcome indicators that should be tracked.

Other Potential Problems in Data Collection

These problems include the following:

- Definitions that are unclear to those responsible for collecting the information.
- Missing data. For example, an economic development program might not have a complete list of businesses served. If missing data are a major problem, the program may need to modify its record-keeping.
- Confidentiality requirements, such as permission from parents to survey their children. Such requirements can add considerably to the effort required to obtain data.

Resolutions may involve correcting the problem, deciding to delete an outcome indicator, or accepting less accuracy.

Frequency of Data Collection and Reporting

Programs need to think hard about how frequently their performance measurement data should be collected. Frequent collection and reporting is important for making the data useful to operating managers. However, higher frequency typically leads to higher cost. Some data need to be collected less frequently than others. For example, some information obtained from customer surveys, such as victimization rates, might not be expected to change for relatively long periods. Other indicators, such as number of traffic accidents or crimes reported, are tabulated and reported perhaps weekly but at least monthly. At the other end of the frequency scale, some data might be collected every other year.

The drive for accountability and performance information for budget planning has led agencies to focus on annual reporting. But *for the basic performance measurement purposes of helping managers monitor and seek continual program improvement, data collection at least quarterly should be the goal.* Quarterly program reporting has been common in government agencies for many years, but until recent years little reporting has included systematically collected data on outcomes.

With careful planning, quarterly data collection does not need to add substantially to costs. With agency records, for example, once the data have been computerized, frequent tabulations are feasible at minimal additional cost. Routine follow-up questionnaires sent to customers a certain period after service receipt (say, nine months) also may yield year-round data at little added cost.

For customer surveys, if sampling is used, consider splitting the annual sample size—defined by a budget constraint—into, say, four quarterly subsamples. A questionnaire would be administered to one-quarter of the eligible population during each quarter. This would give managers *more timely feedback and seasonal information.* The annual cost of the survey work would increase somewhat, about 10 percent more than if one large survey were conducted. The findings for each calendar quarter would be statistically less precise because the samples are smaller, but accumulating the data would yield annual data as precise as if the whole sample had been surveyed at a single point in time.[18]

Some outcomes need to be measured at a specific time after service started or was completed, as is the case for many social service programs. In these situations, the programs will probably need to collect outcome data throughout the year. The data can be tabulated at any useful intervals, such as monthly, bimonthly, or quarterly.

Questions whose responses are not expected to change appreciably from quarter to quarter, or even year to year, need not be asked every time. Agencies and their programs may also want to reserve space on the questionnaire for a small number of especially timely questions that are asked only once. These need not be performance measurement questions: they might seek opinions from citizens on policy or program changes that the agency or program is considering.

Final Comment

When choosing among data collection procedures by cost and accuracy, programs need to trade off a high degree of accuracy against less statistical precision. *It is better to be roughly right than precisely ignorant.*

References and Notes

1. Obtaining quantitative data is not always possible for all indicators. The program needs to be explicit about important outcomes for which there is no quantitative performance information and provide qualitative judgments about performance on those outcomes.
2. The term "archival data" is sometimes used to refer to the use of records.
3. Numerous reports are available that much more fully address the technical issues of surveys, such as sample size and selection, administrative procedures, data accuracy, and response rates. Some suggested readings are listed in the appendix.
4. In the authors' experience, questions asking for explanations for "good" ratings seldom yield much useful information. Every question is an added burden on respondents and requires added coding time by those processing the responses. Therefore, only asking respondents why they gave unfavorable responses is likely to be more practical.
5. Attendance counts are useful but do not indicate how many *different* people or households used the service during a particular reporting period unless the names of particular users are available and can be analyzed.
6. For administration at a facility that is not under the agency's immediate control, permission from the facility is required. For surveys of minors, parental permission may be required.
7. The American College of Mental Health Administration, in the 2001 report of its Accreditation Organization Workgroup, included as one measurement "The rate of persons served who are better, worse, or unchanged at a standard interval following the termination of treatment compared to the termination of treatment" ("A Proposed Consensus Set of Indicators for Behavioral Health," page 35). Similarly, CARF, the Rehabilitation Accreditation Commission (Tucson, AZ), in both its 2001 Medical Rehabilitation and its 2001 Employment and Community Services standards manuals, called for accredited service organizations to follow up with their former clients.
8. One of the few documents that addresses the issue of follow-ups for performance measurement is *Finding Out What Happens to Former Clients* by Ritu Nayyar-Stone and Harry Hatry (Washington, DC: The Urban Institute, 2003).
9. For further details on trained observer procedures, see John Greiner, "Trained Observer Ratings," chapter 8 in *Handbook of Practical Program Evaluation*, 2nd edition, edited by Joseph S. Wholey, Harry Hatry, and Kathryn Newcomer (San Fran-

cisco: Jossey-Bass Publishers, 2004); and Harry Hatry and others, *How Effective Are Your Community Services? Procedures for Measuring Their Quality*, 3rd edition (Washington, DC: International City/County Manager's Association and the Urban Institute, 2006), especially chapter 10 and appendix 6.

10. See New York City Department of Parks and Recreation, "Park Inspection Program Standards: Guide to the Parks Inspection Program and Official Inspection Standards," Office of Operations and Management Planning, March. Every two weeks upper-level management reviews the inspection-summary reports to discuss problem areas and what can be done to improve them. Some of the data are also included in the annual Mayor's Management Reports to citizens. As of early 2006, the department was developing a similar trained observer process for its recreation centers. For San Francisco, see San Francisco Recreation and Park Department, "Park Maintenance Standards: The Manual and Evaluation Form," May 3, 2005.

11. Kelly Maxwell, Donna Bryant, Lynette Keyes, and Kathleen Bernier, *Kindergartners' Skills in Smart Start Counties in 1995: A Baseline from Which to Measure Change* (Chapel Hill: The University of North Carolina, 1997). The checklist was adapted from the Maryland Systematic Teacher Observation Inventory, an instrument developed by the Maryland Department of Education.

12. Georgia Department of Education, "Kindergarten Assessment Program–Revised (GKAP-R)," Atlanta, Georgia, revised April 2003.

13. See http://www.straphangers.org for a description of New York City's Straphangers Campaign scorecard.

14. The Straphangers Campaign web site (http://www.straphangers.org) describes the methodology.

15. Fund for the City of New York, *Computerized Neighborhood Environment Tracking* (New York: Fund for the City of New York, 1999).

16. For more extensive details on the procedures and their application, see Margery Turner and Wendy Zimmermann, "Role Playing," chapter 11 in *Handbook of Practical Program Evaluation*, 2nd edition, edited by Joseph Wholey et al. (San Francisco: Jossey-Bass, 2004).

17. Fund for the City of New York, Center on Municipal Government Performance, *How Smooth Are New York City's Streets?* (New York: Fund for the City of New York, September 1998).

18. For example, an annual sample of 1,000 customers might be split into quarterly samples of 250 each. At a 90 percent confidence level, the sample size of 250 would yield a confidence interval of approximately +5.4 percentage points, versus +2.7 percentage points for the full sample of 1,000. If 50 percent of those sampled gave a certain rating to a particular service characteristic, the confidence intervals would be 44.6 percent to 55.4 percent for the quarter and 47.3 percent to 52.7 percent for the combined four quarters. If the first two quarters are added together, giving a total sample of 500, the confidence interval would be +3.8 percentage points. Further data and information on the trade-offs among sample sizes, confidence intervals, and confidence levels are given in Hatry et al., *Customer Surveys for Agency Managers*.

Part
III

Analysis and Use of Performance Information

Making Outcome Information Useful: Providing Indicator Breakouts

Producing data does not mean that they will be useful. The following elements should be included in a performance measurement system to help transform outcome data into really useful information:

- *Breakouts* (disaggregations) of the outcome data for each indicator
- *Comparisons* of the program's data to benchmark data
- *Explanations* of why the data are the way they are—particularly when they do not meet expectations
- *Clear presentation of the information* in understandable, user-friendly formats

This chapter discusses the first of these elements—how to choose outcome indicator breakouts for a program.[1]

Why Are Breakouts Important?

> **Caution:**
> Watch Out for Overly Aggregated Data!

Breakouts can reveal highly useful findings on performance that are hidden by aggregation. The average depth of a lake may be accurate, but can mislead as to how dangerous it is for swimming. Two functions of breakouts are particularly important.

First, breakouts can distinguish *differences in performance among relevant subgroups*. Identifying such differences is the first step toward asking

- why is *high* performance occurring in some places and not others? Answers to this question can lead to transferring successful practices to less successful work.
- why is *low* performance occurring in some places? Answers to this question can ensure that appropriate improvement options are identified and addressed.

Second, breakouts can help identify *inequities* among customer groups—situations in which some groups had significantly better outcomes than others. An agency or program can also use performance indicators that reflect the size of the gap between groups. For example, Minnesota's Department of Health had as a specific objective reducing the disparity in infant death rates between racial groups. The department periodically issued a "Populations of Color" report that included disparities by race and ethnicity on rate of low birth weight births, infant mortality, adequacy of prenatal care (an index based on the month care began, number of prenatal visits, and gestational age of the infant/fetus at the time of birth), teen birth rates, overall death rate, death rate by individual cause, cancer incidence rates, and percent without health insurance (for both all ages and for children).[2] The department used these data to help guide its allocation of resources.

Here are two examples of the questions programs need to address as they determine their breakouts:

- **For a state or local school system.** For which specific grades should outcome data be provided: groups of grades, such as K–6, 7–9, 10–12; every grade; or just those grades for which academic testing is commonly done? Should the data be divided by age groups rather than by grade, and if so, which ones? Should the outcome data be broken out by individual school districts? Individual schools?
- **For a water quality protection program.** If the Environmental Protection Agency wants intermediate outcome data on state progress, should the data be broken out by state, or is region sufficient? If region, how should the states be grouped? Should the data be provided by pollutant? If so, which ones? Should some outcomes be broken out by industry or business type?

Exhibit 8-1 lists basic breakout categories.

Each program is likely to have multiple performance indicators. Individual performance indicators can have different outcome data breakouts. For example, for police services, the performance indicator "counts of reported crime" might be broken out by type of crime, location, and time of day and day of week when the crime occurred. For "number of crimes cleared," however, breakouts probably would not be important for location of the crime or time of day or week.

By Organizational Unit or Project

Each manager or supervisor should have outcome information for his or her area of responsibility. Outcome data that lumps together the service responsibilities of more than one manager or supervisor limits considerably the value of performance information.

Similarly, if a program sponsors different projects—perhaps using different grantees or contractors—providing outcome data for each project, available both to the program and to the grantees or contractors for their respective projects, will greatly increase the usefulness of the data.

Examples of organizational units for which breakouts are likely to be relevant include the following:

- Individual facilities (such as individual hospitals, libraries, recreation centers, parks, prisons, or jails)
- Particular offices that are each the responsibility of a specific supervisor or manager (such as federal, state, or local public assistance or health offices)
- Groupings of offices or facilities that are an upper-level manager's responsibility (such as groups of parks, fire stations, or any service organized by district)

EXHIBIT 8-1

Basic Types of Breakouts for Outcome Data

■ Organizational unit or project	■ Difficulty of workload
■ Workload or customer characteristics	■ Type and amount of services provided
■ Geographical location	■ Reason for outcome or rating

Exhibit 8-2 displays data on callback timeliness for a federal computer facility with six different supervisory divisions. Each unit reported data on the response time of its own activities. The supervisor used this form to provide the information to each division so each division was able to compare its performance to that of the others.

Exhibit 8-3 compares three units of a family services program.

Providing outcome data on every organizational unit can become expensive. Customer surveys, in particular, can become expensive if the number of organization units is large and/or large samples are needed for each unit. In such cases, the program needs to make a choice: be satisfied with less than complete coverage of all individual units or use smaller sample sizes (and obtain less precise data). An option is to provide individual breakouts for the units with large workloads (such as units with large numbers of customers) and combine into one breakout units with small workloads.

By Workload or Customer Characteristics

Breakouts by categories of customers or other forms of program workload are likely to be very useful in providing information to program personnel about whether particular categories are achieving the desired outcomes (and which categories are not). Such breakouts also provide important information about *the distribution (and therefore equity) of benefits.*

EXHIBIT 8-2

Computer Facility Callback Timeliness

	Percent of Customers Called Back the Same Day[a]	
Division	March 1998	April 1998
1	98	88
2	52	59
3	88	97
4	67	100
5	30	38
6	60	52
Overall	**61**	**59**

Source: Adapted from a report of a U.S. Department of the Navy computer facility.

[a] Information on the number of calls received from customers by each division should also be provided. If the number is very small for a division, the percentage may not be meaningful. In this example, division 4's percentage for April (100 percent) was based on very few calls.

Performance Measurement: Getting Results

EXHIBIT 8-3

**Outcomes by Organizational Unit and Difficulty
of Preservice Problems (Family Services Program)**

| Difficulty of problems at intake | Percent of Clients Whose Adjustment Level Has Improved 12 Months after Intake[a] | | | |
	Family services unit 1	Family services unit 2[b]	Family services unit 3[c]	All units
Minor	52	(35)	56	47
Moderate	35	30	(54)	39
Major	58	69	61	63
Total	**48**	**44**	**57**	**50**

[a] Tables such as these should also identify the number of clients in each cell. If a number is very small, the percentages may not be meaningful.

[b] Unit 2 clients with minor problems at intake have not shown as much improvement as hoped. Unit 2 should look into this (such as identifying what the other units are doing to achieve their considerably higher success rates), report on their difficulties, and provide recommendations for corrective actions.

[c] A substantial proportion of unit 3 clients with moderate problems at intake showed improvement. The program should attempt to find out what is leading to this higher rate of improvement so units 1 and 2 can use the information. Unit 3 should be congratulated for these results.

Programs for which **individuals** are customers should consider such breakout categories as the following:

- Age
- Gender
- Race or ethnicity
- Household income
- Household composition (such as size and number of children)
- Disability status
- English-speaking capability
- Amount of formal education
- Other special status (such as migrant worker family)

Programs for which **businesses** are customers might use such breakout categories as the following:

- Business size (e.g., number of employees and annual sales volume, each grouped into a manageable number of size ranges)
- Product type (using standard industry classifications, for example)

- Ownership characteristics (e.g., whether minority- or female-owned and whether classified as a small business)
- Location

For some programs, outcomes may focus on *types of workload rather than customers*. For example, for road maintenance programs, road condition might be grouped according to one or more of the following characteristics:

- Amount of traffic and the proportion that is truck traffic
- Type of pavement
- Soil conditions
- Historical weather conditions

For water and sewer programs, the condition of various parts of the distribution network might be grouped by these characteristics:

- Pipe size
- Pipe materials
- Soil conditions

For federal and state education programs, outcome data breakouts for groups of school districts or schools might be based on these characteristics:

- Size (student enrollment or number of teachers)
- Urban, rural, or suburban location
- Percent of student body enrolled in subsidized meal programs (as a surrogate for family income)
- Status of educational reform

For some programs, outcome data breakouts by time of day and day of the week (such as for emergency services and public transit) or by season (such as for recreation and library programs) can provide data important for such decisions as allocating resources.

For each breakout used, a program will need to select the particular breakout categories, bearing in mind the need to have a manageable number of categories. For example, a program interested in breaking out its outcomes by customer income will need to decide how many income categories should be used and what income range should define each category. If services are targeted to low-income households, for example, suitable income categories might be less than $5,000 a year, $5,000–$15,000, and over $15,000. For a clientele that is typically middle-income, better categories might be less than $15,000 a year, $15,000–$29,999, $30,000–$44,999, and $45,000 and over.

By Geographical Location

This will be a key breakout for many, probably most, programs. Knowing the outcome of services in each geographical area will provide information about where performance is good and where it is not. (Recent developments in Geographical Information Systems, or GIS, have greatly increased the practicality of breakouts by geographical area, including neighborhood, by facilitating the coding of geographical coordinates.[3])

For example, a state might track indicators of health, employment, and education test scores—not only for the state as a whole but also for each of its counties and cities and for various regions within the state. The state can use such data to identify assistance needs for those areas where performance has been subpar. Each county or city, in turn, may want such data broken out by key districts or neighborhoods.

Useful geographical breakouts include

- neighborhoods,
- areas within organizational boundaries (such as districts or precincts),
- political boundaries (such as electoral districts),
- counties or cities,
- Zip codes,
- regions, and
- states.

Neighborhood breakouts, neglected in the early days of performance measurement, *are likely to become a major form of outcome information for local governments and private nonprofit organizations.* Such information will likely be of considerably more interest to the typical citizen than federal, state, or citywide data.

Portland, Oregon, provided findings from its 2005 citizen survey for both its seven "coalition"-level geographical groups as well as for its smaller 75 neighborhoods. Its formal reports present the coalition-level data. The small neighborhood data are reported on the city's web site. Portland was able to obtain returns from an average of about 300 households in each small neighborhood by mailing questionnaires to a very large number of randomly selected addresses.[4]

Exhibit 8-4 is an example from New York City's street cleanliness rating. Such a map had been published for many years by the city in its

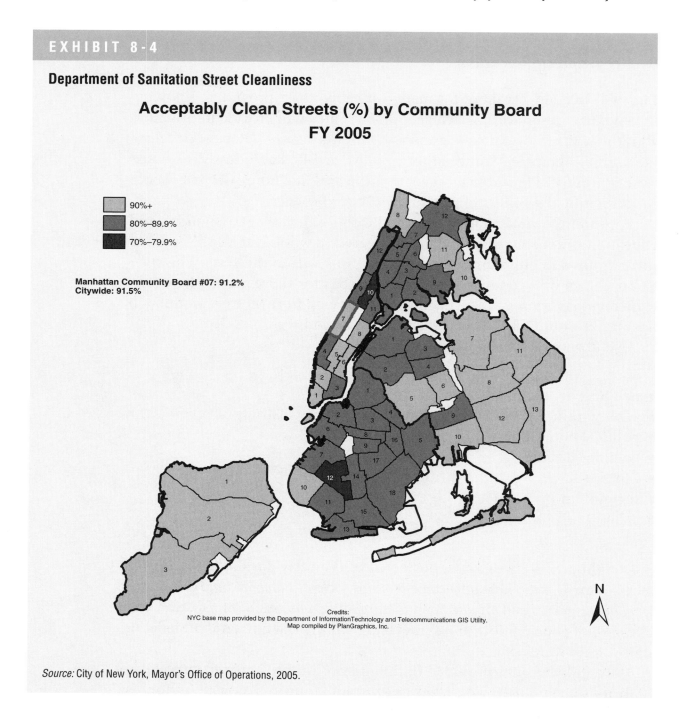

EXHIBIT 8-4

Department of Sanitation Street Cleanliness

Acceptably Clean Streets (%) by Community Board
FY 2005

90%+

80%–89.9%

70%–79.9%

Manhattan Community Board #07: 91.2%
Citywide: 91.5%

N

Credits:
NYC base map provided by the Department of InformationTechnology and Telecommunications GIS Utility.
Map compiled by PlanGraphics, Inc.

Source: City of New York, Mayor's Office of Operations, 2005.

annual *Mayor's Management Report* to the public. It now is available on the city's web site. The darker the shading on the map, the dirtier the streets. The data simultaneously show the outcomes of cleaning efforts and where cleanup activities are most needed. The city uses such cleanliness ratings to help allocate crews to areas most in need. Reviewing the differences in data over time indicates the extent to which long-term progress is being made in each geographical area. Since 1990, the number of dirty and marginal districts has shrunk dramatically.

Exhibit 8-5 presents data from a Portland, Oregon, annual household survey, administered as part of its annual performance measurement process. The data identify differences by geographical area in residents' feelings of security in their neighborhoods during the day.

By Difficulty of Workload

All programs receive work that covers a range of difficulty. The proportion and degree of difficulty are likely to vary from one reporting period to another and from one organizational unit to another. The more difficult the workload, the more time-consuming, and probably the more expensive, it is to achieve desired outcomes. For example,

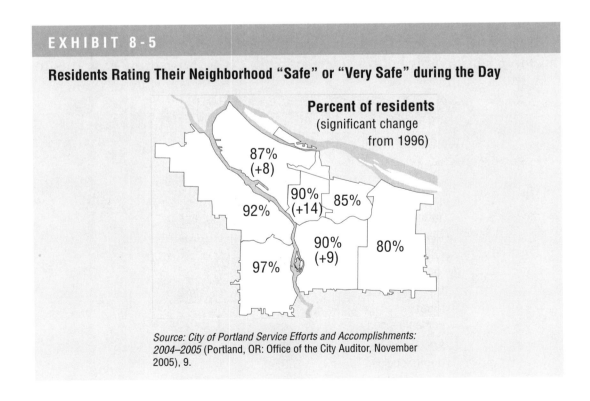

EXHIBIT 8-5

Residents Rating Their Neighborhood "Safe" or "Very Safe" during the Day

Percent of residents (significant change from 1996)

87% (+8)
90% (+14)
85%
92%
90% (+9)
80%
97%

Source: *City of Portland Service Efforts and Accomplishments: 2004–2005* (Portland, OR: Office of the City Auditor, November 2005), 9.

- some customers are more difficult to help than others, perhaps because of limited education or language problems.
- some roads are more difficult to keep in good condition than others, perhaps because of the amount of total traffic, the amount of truck traffic, soil conditions, and/or weather conditions.
- some applications are much easier to process than others. Some applications for eligibility to participate in a program (or for permits or licenses) may be straightforward, while other applications involve complex eligibility issues that require staff to obtain confirmations and perform other checks before accepting or denying the application.

For some programs, "risk factors" may be a good way to capture workload difficulty. For example, to the extent that smoking, lack of exercise, and existing health problems (such as diabetes) are risky conditions that lead to more severe health problems, clients with more risk factors will be more difficult to help.[5] In this case, outcome indicator breakouts reflecting the condition of patients after they have participated in health care programs should be reported by degree of risk when they entered the health program—with higher percentages of success expected for patients at less risk.

Warning on Workload Difficulty Breakouts
For public credibility, the assignment of the workload difficulty rating should be done *as soon as possible upon receipt of the work* (or arrival of a customer). Later assignment is vulnerable to the charge that agency or program personnel are manipulating the data to make themselves look good.

Aggregate outcomes can be misleading and unfair if the difficulty of the incoming workload is not considered. Exhibit 8-6 shows how easy it is to

---

EXHIBIT 8-6

Workload Difficulty Breakout (Clients)

	Unit 1	Unit 2
Aggregate data		
Total clients	**500**	**500**
Number helped	300	235
Percent helped	60%	47%
Breakout data		
Difficult cases	**100**	**300**
Number helped	0	75
Percent helped	0%	25%
Routine cases	**400**	**200**
Number helped	300	160
Percent helped	75%	80%

jump to the wrong conclusion if only aggregate data are reported. Over-all, unit 1 helped a higher proportion of its total cases (60 percent versus 47 percent) than unit 2. However, the breakout data show that unit 2's percentages are better than unit 1's for both difficult and routine cases. How could this occur? Because unit 2 had a much higher proportion of difficult-to-help cases than unit 1 (60 percent versus 20 percent). (See exhibit 8-3 for another example of breakouts by difficulty.)

Reporting breakouts by workload difficulty will also reduce the temptation for service delivery agencies (public or private) to *cream*—that is, focus on easier-to-help (and less costly) customers—to get their ratings up.

How to develop workload difficulty categories. The key challenge is to establish reliable difficulty categories, usually at or near intake. All staff persons responsible for assigning difficulty categories should be able to assign similar categories for similar sets of conditions.

The easiest and least costly strategy for developing such categories is to have a group of key personnel familiar with program agency operations develop a set of categories—at least two and probably no more than five—and detailed definitions of each category. The category names might be simple ones, such as high, medium, and low difficulty, but each category should be defined thoroughly. The definitions need to be based on the specific workload characteristics for which information is expected to be available at the time of the assessment.

The categories and their definitions should then be pilot-tested on a small number of workload units (such as customers, loan applications, or road sections).

Various program personnel, including some of those who will be responsible for assigning the difficulty categories to the workload units, should be asked to select which category is most appropriate for each sampled case. The categories chosen by each person for each test workload unit should then be compared to determine whether they are sufficiently similar to represent reliable categorizations. If the level-of-difficulty categories selected for each case are not similar, the definitions will need to be reworked (and/or the people assigning the categories given more training).

This procedure will be sufficient for many agencies and programs. A more sophisticated approach is to use statistical analysis to relate available data on outcomes to the characteristics. For example, statistical regression analysis might be used to determine the relationship between past data on outcomes for individual clients and the characteristics believed to be related to difficulty in achieving successful outcomes. For human service programs these characteristics might include educational level and household income.

The federal Job Training Partnership Act program, for example, used such statistical procedures to enable states to take into account local economic conditions when comparing the success of programs in getting their customers employed. The U.S. Health Care Financing Agency also used statistical analysis to take the entering condition of patients (an indicator of difficulty) into account in comparing mortality rates among hospitals.

By Type and Amount of Service

Outcomes can be grouped by the amount, type of service provided, and/or the procedure used to deliver the service. This provides managers and their staff with information to help them assess which service delivery approaches are accomplishing desired outcomes and which are not. This breakout applies when the program varies the service given to individual items in its workload. In a social service program, for example, the agency might apply more caseworker time for some clients, use a greater proportion of telephone rather than in-person assistance for some clients, use more paraprofessionals for some clients, use both group and individual counseling, and so on, depending on resources available on a given day or during a given week. Another example is a program that contracts some of its work but also uses its own personnel to perform similar work. *As long as the type of assistance is not tailored to particular categories of clients, breakouts by type of assistance can be helpful.*

If the agency classifies each item of workload by the particular type, or amount, of service applied to the item and then links that information to the outcome data on the item, program personnel can subsequently obtain and compare outcome information for each type or amount of service.

Exhibit 8-7 is a version of exhibit 8-3 but here comparing outcome data by number of counseling sessions provided to individual clients (adapted from performance measurement data for social service programs in North Carolina local governments). In these data, the number of sessions (and the severity of problems at intake) does *not* appear to be related to the percentage of clients whose condition improved. (Program analysts would

---

EXHIBIT 8-7

Outcomes by Level of Service Received

	Percent of Clients Whose Problems Improved after Nine Months			
Problems at intake	1 session	2–10 sessions	Over 10 sessions	Total
Minor	50	36	0	28
Moderate	57	53	56	55
Major	67	77	47	63
Total	60	58	45	53

Performance Measurement: Getting Results

need to investigate further to understand the relationship between client difficulty, number of sessions, and successful outcomes.)

A good example of what breakouts by type of procedure can reveal is Hawaii's audit of procedures for licensing nurses. The audit examined complaints involving nurses' use of drugs. It broke out the complaint data by procedure used to check on the nurses' license applications. It found that 81 percent of all such complaints involved nurses who had been licensed by an endorsement procedure rather than by a check of the applicant's nursing history. The audit recommended altering the endorsement procedure.[6]

Outcome breakouts by type and amount of service can be used to encourage innovation. Managers who want to test new service delivery procedures can try the procedures on a segment of their workload while continuing to use existing procedures on the remainder. This will help them determine which procedures are leading to better outcomes. To ensure against bias, the workload should, when feasible, be randomly assigned to each candidate procedure.

Outcome data obtained during the test period can then be tabulated for each procedure. Here is the basic sequence of steps to be followed in such a test:

1. Identify the procedures to be compared.
2. Choose a method for selecting which incoming unit of workload will be served using each procedure. The purpose here is to select a *representative* sample of the workload for each procedure (and thus maximize the likelihood that the same proportion of difficult workloads will be included in each group). For this purpose, a coin toss (or random number table) can be used to ensure representativeness. If the arrival of workload is essentially random, assigning every unit of incoming workload on a rotating basis to each procedure would serve the

Cautionary Tale

Avoid assignment procedures that lead to different types of workloads being assigned systematically to different procedures. Many years ago, one city government wanted to compare its existing process for maintaining city vehicles in-house to a second process that involved more preventive maintenance and to a third process that used private contractors to provide the vehicle maintenance. The agency assigned one-third of its vehicles to each of these three methods—a fine idea. Unfortunately, the city chose to assign all Fords to the first process, all General Motors cars to the second, and all Chryslers to the third. By choosing this assignment process, the city eliminated the possibility of telling whether different outcomes were due to the particular procedure or to the make of car.

same purpose. For some services, the new procedure might be implemented in randomly selected geographical areas of the jurisdiction.

3. Assign each unit of incoming workload to a procedure, based on the randomizing scheme.
4. Record the procedure used for each workload item.
5. Track the outcome indicators for each item.
6. Tabulate the value of each outcome indicator for each procedure.

By Reason for Outcome or Rating

If information is available on reasons for outcomes, particularly reasons for poor outcomes, *breakouts by reason can be used to suggest actions needed to correct problems.*

For example, some government civil or criminal litigation cases will be unsuccessful. This may have been for such reasons as witnesses died, evidence became contaminated, adequate staff time was not available to handle the case, or litigation work was poor. Health treatment may be unsuccessful because patients did not follow the regimens prescribed, physicians or nurses made errors, or the health problems were essentially incurable. Tabulating outcomes for each such reason can help the program identify corrective actions.

In customer surveys, respondents can be asked why they expressed dissatisfaction with a particular service or why they did not use it. For example, respondents might not have used a service for any of these reasons:

- Location not convenient
- Location not safe
- Hours of operation not convenient
- Had a previous bad experience with the service
- Did not know the service was available
- Had no time available to use the service
- Had no need for the service

For traffic accidents, agencies usually identify a reason, such as weather, car defects, traffic signal or sign problems, or driver or pedestrian error. Tabulations by cause (perhaps also tabulated for each location and time) can be important information for deciding corrective actions.

For all these situations, recording and tabulating reasons for each case allows agency and program managers to identify prominent reasons and decide what corrective actions are appropriate. *To be most useful, reasons should be grouped into those reasons the program can do something about and those it cannot.* In the example above about reasons for nonuse, no time available for use and no need for a service are reasons over which the program typically has little or no influence. If substantial numbers of respondents identify the other reasons for nonuse, the program may be able to alleviate the

Be Wary of Breakouts of Outcomes by Individual Staff Members

Reporting breakouts by individual staff members carries great danger of causing animosity and contention, which can be destructive to good performance. They should be used only internally—and even then only when a program has substantial confidence in the data. As discussed in chapter 11, breakouts by work group (organizational unit) are less likely to cause animosity and contention among workers than breakouts by individual employees.

Some agencies and their programs will want to track such information for internal use—particularly when individual employees have considerable direct influence over outcomes (such as caseworkers, loan application and tax return processors, and teachers). Such information can be useful in motivating personnel and in performance appraisals. It provides appraisers who need to justify performance ratings (especially low ratings) with relatively objective information, which is likely to be accepted more readily by the employees being appraised than are subjective ratings by supervisors.

problems and subsequently increase usage.

Exhibit 8-8 shows reasons that students who needed help for substance abuse found it difficult to get (based on survey data). The performance indicator is "percent of students who needed help but found it difficult to get." All the reasons are ones over which agency actions can be taken, but in different ways. The first two reasons indicate the need to get information to students on sources of help. The other reasons indicate the need for specific changes in program approaches. (The exhibit also indicates the use of breakouts by grade, usually important for educational outcomes.)

Other Types of Breakouts

Programs should examine each of their outcome indicators to determine what additional breakouts would help them identify where the desired outcomes are occurring and where they are not. Examples of special breakout characteristics include the following:

- Vehicle ownership—for transportation programs in which accessibility to transportation is important
- Home ownership and type of dwelling—for housing-related programs that base benefits (or regulations) on criteria such as owner or renter, single-family or multifamily dwelling

EXHIBIT 8-8

Reasons Students Who Needed Help for Their Alcohol and Other Drug Use Found It Difficult to Get, Hawaii, 1989–1996, by Grade (percent)

Reason	6 (*N*=164)	8 (*N*=229)	10 (*N*=183)	12 (*N*=109)
1. Had no idea who to ask or where to go for help	54	57	50	60
2. Didn't think that people your age could get counseling/treatment	47	39	28	24
3. Were afraid to talk to a counselor or anyone else because your parents or teachers would find out	43	58	57	52
4. Were afraid of getting in trouble with the law	46	38	28	27
5. Were afraid of what your friends would think	43	38	28	27
6. Thought you could handle the problem yourself	41	55	58	61
7. Could not get the kind of help that you needed or wanted	27	31	25	24

Source: Adapted by the Center for Substance Abuse Research (CESAR), University of Maryland, from data from Renee Klingle and Michael Miller, *Hawaii Adolescent Treatment Needs Assessment Results from the Hawaii Student Drug Use Study, 1989–1996* (Honolulu: The University of Hawaii Speech Department for the Hawaii Department of Health, Alcohol, and Drug Abuse Division, 1996).

- The extent of business customers' past experience in exporting—for interpreting the outcomes of export promotion programs
- Length of residence in the city/county/state—perhaps to identify the type of message needed to appeal to one group or the other

Procedures for Choosing Breakouts for a Program

Final decisions on which breakouts are needed should be made before final decisions on data content and procedures. This is to ensure that the data collection needed for the preferred breakouts is built into the final data collection plan. Going back after the fact and trying to reconstruct data from records, for example, is usually very inefficient and can be expensive.

The program should consider the breakout categories such as those discussed earlier in this chapter and determine which are applicable. A sensible approach is to have program staff select categories with input from other parts of the agency. (The sources discussed in chapter 6 for identifying outcome indicators can also help identify breakout candidates.)

References and Notes

1. Comparisons are discussed in chapter 9, explanations in chapter 10, and presentation formats in chapter 11.
2. See, for example, "Populations of Color in Minnesota: Health Status Report Update Summary" (St. Paul, MN: Center for Health Statistics, Minnesota Department of Health, spring 2005).
3. For discussions of using geographical information, especially at the community level, see U.S. Department of Housing and Urban Development, *Mapping Your Community: Using Geographic Information to Strengthen Community Objectives,* HUD-1092-CPD (Washington, DC, October 1997); and Josh Kirschenbaum and Lisa Russ, *Community Mapping: Using Geographic Data for Neighborhood Revitalization* (Oakland, CA: PolicyLink, 2002), http://www.policylink.org/pdfs/Mapping.pdf.
4. "City of Portland Service Efforts and Accomplishments: 2004–2005" (Portland, OR: Office of the City Auditor, November 2005).
5. For more discussion of risk factors, see National Research Council, *Assessment of Performance Measures for Public Health, Substance Abuse, and Mental Health,* edited by Edward B. Perrin and Jeffrey J. Koschel (Washington, DC: National Academy Press, 1997).
6. Auditor, State of Hawaii, *Sunset Evaluation Update: Nurses: A Report to the Governor and the Legislature of the State of Hawaii* (Honolulu, October 13, 1994).

Jose Canseco and Rickey Henderson went on a camping trip to Alaska. They were awakened one night by a crash and a growl. A great big grizzly bear was lumbering toward them. Rickey put on his running shoes and took off. Jose shouted, "Idiot! You can't outrun a bear." Rickey responded, "I don't have to outrun the bear. I only have to outrun YOU!"

Making Outcome Information Useful: Comparing Findings to Benchmarks

Once a program has outcome data, how can it determine whether the level of performance the data reflect is good or bad? Comparing the outcomes to benchmarks is a fundamental, and essential, element of performance measurement and performance management systems. This chapter identifies the benchmarks likely to be useful for comparisons.

Major types of benchmarks used to assess performance for a particular reporting period are

1. performance in the previous period,
2. performance of similar organizational units or geographical areas,
3. outcomes for different workload or customer groups,
4. different service delivery practices,
5. a recognized general standard,
6. performance of other jurisdictions,
7. performance of the private sector, and
8. targets established at the beginning of the performance period.

The breakout data discussed in chapter 8 provide the information for comparisons using benchmarks 2, 3, and 4. Other data sources are needed for comparisons using benchmarks 1, 5, 6, 7, and 8. Each of these benchmarks is discussed in detail below.

Performance in the Previous Period

These comparisons are almost always relevant and important. Comparisons to previous performance are the most common type of comparison and are applicable to all programs. They help agency officials assess whether performance in a given service environment has improved or deteriorated over time. Comparisons to previous periods can also help assess the impact of a new procedure on performance.

Data on past performance should be readily available, except for first-time performance indicators. Reporting periods compared should be of the same length, whether monthly, quarterly, annually, or whatever.

An agency needs to answer two important questions in establishing its performance measurement system: How frequently should the data for each indicator be reported? To which particular past period should the current period be compared?

Frequency

The more timely the feedback, the more useful it is for program managers and staff. Many agencies prepare internal program reports on process and output indicators on a quarterly, if not a monthly, basis. This same frequency is likely to be desirable for data on outcomes and efficiency. For data already in administrative records, greater frequency can be obtained at minimal cost. As noted in chapter 7, the timeliness problem can often be solved at only a small additional cost. If survey data are desired quarterly, for example, a quarter of the annual budget can be devoted to collecting a quarter of the anticipated annual data. The quarterly data will be less precise than surveying all respondents at once, but the desired precision for the annual figures will still be achieved when the quarterly observations are combined into annual estimates. The total additional cost will be about 10 percent.

Two exceptions sometimes occur. The first is for performance indicators for which even annual data are inherently too expensive to collect. The second covers indicators whose values are not expected to change significantly over a 12-month period, such as some water quality measurements.

Comparison Period

Comparing a particular 12-month period with the previous 12-month period is almost always appropriate. Should comparisons of quarterly data also be made? If so, should the latest quarterly data be compared with the previous quarter, or with data from the same quarter of a previous year, or both? Programs whose outcomes are believed to be significantly affected by seasonal factors should compare data for a particular quarter with data for the same quarter in previous years.

To track changes in outcomes after the introduction of new program practices, data for several periods after the introduction of the new practices should be compared to data for several periods before their introduction.

Performance of Similar Organizational Units or Geographical Areas

An important use of breakouts by organizational units and geographical areas (see chapter 8) is to enable comparisons among organization units, or geographical areas, providing essentially the same service to essentially the same type of customers. Such comparisons indicate which units or areas are performing well and which are performing badly relative to one another. In addition to the monitoring value of such comparisons, they can have motivational value for program personnel in each unit and be a source of "best practice" information. Organization units that might be compared include

- offices,
- service districts,
- facilities (such as libraries, parks, community centers, hospitals, correctional facilities, day care centers, landfills), and
- regions.

For such comparisons to be valid (and fair), the missions and types of customers should be reasonably similar across units. Exhibit 8-2 in chapter 8 compares operating divisions of a computer facility. Exhibit 8-3 compares service units of a family services program.

Some programs will want to compare performance across small geographical areas of the program's jurisdiction. For example, many local programs, such as street cleaning, road maintenance, parks and recreation, and libraries, find it useful to examine outcomes across neighborhoods. Exhibits 8-4 and 8-5 illustrate comparisons by geographical area.

Outcomes for Different Workload or Customer Groups

When workload and customer breakouts of performance data are available (such as those discussed in the previous chapter), categories can be compared so managers can focus on the groups that seem to need special actions.

In other words, comparisons indicate whether the program is more or less successful on particular outcome indicators with certain categories of customers or workload than with others—men compared to women, the young compared to the elderly, Hispanics compared to whites, blind customers versus wheelchair customers, rural roads versus urban roads, and so on.

Exhibit 8-3 in chapter 8 shows comparisons across both organizational units and customer difficulty levels for a social service agency. Family services unit 3 had a substantially higher overall success rate than units 1 and 2, but, as usual, the outcome data do not tell why unit 3 did better. Program staff can use a breakout by difficulty to help explore the whys, as in these two examples:

- Compared to the other units, unit 2 did very well with clients who had major problems but not so well with clients who had minor or moderate problems. Unit 2's procedures for clients with minor and moderate problems should be looked into to ascertain whether its procedures differ significantly from those of the other two units and whether unit 2 might be able to obtain improvement ideas from those other units.
- Unit 3 had substantially better outcomes on clients with moderate problems and did relatively well on other clients. Can and should this unit's practices be transferred to the other units?

Different Service Delivery Practices

Programs periodically consider new or different practices. As discussed in chapter 8, the outcome measurement process can be used to help programs assess the results and outcomes of different ways of delivering services, such as

- different operating procedures,
- different technologies,
- different staffing arrangements,
- different amounts or levels of service provided to individual customers, or
- different providers (such as private contractors).

When using outcome measurement to compare alternative policies, processes, or procedures with those in use, the two principal approaches are

- introducing new practices *across the board* to replace the old practice; and

- introducing new practices into *part of an operation* and running the old and new practices side by side for a period of time.

When introducing new practices *across the board,* outcome data for a period before the change should be compared with outcomes for a period after the change. Exhibit 9-1 illustrates such data for the introduction of automated dispatching equipment. The new equipment appears to have improved response times. According to this comparison, the new equipment should be continued (other factors being equal) and even added to other parts of the system, assuming its costs are reasonable.

When introducing new practices in just *part of the program,* outcome data for the old process should be compared with outcomes for the new process over the same period. This type of comparison helps managers test alternative procedures and innovative ideas without making a full (and irreversible) commitment. Exhibit 9-2 illustrates outcome data obtained for a computer versus manual loan-processing comparison. (Chapter 8 describes how to set up an experiment to generate the data needed for such a comparison.)

The data in exhibit 9-2 indicate that computer processing is considerably faster but that error rates are slightly higher. This outcome information may lead the agency to review the errors made under the new procedure to identify and correct problems and then run the experiment again to check error rates. If the error rates fall, the program may choose to move completely to computer processing. If error rates do not fall, the program must decide whether to tolerate higher error rates in return for greater speed or look for an automated system that is less error-prone.

EXHIBIT 9-1

Comparison of Outcomes before and after Procedure Change

	1998 Quarters				1999 Quarters				2000 Quarters				5-qtr. average before	6-qtr. average after
	1st	2nd	3rd	4th	1st	2nd	3rd	4th	1st	2nd	3rd	4th		
Average response time (minutes)	5.2	5.7	5.8	5.3	5.5	5.6	4.8	4.5	4.5	4.4	4.8	N/A	5.5	4.8

↓

Introduction of automated dispatching equipment

EXHIBIT 9-2

Computer versus Manual Procedures for Processing Eligibility Determinations

Processing procedure	Error rate (%)	Applications taking more than one day to process (%)
Computer	9	18
Manual	8	35

Note: About 250 applications processed by each procedure.

Exhibit 8-7 compared various levels of service provided to customers of a social service program. This is an example of a "natural" experiment. The program did not purposely set up an experiment to test whether more sessions made a difference. Rather, in the normal order of doing business, incoming clients varied in the scale of their problems and staff had more sessions with some clients than others, regardless of the difficulty of the client's problem. Natural experiments can provide useful comparisons if the requisite outcome data are recorded.

The exhibit presented data on clients' number of sessions and problem difficulty. The data suggest that more sessions are not associated with improved outcomes. However, these data are not sufficient to draw a firm conclusion. In-depth analysis is needed before a program takes action based only on this type of pattern. Other factors that should be investigated are customer age, ability to speak English, and so on.

The Minnesota Department of Revenue's Tax Collection Division tested the procedure of mailing a letter to individual taxpayers with unpaid liability, giving them the opportunity to resolve the liability before being billed. The agency randomly selected 100 such taxpayers to be sent the letter and 100 not to be sent the letter. The department found that approximately 75 percent of respondents sent the letter responded appropriately, compared with less than 25 percent not sent the letter.[1]

The State of Virginia compared the collection performance of its existing publicly operated child support enforcement offices with that of privately run offices contracted for the purpose. The state's performance measurement process compared total dollars collected for the two groups of offices in FY 1997, finding that the privately operated offices had done better. But when the state broke out the collections data by type of household, it found that publicly operated offices had larger collections for families on welfare than did the privately run offices. On another indicator, number of support orders established, the publicly run offices also did better, although their operations cost somewhat more. After two years, the agency concluded that the overall difference between the two approaches was small. As a result, the General Assembly approved outside contracting as an option *but did not mandate its use.*[2]

When another level of government or a professional association has developed a standard for an outcome indicator, this standard can be used to assess performance, as in the examples below:[3]

- The federal government periodically sets standards on drinking water quality and on emissions from wastewater treatment plants. Some of these are mandated; some are not. Individual jurisdictions can use these standards as a benchmark against which to compare their own levels.
- The U.S. Department of Labor's performance measurement process for its old Job Training Partnership Act (JTPA) program calculated and disseminated annual national performance standards based on the most recent outcomes data from local programs. Individual programs at both state and local levels have used these national standards to assess their own performance.[4]

Exhibit 9-3 lists the six indicators JTPA used as the primary outcome measurements. (The first five are end outcomes. The last is best considered an intermediate outcome.) JTPA recommended adjusting these standards (statistically) to reflect local difficulty conditions, including economic factors and participant characteristics.

Under the current Workforce Investment Act, however, the Department of Labor negotiates standards with each state, recognizing that different states will have different circumstances. This results in different targets for each employment and training outcome indicator. In effect, the department

---

EXHIBIT 9-3

Job Training Partnership Act Performance Indicators and National Standards

	Performance indicator	National standard
Adult	Employment rate at follow-up[a]	62%
	Weekly earnings at follow-up[a]	$204
Welfare	Employment rate at follow-up[a]	51%
	Weekly earnings at follow-up[a]	$182
Youth	Entered employment rate	45%
	Employability enhancement rate	33%

[a] The follow-up period was defined as 13 weeks after employees had finished the training or employment program.

has switched from the use of a standard to the use of tailored targets, discussed later in this chapter.

Another type of standard is the "rule of thumb." For example, what levels of citizen satisfaction in citizen surveys should be considered "acceptable." Many governments and agencies are surveying their customers. If 10 percent of respondents rate a service characteristic as only "fair" or "poor," rather than "excellent" or "good," is this bad? Should the 10 percent be a major concern for the agency?

There is no widely acceptable standard. Based on a review of many such surveys, however, *a suggested rule of thumb is that if more than 15 percent of respondents give low ratings, the issue warrants attention.* Typically, for most public services, most customers have given high ratings to agency service providers (such as to their helpfulness and courteousness). However, typically, for most services, considerably smaller percentages of respondents have reported that their condition has improved significantly since receiving the service.

Of course, all such rules of thumb have to be considered in light of the particular service being rated. For example, if past experience indicates that customers have been very unhappy with a service, the agency might want to use a higher level than 15 percent, perhaps 20 or 25 percent, as the level to which it wants to improve.

Performance of Other Jurisdictions

For some outcome indicators, comparable outcome data might be available from other jurisdictions. This type of comparison can be useful as long as (a) the activity of the other jurisdictions is sufficiently similar to that of the program being evaluated, (b) compatible data on the indicators are available, and (c) the data cover approximately the same period.

For many such comparisons, if the outcome values are not already expressed as a percentage, the numbers will likely need to be "normalized" to produce meaningful (and fair) assessments. That is, the outcome values need to be related to some factor that adjusts for differences in scale, often a population count. This is why national crime reports are expressed as crime rates (number of reported crimes *divided by the relevant population*) so the crime data can be reasonably compared across jurisdictions of different sizes. Another example is that of comparing road conditions among states. The "number of lane-miles of road in good condition" needs to be divided by the number of lane-miles to provide meaningful comparisons across states.

Making these comparisons has the added benefits of (a) indicating what performance level is realistic to target and (b) identifying exemplary practices of high-performing organizations that can be adapted by managers in other jurisdictions to enhance their own agency's performance.

Certain comparative outcome indicator data have been available to local or state jurisdictions for many years:

- Number of traffic accidents, injuries, and fatalities
- Crime rates (aggregate clearance rates for various categories of crime are also reported annually for local governments in various population-size categories)
- Fire incident rates and losses
- Levels of air and water pollution (for larger cities and counties)
- Health statistics
- Standardized test scores for school districts within a state, collected and reported by districts and state education agencies

In recent years, some countries have begun formal efforts to compare public agency performance measurements, especially comparisons of local government agencies. The latter include efforts in the United Kingdom, Germany, and the United States. The Australian government has begun comparing various performance data from its states. Exhibit 9-4 illustrates such comparisons using U.S. public library data.

A problem here is obtaining the outcome data in a timely way. Regular reports providing intergovernmental data may not be available for many months, if not years, after the reporting period. Programs and agencies may be able to shorten this lag considerably by arranging to share data before public release.

Another major concern is that each jurisdiction has its own special circumstances, some which could have substantial effects on the performance data. For example, the amount of precipitation varies substantially across the country. The amount can affect the outcomes and efficiency of many services, such as road conditions and park usage. A common way to alleviate this problem is to group jurisdictions into ones that appear similar to each other, and then focus comparisons on the jurisdictions in each group.

Performance of the Private Sector

Some private businesses provide services similar to publicly provided services—and therefore have outcomes that can provide useful benchmarks.

EXHIBIT 9-4

Per Capita Circulation Rates for Libraries, 2004

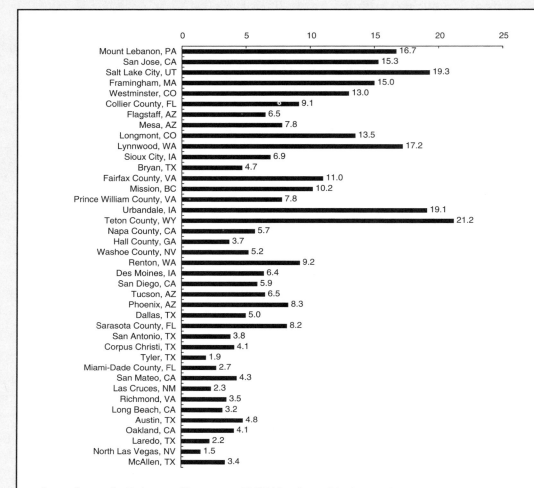

Source: *Comparative Performance Measurement: FY 2004 Data Report* (Washington, DC: International City/County Management Association, 2005).

Notes: Circulation includes all items of any format (e.g., written and audiovisual materials), including renewals that are checked out for use outside the library. Circulation per capita includes combined circulation reported by jurisdictions from central libraries, branches, and bookmobiles. Some of the variation in circulation rates among jurisdictions my be due to differences in factors such as the availability of branch libraries, the overall number of facilities, number of hours open, size and scope of library holdings, and economic or demographic characteristics of the population served.

Such businesses include private bus companies, solid waste collection firms, vehicle maintenance shops, and food service companies.

Can comparable performance data be obtained from these businesses? Data on frequency of in-service breakdowns, response times, and/or unit cost might be available to provide relevant benchmarks for comparisons.

Targets Established at the Beginning of the Performance Period

Establishing targets (or at least projected values) for each outcome indicator for the coming performance period is a highly useful management tool. Since fiscal year 1999, the Government Performance and Results Act has required federal programs to set targets at the beginning of each year for that year—and to report to the president and Congress after the end of the year the actual values and how they compared to the targets. Many states and local governments include targets ("projections") for each performance indicator in budget submissions.

Experience with an indicator is important in setting firm targets. If an outcome indicator is new, it is wise to defer setting firm targets until the program has collected enough data to be confident of setting plausible values. Alternatively, a program might set targets for the initial data collection periods and be explicit in labeling them experimental.

Annual targets (or projections) are likely to be required for an agency's budget preparation process. These projections should be compatible with any goals or targets in the program's strategic plan, if one exists. *Programs will typically find it useful to set not only annual targets but also targets for shorter reporting periods, such as quarters.*

Out-year targets, perhaps for five years into the future, can encourage program personnel to think in the long term and reduce the temptation to overemphasize current results at the expense of future progress.

In deciding on out-year targets, managers need to consider the timing of outcomes in relation to program activities. Some outcomes, especially end outcomes, should not be expected until one or more years after the year in which the activity takes place. This is particularly true for federal and state programs that work through lower levels of government. (In such instances, a program's current-year outcomes may be based primarily on expenditures and activities undertaken in previous years.)

Preferably, *different targets should be established for each outcome indicator in each breakout category* (see chapter 8). This is especially important for level-of-difficulty categories. Different targets will make comparisons much more useful, more meaningful, and fairer if the targets take into consideration case difficulty. This will also reduce the temptation for program personnel to concentrate on easier cases in order to show high performance.

Things to Keep in Mind When Selecting Targets

Targets can be set in many different ways. Chapter 13 discusses the process in more detail. In the meantime, here are some pointers:

- *Consider previous performance.* This is almost always a major factor in determining targets.
- *Consider benchmarking against the best.* If the program has more than one unit that provides the same service for the same types of customers, consider using the performance level achieved by the most successful managerial unit as the target for all units. In exhibit 8-6 of chapter 8, for example, benchmarking against the best would select unit 2's outcome rate for both difficult and routine cases (25 percent and 80 percent, respectively) as the next year's target—at least for internal agency reporting. Reports going outside the agency might use only the aggregate success rate as the target. Since aggregate targets are based, at least implicitly, on some assumption about the distribution of workload by difficulty category, the program should explicitly estimate the percentage of customers expected to fall into each difficulty category in the next reporting period.
- *If benchmarking against the best is considered too great a challenge, use the average performance of all units.* If the program wants to be even more conservative, it could use the worst value as the target, to emphasize the need to achieve at least that minimum level of success. However, avoid the temptation to underestimate targets in order to look good each year; program reviewers will eventually catch on.
- *Consider the outcomes achieved in the past for different customer or workload categories.* For example, use the highest or average outcome achieved for any one demographic category as the target for all categories. If a program indicated successful outcomes for, say, 53 percent of men and 48 percent of women, setting a future overall target of 53 percent— for each gender and in the aggregate—would encourage high performance with all customers.
- *Consider the performance levels achieved by other jurisdictions or by private firms with similar activities and workload or customer compositions.* Benchmarking against the best in this case means setting targets at or near the best outcomes achieved by other organizations.

- *Make sure the targets chosen are feasible, given the program's budget and staffing plan for the year.* Keeping the same target despite reduced budgets can probably be achieved up to a point, but eventually cutbacks in resources should be reflected in reduced targets.
- *Identify any new developments—internal and external—that may affect the program's ability to achieve desired outcomes.* For example, legislative changes (whether affecting policy or budget) that have just occurred or are expected to occur during the next reporting period may make it more or less difficult to achieve desired outcomes.
- *Target setting for periods shorter than a year needs to be done in the context of seasonal factors*—job availability, changes in service demand, and so on.
- *A target does not have to be a single value.* A range is a reasonable alternative, especially if a substantial amount of uncertainty exists. For example, if the outcome indicator is expressed as a percent, the target might be expressed as the most likely achievable percent, plus or minus 5 percentage points.

References and Notes

1. Reported in Blaine Liner, Harry P. Hatry, Elisa Vinson, Ryan Allen, Pat Dusenbury, Scott Bryant, and Ron Snell, *Making Results-Based State Government Work* (Washington, DC: The Urban Institute, 2001), 54.
2. Reported in Diane Kittower, "Counting on Competition," *Governing Magazine* 11, no. 8 (May 1998).
3. For the purpose of outcome measurement comparisons, however, these standards need to be *outcome* standards. Most professional standards pertain to process and staffing characteristics, which do not help calibrate outcomes.
4. The Workforce Investment Act of 1998 (P.L. 105-220, August 7, 1998) replaces JTPA, but it appears to call for quite similar outcome-tracking procedures.

Analysis of Performance Information

U sing performance measurement only for accountability to higher levels would be a great waste. Performance measurement data should be used to help improve programs. After an agency has collected all these data, *it needs to analyze the data to identify appropriate actions that may be needed.* This chapter suggests ways in which agencies can analyze performance data to help make such improvements. This chapter does not, however, discuss the subsequent analysis needed when considering cost and other considerations for planning and budgeting purposes. These matters are discussed in chapters 12 and 13.

How Performance Data Can Help

Analysis of data from a well-conceived performance measurement system can help an agency

- identify the conditions under which a program is doing well or poorly and thus stimulate remedial actions,
- raise key questions regarding a service that can help staff develop and carry out improvement strategies,
- provide clues to problems and sometimes to what can be done to improve future outcomes, and
- assess the extent to which remedial actions have succeeded.

Chapters 8 and 9, respectively, identified breakouts a program should consider for each outcome indicator and potentially useful comparisons the program might make to interpret its outcome data. Such breakout and comparison information should be a major focus of a program's analysis effort.

Always keep in mind that almost all performance data have substantial limitations. The major limitation is that data on outcomes seldom, if ever, tell what caused the outcomes, especially end outcomes. Other information and other procedures, such as in-depth program evaluation, are needed to identify the extent to which the program contributed to the outcomes. Similarly, *outcome information does not indicate what should be done to improve the program, but a well-designed performance measurement system can often provide highly useful clues.*

Analyzing Performance Data

Considerable literature exists on procedures for in-depth, ad hoc program evaluations. However, little guidance exists on procedures for examining outcome data obtained from a regular, frequent schedule. Many examinations of performance measurement data by agency personnel appear to be overly quick and casual. This chapter focuses on ways to examine outcome information to help agencies determine what changes, what steps toward improvement, if any, should be taken. The focus is on *basic steps* that all agencies can take, not on more sophisticated, high-powered steps such as extensive statistical analyses and in-depth program evaluations.

Exhibit 10-1 lists a number of steps for analyzing program outcome data. Each step is discussed below.[1]

The initial step, of course, is to tabulate the data for each performance indicator. As discussed in chapter 6, decide for each indicator the numeric form in which the results will be presented. (For example, should percentages, ranges of numbers, or averages be presented?)

Step 1. Compare the Latest Overall Outcomes to Outcomes from Previous Time Periods

Examine changes over time. After performance information becomes available for more than one reporting period, the latest findings can be compared with findings for prior reporting periods to detect trends and other significant changes. If the data indicate major improvement or deterioration, the agency should identify why it occurred. The following are examples of questions that might be asked to help identify reasons for changes:

Basic Steps for Analyzing Program Outcome Data

Examine the Aggregate Outcome Data

Step 1.   Compare the latest overall outcomes to outcomes from previous time periods.

Step 2.   Compare the latest overall outcomes to preestablished targets.

Step 3.   Compare the program's outcomes to those of similar programs—and to any outside standards.

Examine Breakout Data

Step 4.   Break out and compare outcomes by workload (demographic) characteristics.

Step 5.   Break out and compare outcomes by service characteristics.

Step 6.   Compare the latest outcomes for each breakout group with outcomes from previous reporting periods and to targets.

Examine Findings across Indicators

Step 7.   Examine consistency and interrelationships among inputs, outputs, and outcomes.

Step 8.   Examine the outcome indicators together to obtain a more comprehensive perspective on performance.

Make Sense of the Numbers

Step 9.   Identify and highlight key findings.

Step 10.   Seek explanations for unexpected findings.

Step 11.   Provide recommendations to officials for future actions, including experimentation with new service delivery approaches.

- Have external factors significantly affected outcomes?
- Have special events during the reporting period significantly affected outcomes?
- Have resources been reduced (or increased) to a degree that affected outcomes?
- Have legislative requirements changed in ways that affected the ability of the program to produce outcomes?
- Have the program staff changed their procedures (strategies) in a way that affected outcomes?

An important use of data collected over time is to detect patterns of deterioration in outcomes. Such patterns alert the agency to consider modifications to the program. For example, if the number of fires and loss of life and property have been increasing for several years, the relevant agency needs to determine the causes and the extent to which they can be prevented, such as by increasing inspections or strengthening fire codes.

Caution and suggestion: Sometimes, performance indicator values can be substantially affected by infrequent events. These cause distortions in the data for a particular reporting period (such as might happen with fire statistics if only one or two major fires occurred during a reporting period). For such indicators, multiyear averages can smooth the data to highlight persistent trends. For example, suppose the fire rate data show 2.6, 9.7, 3.6, 1.5, 18.7, and 3.9 major fires per year, respectively, for six annual reporting periods. A series of three-year running averages, starting with the first three periods, would show rates of 5.3, 4.9, 7.9, and 8.0. This smoothes out the effect of outlier values.

Reminder: When comparing reporting periods of less than one year, seasonal factors can be present and can affect such outcomes as the condition of roads, the amount of crime, and the rate of unemployment. In such cases, as noted in chapter 9, the program should *compare performance data for a given season with data for the same season in previous years.*

Comparing performance indicator values that occurred before new procedures or policy changes were made to values that occurred afterward is a way to assess the success of changes. For example, A state legislature might stiffen the requirements for obtaining driver's licenses in the hope of reducing state accident and injury rates. Computing a trend line showing accident rates before and after the new legislation would help assess whether accident rates had improved significantly. If not, the state would need to consider other actions.

Exhibit 10-2 (a variant of exhibit 9-1) shows that average response times for processing loan requests after an automated process was introduced declined from 52.4 to 46.8 days. Whether this improvement is worth the investment is a judgment for the agency to make. However, analysis is desirable to assess the likelihood that the difference occurred by chance.

Caution: Before-and-after values provide evidence of successful or unsuccessful attempts at improvements. Such evidence is weak, however,

---

EXHIBIT 10-2

Comparison of Outcomes before and after Process Change

	1997 Quarters				1998 Quarters				1999 Quarters				Average before change	Average after change
	1st	2nd	3rd	4th	1st	2nd	3rd	4th	1st	2nd	3rd	4th		
Average response time (days)	53	51	56	49	53	53	49	47	43	45	44	N/A	52.4	46.8

Introduction of
automated process

and should not be relied on exclusively in making agency decisions about change. Almost always other factors will be present that could have caused the change, and they should be considered before deciding what to do next. In the case of legislation changing driver's license eligibility in order to reduce traffic accidents, the downward trend in accidents might also be explained by stepped-up enforcement of speed limits or higher safety standards in vehicle manufacture.

Step 2. Compare the Latest Overall Outcomes to Preestablished Targets

Actual values for each performance indicator should be compared to the target. Indicators with substantial differences, whether the actual values are much better or much worse, should be identified. An attempt needs to be made to identify why the difference occurred.

The Texas and Louisiana legislatures have required state agencies to provide quarterly variance reports. An explanation is required for any performance indicator (output or outcome) if the difference between the actual and expected value is not within 5 percent.

Not surprisingly, the helpfulness of explanations varies considerably. For example, in a Texas Commission on Environmental Quality quarterly variance report, the actual values for the outcome indicator "percent of Texans living where air meets federal air quality standards" was 94 percent of the projected value. The explanation given was, "The lower than expected performance probably correlates with a shift in population from rural areas of the state to urban areas." A substantial shortfall in "tons of hazardous waste reduced because of pollution prevention planning" was explained with "Due to a slow economy, companies may not have invested in pollution reduction projects" and "Complete data may not have been included on annual progress reports submitted to the agency."[2] Such conjectures are less helpful, and less convincing, than the more factual explanations the Commission provided in other instances.

Step 3. Compare the Program's Outcomes to Those of Similar Programs—and to Any Outside Standards

If comparable data are available on any performance indicators from other programs, other agencies, other jurisdictions, or the private sector (as discussed in chapter 9), these data can be used for comparisons. If substantially better outcomes have been achieved elsewhere, ask program staff to assess why. Ask them to justify their lower past performance or performance targets. If services and conditions appear sufficiently similar, the program might also choose to use these other programs' values as future targets for itself.

In addition, the identification and reporting of practices found particularly successful in one or more other jurisdictions can be a valuable by-product of a performance measurement activity.

In some instances, external standards will be available for comparisons, such as federal water and air quality standards. Sometimes these standards are actually built into the outcome indicator used by programs. For example, many jurisdictions have used an indicator such as "Percent of days in which air quality did not meet federal standards." If not already built into the performance indicator, the level measured (such as the amount of a certain pollutant in the air or water) can then be compared to the standard (such as the amount of the pollutant that the EPA has labeled as unsafe).

Steps 4, 5, and 6. Break Out and Compare Outcomes by Workload and Service Characteristics, to Previous Reporting Periods, and to Targets

These three steps are likely to be done jointly and so are discussed together. Chapters 8 and 9 have discussed such breakouts and comparisons. This section discusses ways to examine that information.

Examine the breakouts for each outcome indicator to assess where performance is good, fair, or poor. Compare the outcomes for various breakouts, such as customer characteristics, organizational units, workload difficulty, and type and amount of service. Identify those categories where performance seems particularly good or particularly bad.

For subgroups whose performance appears to have been particularly *bad,* the agency should seek out the reasons and take corrective action. (This will be discussed further under step 10.)

For subgroups whose performance appears to have been particularly *good,* the agency should also seek explanations to assess whether these successes can be transferred to other groups. For example, if the outcomes for younger clients are particularly good, the agency should find out why in order to determine whether any program changes are appropriate. The agency might consider actions directed toward improving the outcomes for the elderly, or it might reconsider whether the program is well-suited to helping the elderly in the first place.

Comparing breakouts across organizational units can indicate which units have particularly weak outcomes—and need attention, such as training or technical assistance. This information can also be used as a basis for rewards (whether monetary or nonmonetary) to people or organizations with particularly good outcomes or efficiency levels.

Exhibit 10-3 lists a number of the "standard" breakouts of programs, those for which people are the primary workload (and not, for example, roads and their condition). The exhibit lists typical breakouts and comparisons for both client and service characteristics. Exhibit 10-4 shows a report for a mental health program that provides comparisons across three client demographic characteristics (gender, age group, and race/ethnicity) and three service characteristics (number of sessions clients attended, the facility used, and the attending caseworker).

Comparisons can be made of outcomes *both within and among each characteristic*. For example, exhibit 10-4 indicates that, for the reporting period, the mental health program achieved considerably poorer outcomes for females than males. (Why did this occur? Has this also been the case in previous years? How close were these actual results to the targets set for these groups?) The exhibit also indicates that most clients who had attended only one or two sessions showed little or no improvement. Most clients of therapist C also showed little or no improvement. It appears likely that many females only attended one or two sessions and had therapist C. These possibilities can be checked by cross-tabulating theses characteristics.

This example also illustrates the danger of jumping to conclusions too soon. Does the data in exhibit 10-4 show that therapist C is a poor therapist? Not necessarily. This possibility needs to be checked. However, it is also possible that therapist C by chance was asked to help a large group of females under circumstances where they could only attend one or two sessions. *As is typical, the data indicate what has happened; more information on why it happened is almost always needed before actions should be taken.*

Exhibit 10-5 illustrates another way that such tabulations can be useful. Using data from a program that seeks to help train customers for employment, the exhibit cross-tabulates one customer demographic characteristic (whether the customer had completed high school) against one service characteristic (whether the customer attended the program's short or long course).

Without this two-way breakout, users of the outcome data might not realize the full importance of encouraging clients who came in without a high school diploma to take the long course and of encouraging high school graduates to take the short course because it is cheaper than the long course and gets roughly the same results.

To make comparisons more meaningful, and to be fair to the organizational units, the analysis should examine the disaggregation of each unit's outcomes by a variety of relevant breakout characteristics, such as customer

EXHIBIT 10-3

Possible Client and Service Characteristic Breakouts

Client Characteristics (at intake)

Gender	Examine outcomes for men and women separately.
Age	Examine outcomes for different age ranges. Depending on the program, the age groups might span a large range of ages (such as examining clients under 21, between 21 and 59, and 60 and older), or the program might focus on a much smaller age range (such as youth programs wanting to compare outcomes for youth under 12, 13–14, 15–16, and 17 or older).
Race/Ethnicity	Examine outcomes for clients based on race/ethnicity.
Disability	Examine outcomes based on client disability. For example, some programs might want to determine whether clients with disabilities rate services differently than those without disabilities, as well as the outcomes for clients with various types of disabilities.
Educational level	Examine outcomes for each client based on the educational level achieved before starting service.
Income	Examine outcomes for clients grouped into specific income ranges based on the latest annual household income at the time clients began service.
Household	Examine outcomes for households of various sizes, generations, and numbers of children.
Difficulty of problem at intake	Examine outcomes by incoming status based on expected difficulty in being able to help the client. Inevitably, some clients are more difficult to help than others. For example, an employment program might want to consider the literacy level of its new clients. An adoption program might want to relate outcomes to the age and health of the children.

Service Characteristics

Facility/Office	Examine outcomes for individual facilities or offices.
Service provider	Examine outcomes for clients of individual service providers, such as caseworkers.
Type of procedure	Examine outcomes for clients who were served using each distinct procedure. For example, a youth program might have used workshops, fieldtrips, classes, and so on.
Amount of service	Examine outcomes for clients who received varying amounts of service. This might be expressed as number of "sessions" a client attended, the number of hours of service provided each client, or whatever level of service measurement the program uses.

Source: Harry Hatry, Jake Cowan, and Michael Hendricks, *Analyzing Outcome Information: Getting the Most from Data* (Washington, DC: The Urban Institute, 2004), exhibit 8.

EXHIBIT 10-4

Sample Comparison of All Breakout Characteristics

Clients That Reported Improved Functioning after Completing Group Therapy

Characteristic	Number of clients	Considerable improvement (%)	Some improvement (%)	Little improvement (%)	No improvement (%)
Gender					
Female	31	10	19	55	16
Male	43	30	40	21	7
Age group					
21–30	13	23	31	31	15
31–39	28	21	32	36	11
40–49	24	21	29	38	13
50–59	9	22	33	33	11
Race/Ethnicity					
African American	25	32	20	32	16
Asian	5	0	60	20	20
Hispanic	20	15	40	40	5
White/Caucasian	24	21	29	38	13
Sessions attended					
1–2	13	15	8	54	23
3–4	21	24	33	33	10
5+	40	23	38	30	10
Facility					
Facility A	49	24	27	35	14
Facility B	25	16	40	36	8
Caseworker					
Therapist A	19	26	26	42	5
Therapist B	18	11	39	33	17
Therapist C	18	6	17	56	22
Therapist D	19	42	42	11	5
All clients	**74**	**22**	**31**	**35**	**12**

Source: Harry Hatry, Jake Cowan, and Michael Hendricks, *Analyzing Outcome Information: Getting the Most from Data* (Washington, DC: The Urban Institute, 2004), exhibit 9.

demographic characteristics and difficulty of the incoming workload. Exhibit 8-3 illustrated a workload difficulty breakout for a social service organization providing counseling to low-income families. As shown, the units achieved significantly different outcomes for different levels of difficulty. The footnotes in exhibit 8-3 indicate the type of action a program might take in light of such outcome data.

EXHIBIT 10-5

Sample Two-Characteristic Breakout

Percent of Clients Employed Three Months after Completing Service

Education level at entry	N	Short program	Long program	Total
Completed high school	100	62% employed	64% employed	63%
Did not complete high school	180	26% employed	73% employed	48%
Total	280	39%	70%	54%

Source: Harry Hatry, Jake Cowan, and Michael Hendricks, *Analyzing Outcome Information: Getting the Most from Data* (Washington, DC: The Urban Institute, 2004), exhibit 12.

Statistical analysis can help with this examination by

- estimating the likelihood that observed differences occurred by chance rather than being real differences, and
- estimating the extent to which outcomes are related to particular service characteristics.

Statistical tests can be used to estimate the likelihood that observed differences in outcomes between *organizational units* or *customer categories* are due to chance rather than to real differences.[3] If the analysis indicates, for example, that an observed difference could have occurred by chance more than 10 times out of every 100, that difference should be interpreted with caution. The likelihood that an observed difference is a real difference increases as the number of observations grows. If the numbers in each group being compared are in the hundreds, for example, the probability that an observed difference is a real one is high. As the number of observations gets smaller, the chances that an observed difference of a given size is a real difference goes down.

In exhibit 8-3, for example, the number of clients in each box is not given. If the program is large and the number of clients in each category is in the hundreds, observed differences among the units are likely to represent real differences. If the number of clients in each category is small, it is more likely that the differences between the 35 percent improvement rate for clients with minor problems in unit 2 and the 52 and 56 percent improvement rates for clients in the other two units are due to chance.

Statistical tests can also assess the likelihood that differences in outcomes for *different service approaches* are due to chance, rather than being real differences. If, for example, a program used two different methods to deliver services (such as contracting for part of the service and using agency employees to deliver the remainder of that service), those outcomes can be compared statistically to identify the likelihood that any difference might have occurred by chance.

Statistical analysis can help identify the strength of the relationship between potential causal factors and the outcome observed. For example, if a program has provided different services or service intensities to numerous customers, such analysis can estimate how much of the outcome is related to the type and amount of service provided. If the characteristics of the customer population vary, statistical analysis can estimate how strongly different customer characteristics are associated with differences in outcomes. (As with all outcome data, discerning the *implications* of such relationships for program improvement is a matter of judgment.)

Even the news media get this point on occasion. In a May 1999 article, the *Washington Post* estimated (using a statistical technique called multiple regression analysis) how closely Maryland School Performance Assessment Program scores correlated with student income and other factors beyond the control of educators. It then used the results of that study to estimate how much higher or lower each school's actual scores were on the MSPAP tests than the schools' "predicted" scores. Schools whose actual scores topped their predicted score by a big margin may well be doing a good job of educating their students—even if the actual raw scores were only average.[4]

In this Maryland example, the outcome data from regular test scores at different schools (breakout data), along with explanatory characteristics (such as the proxy for student income "percent of students eligible for free or reduced-price lunches"), were used to provide fairer and more informative information on school performance. States and their individual school districts can and should use such analysis. Public and private organizations can undertake similar analyses.

Step 7. Examine Consistency and Interrelationships among Inputs, Outputs, and Outcomes

The amount of input (e.g., funds and staffing) should be consistent with the amount of output. The amount of output, in turn, should be consistent with the amount of intermediate and end outcomes achieved.

If an agency was unable to produce the amount of output anticipated, the amount of subsequent outcomes that can be achieved is also likely to be less than expected.[5] Similarly, if the expected intermediate outcomes did not occur as hoped, subsequent end outcomes can be expected to suffer as well. These relationships do not always hold, but they sometimes can help explain why measured outcomes were not as expected. For example, one reasonable explanation for a reduced number and percent of successful outcomes is staff cutbacks during the year that resulted in working with fewer clients (thereby producing less output and fewer outcomes).

Another example: If the "number of persons counseled" by program caseworkers has declined (or increased), it can be expected that the "number of counseled persons whose situation improved" would also decline (or increase). However, declines in number counseled might also lead to improvements in other outcomes. In the counseling example, smaller numbers of persons counseled might lead to higher rates of success, because caseworkers might then have more time to spend with each person.

Step 8. Examine the Outcome Indicators Together to Obtain a More Comprehensive Perspective on Performance

Most programs will have more than one outcome indicator they need to track. It is tempting to only examine these indicators separately. However, programs should also examine the *set of outcome indicators* together to better understand recent performance and, thus, what improvements may be needed.

For example, the manager of a traffic safety program might find that an indicator based on trained observer ratings showed traffic signs were in satisfactory condition, while another indicator, based on findings from a citizen survey, found that a substantial percentage of citizens had problems with the signs. A third indicator showed increasing traffic accidents. A fourth indicator reported a high percentage of delayed response times to requests to fix traffic sign problems. The agency would need to consider all these findings (and others) in determining what action, if any, is needed.

Another example: a program might want to better understand the relationship between overall customer satisfaction and individual indicators of the quality with which the service is delivered, such as response time. Program analysts could cross-tabulate data on individuals' overall satisfaction against the records on response times or customer ratings of the adequacy of the response times. To what extent did dissatisfied customers also express dissatisfaction with the timeliness of the program's response?

A program's performance may improve on some indicators and deteriorate on others. For example, the road condition measurements might indicate improved road surfaces but, over the same time period, larger proportions of customers giving poor ratings for the quality of their rides. Program staff then need to look for reasons for the apparent conflict. Examining breakout information might reveal that the program's road maintenance had focused on primary roads and not neighborhood roads or had neglected certain areas of the jurisdiction where a large amount of dissatisfaction was present. The pattern of reasons for dissatisfaction given by survey respondents might also identify a problem to which the program had not directed much maintenance or measurement attention.

A program sometimes has directly competing objectives. In such cases, the outcomes relating to these multiple objectives need careful examination to achieve a reasonable balance. For example, reducing high school dropouts might lower average test scores because more students with academic difficulties are being tested. Improved water quality might be associated with reduced economic performance in an agricultural industry. Analysts need to examine these competing outcomes together to assess overall program performance.

Step 9. Identify and Highlight Key Findings

Performance measurement systems are likely to provide large amounts of data each reporting period—too much data for many, probably most, managers and staff to absorb. Therefore, an important element of data analysis is to highlight the performance data that most warrants attention.

A simple step is to ask someone in the program to examine the comparisons, such as those described above (and in chapter 9), and judge what performance information is important. The examiner might provide written highlights or merely flag the data (such as by circling or marking the flagged data in red).

Legislative analysts of the states of New Mexico and Utah have been experimenting with summary reports that review outcomes and fiscal information for selected programs of particular interest to their legislators.[6]

A more formal procedure is to establish an "exception reporting" process. The program establishes target *ranges* (also called *control limits*) within which it expects the values for its indicators to fall and concentrates on indicators whose values fall outside those ranges. This approach is an adaptation from the field of statistical quality control, often used by manufacturing organizations.

Exception reporting has the advantage of enabling the program to focus its subsequent analysis on a relatively small number of indicators for each reporting period, rather than having to review the data on each and every one. In manufacturing, statistical procedures are used to establish the target ranges. For most public and private services, in contrast, these ranges have to be set by staff judgment about what values of a given indicator can be safely ignored.

Once chosen, the target ranges can be programmed into the performance report software so a performance indicator value falling outside them is automatically highlighted for program attention.

The Florida Department of Environmental Protection has used a qualitative version of this approach. It puts each of its outcome indicators into one of three categories: the first indicating fully satisfactory outcomes, the second calling for closer monitoring, and the third calling for major attention. The federal government's red light, yellow light, and green light system, applied to track progress in each item of the president's management agenda, is another variation.

Step 10. Seek Explanations for Unexpected Findings

A performance measurement system, whether in government at any level or in the private sector, should explicitly call for explanatory information along with the outcome and efficiency data. This is particularly important in situations where the latest outcome data are considerably worse (or better) than anticipated.

The U.S. Government Performance and Results Act (section 1116 (d)(3)) requires agencies to explain in their program performance reports why goals were not met. New Zealand has required agency heads, as part of their quarterly reports to ministers, to provide explanations for below-standard performance and propose actions to correct it.[7] Similarly, as noted earlier, the states of Texas and Louisiana require quarterly "variance" reports that require agencies to explain any difference of 5 percent or larger between the target for an indicator and the actual value to date. Most performance measurement systems, however, have underplayed the importance of explanatory information.

Sources of explanations include the following:

- Discussions with program personnel
- Discussions or focus groups with program customers
- Responses to open-ended questions on customer surveys
- Examination of the breakout data (as suggested under steps 4–7)
- Examination of the output data (as suggested under step 7)
- Special examinations by teams selected by the program
- In-depth program evaluations

Performance Measurement: Getting Results

Explanatory information can take many forms. Probably the one most used is the *qualitative judgments* of program personnel on why the outcomes were the way they were. Such judgments might be mere rationalizations and excuses, but program personnel should be encouraged to provide substantive information.

At the other end of the spectrum, the agency might sponsor *in-depth program evaluations* that provide statistically reliable information about the reasons for the measured outcomes. Such information can help considerably in understanding what the program has achieved and why. These special studies can be very expensive and time-consuming and, thus, can be done only on a small fraction of an agency's programs in any given reporting period.[8]

Between these two extremes, program personnel should usually be able to provide information, some quantitative and some qualitative, that will reveal the reasons for problems. Likely reasons include the following, each of which requires a different program response:

- Staff and/or funding changes, such as cutbacks
- Legislation or regulatory requirements that have changed or been found inappropriate
- Poor implementation (for example, inadequate training, inexperience, or motivation of staff)—no matter how good the theory and design, weak or poor implementation will usually negate good intentions
- External factors over which the program has limited or no control, such as increasingly difficult workload; significant change in the international, national, state, or local economy; unusual weather conditions (e.g., unusually heavy rains can increase runoff, leading to increased pollution of rivers and lakes); new international pressure or competition; new businesses starting up or leaving the jurisdiction (thus affecting such outcomes as employment and earnings); and/or changes in the composition of the relevant population
- Problems in the program's own practices and policies

Another source of explanatory information is the *responses to open-ended questions on customer surveys*. As noted in chapter 7, when an agency surveys its customers as part of the performance measurement process, the questionnaire should give respondents opportunities to explain the reasons for the ratings they have given (particularly any poor ratings) and to provide suggestions for improving the service. Tabulations of the responses provide clues about the causes of poorer-than-desired performance and may provide suggestions for improvement.

Sometimes only a small percentage of respondents may provide answers to open-ended questions, and some of their responses may not be understandable or useful. Nevertheless, customer responses can be an important source of explanatory information and ideas for program improvements.

Programs with lower-than-expected performance might ask themselves such questions as: Are procedures being implemented as planned? Is the implementation of high enough quality? Are the procedures the right ones? If the problems identified by the performance data are bad enough, the program may need special investigations to identify causes and to suggest specific improvements.

As discussed in chapter 8, *breakouts of outcome data* provide clues by identifying whether specific groups of customers have particularly weak outcomes. Some breakouts can provide direct explanations. If the program breakouts identify the likely reason for failures, these can be tabulated across all customers to identify likely reasons for less-than-satisfactory performance. For example, traffic safety agencies identify the causes of traffic accidents. Performance indicators should identify the total number of accidents and disaggregate the total into categories by cause, allowing the agency to focus on causes it can affect. Traffic accidents due primarily to mechanical failure or bad weather, for example, are much less controllable by public agencies than accidents related to problem intersections.

Similarly, questionnaire response categories for customer surveys can ask respondents to identify reasons for dissatisfaction or the lack of success. Tabulations of reasons by category can help the program obtain insights into why poor outcomes happen and what is likely to improve results in the future.

Surveys that seek information on citizen participation rates (such as the use of public transit, libraries, parks, and other services) can give respondents a list of possible reasons why they did not use the service. Such reasons might include the following:

a. Did not know about the service
b. Service times were inconvenient
c. Service location was inconvenient
d. Heard that the service was not good
e. Had previous bad experiences with the service
f. Don't need the service
g. Don't have time for the service

Responses (a) through (e) refer to things that the program could correct. For example, if a substantial proportion of the respondents indicated that the hours of operation were inconvenient, the agency could consider whether changes in those hours are feasible. (Note that the responses may not indicate what the optimal hours are. To determine that, the program would need to ask about the best times for customers.)

The last two responses, *don't need* and *don't have time for the service*, are reasons over which the agency has little or no influence. No action is likely to be appropriate for these categories.

Another example is provided by the American Nurses Association, which has suggested indicators related to the care nurses provide. Its service quality indicators include the following:[9]

- The rate at which patients admitted to acute care settings develop urinary tract infections (as defined by the federal Centers for Disease Control and Prevention) within 72 hours of admission, assuming the patients showed no evidence of the infection at admission
- The rate at which patients fall and injure themselves during the course of their hospital stay
- The rate at which patients develop skin pressure ulcers—Grade II or higher—72 hours or more after admission
- Patient ratings of
    - care received during their hospital stay
    - how well nursing staff managed their pain
    - nursing staff efforts to educate them regarding their condition and care requirements

An important characteristic of the above example is the precise way most indicators are defined.

Note that an agency may not be able to take direct action itself but may still want to propose legislation or other actions by others to alleviate identified problems. For example, while vehicle mechanical failures are not within the control of local governments, the federal government, and to some extent state governments, can take action if significant patterns of such failures occur. Agencies should recognize the presence of shared and joint responsibility for indicators, particularly outcome indicators. (Sharing may be with other agencies, other levels of government, or with other sectors of the economy.)

The important point here is that by properly designing data-gathering instruments and analyzing the resulting data, the program can obtain important clues about what the problems are and what the program can do about them.

Suggestion: Categorize each outcome indicator by the degree of influence the program has and include this information in performance reports. The degree of influence might be expressed in three categories, such as *little or no influence, modest or some influence,* and *considerable influence.* The agency using such categories should define them as specifically as possible and provide illustrations for each. Such categorization helps users of the information understand the extent to which the agency can affect outcomes. (For an outcome indicator to be included in a program's set, the program should have some influence, even if small.)

Generally, agencies and their programs will be less able to influence end outcomes than intermediate outcomes. Even most intermediate outcomes are not likely to be fully controllable by any agency. Yet this does not absolve agencies from the responsibility to recognize the amount of influence they have.

Step 11. *Provide Recommendations to Officials for Future Actions, Including Experimentation with New Service Delivery Approaches*

People who examine the data, whether they are professional analysts, staff, or managers, probably should also provide recommendations to other officials based on what the performance information shows. Those who examine the data in some detail are likely to gain insights into next steps and possible actions.

Elsewhere, we have emphasized that users of the information should not jump to conclusions and take action based solely on the data. Normally the appropriate recommendations are to further examine the causes and ways to alleviate them. When performance data indicate the presence of problems, the solutions are often unclear.

However, based on the findings from procedures such as those discussed above, analysts should be able to recommend one or more of the following types of actions:

- Specific possible corrective procedures (with provisions that when future outcome data reports become available, these should be assessed to determine whether the actions appear to have resolved the problems)
- An examination of program activities that explanatory information indicated might be causing problems

- An in-depth evaluation to identify causes and what corrective actions should be taken
- An experiment to test a new procedure against the current one
- A wait-and-see strategy in the expectation that the unsatisfactory outcomes are aberrations—the result of a temporary problem rather than a trend—and will correct themselves in the future

The experimental option included above may be particularly interesting to officials who like to innovate. It will be practical under some conditions to design a "simple" experiment with new service approaches and use subsequent performance data to assess the results before committing to any particular approach. A program with an ongoing performance measurement system can use it to help evaluate new or modified procedures or policies, as discussed in chapter 9.

Exhibit 9-2 compared computer to manual processing of eligibility determinations in a program that applied the new process to part of its incoming work. The program then tracked the outcomes separately for an appropriate period and compared the findings across the different procedures. A simpler but less powerful approach to examining new or modified processes is to only compare outcomes for the old service procedures with outcomes after introduction of the new procedures. (See exhibit 10-2 and the associated discussion for this "before versus after" measurement approach.)

These procedures are similar to a variety of standard program evaluation procedures. Exhibit 10-2 is a simple illustration of a pre-post program evaluation. The example in exhibit 8-3 is a basic comparison-group design. Exhibit 9-2 illustrates a (small scale) random assignment controlled experiment. The comparisons of demographic breakout categories discussed in chapters 8 and 9 can provide basic data for comparison-group program evaluations (such as comparing the outcomes for male customers to those for female customers). A *full* program evaluation would use the outcome data but add such steps as more extensive statistical analysis and an intensive search for explanations.

Special Analysis Problem for Programs That Need to Combine Outcome Data from Many Sources

Agencies (particularly federal and state agencies) may obtain data for some outcome indicators from other agencies, such as those in another level of government. This situation can also arise for private, nonprofit organizations, such as a local United Way that wants aggregate counts of progress on an indicator from the many agencies it supports.

Can the data be combined? If so, how? The problem is that the agencies supplying the data are very likely to have used somewhat different data collection procedures.

An agency wanting to combine data for an outcome indicator can often develop some rough aggregate data but will likely need to accept some differences among the data collection procedures used by different sites. Using education as an example, the process might be the following:

1. Data would be obtained from each decentralized site.
2. The data-gathering procedures and specific definitions used would be examined to ascertain whether the coverage of the data from each site is at least roughly comparable. For example, if all states have their own standardized tests of 8th grade mathematics, the number and percentage of students that scored at a certain percentile in a given year might be provided to the aggregating agency.
3. The aggregation could be in several forms, including the following:
   — A calculation of the percent of *students* who scored at or above the X percentile. This number would be calculated from the number of students that took each state test.
   — The number of *states* in which at least X percent of students scored at the Y percentile or above.
4. The report that presents these data should indicate clearly the limitations of the procedure (in this example, how much the subject matter differed from test to test and whether the same criteria were used to exclude students from testing).

This process, while unpleasant to many analysts and other users, nevertheless seems preferable to the alternative of not aggregating at all.

References and Notes

1. A similar set of steps prepared as a guide for state legislative analysts is included in National Conference of State Legislatures, "Asking Key Questions: How to Review Program Results" (Denver, CO, 2005), 8–10.
2. Texas Commission on Environmental Quality, "Fourth Quarter Report on Performance Measures: Fiscal Year 2003," SFR-055/03-04 (Austin, October 2003), 4, 33.
3. It is beyond this book's scope to describe the many statistical procedures that can help an agency analyze performance information. For further information, see, for example, Kathryn E. Newcomer, "Using Statistics in Evaluation," and Dale E. Berger, "Using Regression Analysis," both in *Handbook of Practical Program Evalu-*

ation, 2nd edition, edited by Joseph S. Wholey et al. (San Francisco: Jossey-Bass Publishers, 2004).

4. Amy Argetsinger, "Beating Poverty in the Classroom," *Washington Post,* 16 May 1999, C5. Agencies will need statistical personnel or consultants to use these specialized statistical procedures.

5. Some outputs are closely related to outcomes, such as number of miles of roads maintained and number of clients provided service. Other outputs are not likely closely linked to outcomes, such as number of reports completed and number of training programs held.

6. A pamphlet describing this process has been published by the National Conference of State Legislatures; "Asking Key Questions: How to Review Program Results" (Denver, CO, 2005).

7. The Treasury, Government of New Zealand, *Purchase Agreement Guidelines 1995/96: With Best Practices for Output Performance Measures* (Wellington, April 1995), 20.

8. A description of the procedures for in-depth evaluations is outside the scope of this book. The appendix lists a few publications on this topic.

9. For more details, see American Nurses Association, *Nursing Quality Indicators: Guide for Implementation* and *Nursing Quality Indicators: Definitions and Implications* (Washington, DC, 1996). Data collection on these indicators is currently being pilot-tested. These indicators have been modified somewhat since 1996. See the ANA National Center for Nursing Quality Indicators web site (http://www.nursingworld.org/quality/temp.htm) for more details.

Reporting Performance Information

How the findings are reported is likely as important as what is reported. The importance of good presentation for performance measurement information, especially in public documents, has only recently been fully recognized. In the past few years, the Governmental Accounting Standards Board has issued reports suggesting criteria for external performance reporting.[1] A number of annual awards programs have been established for good public reporting of performance information.

Technological advances continue to make it much easier to provide clear, attractive reports. The use of diverse forms of graphics and even color printing are becoming much easier and less expensive. In addition to the traditional tables, performance data can be provided in bar charts, trend charts, pie charts, maps, other graphics, and, likely one of these days, 3-D charts. Photographs can also be added to illustrate performance results.

Of course, report presentation also needs attention to content. What information needs to be provided to the various audiences? The remainder of this chapter discusses a number of content issues.

The focus here is on written, not oral, reporting. Oral reporting techniques are also important but are beyond the scope of this book. Below, we first address external reporting and then internal reporting.

External Reporting

External reporting or performance information is a major approach to "accountability." It enables elected officials, interest groups, and citizens to see what they are getting for their money—at least to some extent, since the internal organization inevitably will filter the information.

External reporting also has the potential operational benefit of motivating the organization to perform better on the indicators being reported. In addition, more data comparing one agency's outcomes to those of other outside agencies are being reported—data that compare different governments or different nonprofit organizations that provide similar services. These comparisons have dangers. They can be misleading and unfair for many reasons, such as comparing agencies that operate under considerably different environmental conditions, or using questionable performance indicators. On the whole, however, comparisons will continue to be made and can serve a useful motivational, as well as accountability, function.

An example that captures the essence of performance measurement reporting is a statement in a City of San Jose "Budget in Brief" report. In a section called "Service Delivery Impacts," the report includes this statement on the city's airport: "Reduced parking shuttle hours at the airport, resulting in an additional 30 seconds to 1 minute wait for customers during peak traffic."[2] The City and its Airport Services used the public budget report to identify the specific added burden customers faced because of a curtailed service.

Increasingly, governments and their agencies are breaking out and reporting outcome data by geographical areas and other demographic groups. Charlotte, North Carolina, reports quality of life indicators for each of over 170 neighborhoods.[3] San Jose, California, publishes various indicators twice each year on seven City Service Areas.[4] The New Mexico Department of Health reports health profiles for each of its counties. Exhibit 11-1 is a page relating to the health of babies from one of its annual reports.

Web-based reporting is replacing at least some paper reports. Many (if not most) governments (federal, state, and local) and nonprofit organizations have their own web sites. Individual agencies in larger governments also have their own sites. Many of these organizations have placed performance data on their web sites. This trend is likely to continue, making electronic reporting the major way citizens and interest groups will obtain performance information.

The City of Bellevue, Washington, includes "Vital Signs" data, based on 16 key performance indicators for the city as a whole, in its newsletter to citizens and on its web site. The city web site also contains tables present-

EXHIBIT 11-1

Santa Fe County Health Profile

MATERNAL AND INFANT HEALTH - *BIRTH WEIGHT*

RESIDENT LIVE BIRTHS
LOW BIRTH WEIGHT BIRTHS (< 2500 grams)
1992-2002

	1992	1993	1994	1995	1996	1997	1998	1999	2000	2001	2002*
Santa Fe Co.	96	101	98	97	119	115	144	118	124	107	126
New Mexico	2,014	2,032	2,023	2,017	2,041	2,086	2,042	2,078	2,180	2,147	2,224

*2002 data are provisional

SOURCE: NM Department of Health, Office of New Mexico Vital Records and Health Statistics

RESIDENT LIVE BIRTHS
PERCENT LOW BIRTH WEIGHT (<2500 grams)
1992-2002

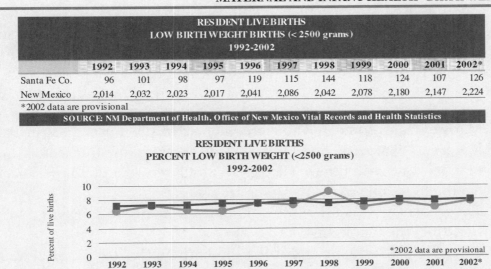

*2002 data are provisional

	1992	1993	1994	1995	1996	1997	1998	1999	2000	2001	2002*
Santa Fe Co.	6.4	7.2	6.5	6.5	7.5	7.3	9.1	7.0	7.6	7.0	7.8
New Mexico	7.2	7.3	7.3	7.5	7.5	7.8	7.5	7.7	8.0	7.9	8.0

SOURCE: NM Department of Health, Office of New Mexico Vital Records and Health Statistics

Low Birth Weight

Low birth weight (LBW) is defined as an infant weight of less than 2,500 grams (5 1/2 lbs) at the time of delivery. Birth weight is one of the most important factors in determining the survival and health of an infant. Low birth weight is a public health problem since infants born LBW have increased infant mortality, morbidity, incidence of learning disabilities, and medical costs. Nationally, the risk factors for LBW include maternal age of less than seventeen and greater than 34 years, Black race/ethnicity, low socioeconomic status, single marital status, lower levels of maternal education, smoking, inadequate weight gain, low pre-pregnancy weight, and a variety of medical risk factors (Source: Data to Action).

Smoking, which retards fetal growth, is the single largest modifiable risk factor for LBW and infant mortality. It is estimated to account for 20 to 30% of all LBW births.

RESIDENT LIVE BIRTHS
VERY LOW BIRTH WEIGHT BIRTHS (< 1500 grams)
1994-2002

	1994-1996		1997-1999		2000-2002*	
	Number	Percent	Number	Percent	Number	Percent
Santa Fe Co.	55	1.2	51	1.1	57	1.2
New Mexico	894	1.1	880	1.1	1,005	1.2

*2002 data are provisional

SOURCE: NM Department of Health, ONMVRHS

High Birth Weight

A woman with a history of gestational diabetes or delivery of a baby weighing >9 pounds is at risk of developing type 2 diabetes. In addition, if the baby has macrosomia (generally defined as a weight of 4000 g or more), he or she is at risk for obesity and also for developing type 2 diabetes later on in life. It should be noted that there is no widely agreed-upon weight definition. Any evaluation of fetal weight must be considered in the context of gestational age.

Sources: *"Diabetes in the Life Cycle and Research,"* Vol. 4. 2003. Editor M. Franz. Published by the American Association of Diabetes Educators, Chicago Illinois. *Diabetes Care Journal*, Supplement 1, January 2003 Vol. (26).

RESIDENT LIVE BIRTHS
HIGH BIRTH WEIGHT BIRTHS (4090+ grams, 9 pounds)
1994-2002

	1994-1996		1997-1999		2000-2002*	
	Number	Percent	Number	Percent	Number	Percent
Santa Fe Co.	205	4.5	160	3.3	187	3.9
New Mexico	4,010	5.2	3,810	4.9	3,674	4.7

*2002 data are provisional

SOURCE: NM Department of Health, ONMVRHS

Source: New Mexico Department of Health, "Santa Fe County Health Profile" (Santa Fe, NM: New Mexico Department of Health, 2003), 17.

ing the values of "effectiveness," "efficiency," and "workload" key performance indicators for each city department. The data presented for each indicator include actual values for the three latest years and the target value for the latest year. The vital sign indicators were developed with citizens in a series of discussion meetings. Exhibit 11-2 is the 2004 vital signs report.

The New York City web site provides data on selected performance indicators on each of its almost 59 citizen community board areas. Citizens can enter their addresses and find the relevant data.

Key issues for web-based performance reporting include the following:

- Many citizens, some of whom are likely to be the most concerned about low levels of service, do not have ready access to the Internet.
- Many people with Internet access are not likely to look for performance data unless some particular issue faces them.
- The information is often not summarized in any way, leaving the user to extract the highlights.
- Often the performance information on the web sites is not kept up to date in a timely manner.

Nevertheless, there is a ton of data out there.

Internal Reporting

Internal performance reporting is vital to stimulating service improvements. Performance data are much more frequently seen and used internally than externally. Regular feedback is a key ingredient of good management. The form, substance, and dissemination of performance reports play a major role in proving useful feedback.

Key issues for internal performance reporting include the following:

- Are the reports clear and substantial?
- Are they timely? Are the data reported with sufficient frequency? When reported, are the data in the reports reasonably up to date? Some performance indicators may need to be reported more frequently than others. (For example, data from household surveys are likely to be needed less frequently, only annually or quarterly, while performance reports containing incidence of crimes, fires, water main breaks, etc., need to be reported considerably more frequently to enable managers to take timely corrective actions.)
- Are the reports adequately summarized or highlighted to allow very busy managers to digest the information in a reasonable amount of time?

EXHIBIT 11-2

Snapshot of Citizen-Based Vital Signs

A snapshot of Bellevue's current vital signs	2002 actual	2003 actual	2004 actual	2004 target	2004 target met or exceeded
Effectiveness					
Residents' overall satisfaction with Parks and Recreation in Bellevue	86%	88%	89%	NA	
Patrol response times to critical emergencies from dispatch to arrival	3.4 min.	3.3 min.	2.1 min.	4.2 min.	✓
Number of violent and property crimes committed per 1,000 population	40	39	43.5	44	✓
% of residents saying they are getting their money's worth when thinking about City of Bellevue services and facilities	84%	80%	82%	85%	
Moody's Investors Service Bond rating	Aaa	Aaa	Aaa	Aaa	✓
Residents rating their neighborhood as a good to excellent place to live	89%	92%	92%	90%	✓
Resident satisfaction rating for clean streets (fairly clean to very clean)	96%	95%	97%	90%	✓
Percent of fires confined to room of origin	86%	93%	88%	85%	✓
Residential street average pavement rating	81%	86%	80%	80%	✓
Violations of state and federal drinking water standards	0	0	0	0	✓
Cardiac arrest survival rate	35%	35%	46%	35%	✓
Residents rating Bellevue as a good or excellent place to live	93%	97%	97%	95%	✓
% of residents fairly satisfied to very satisfied with job City is doing in planning for the future	35%	35%	46%	35%	✓
Water service interruptions per 1,000 service connections	2.9	2.9	2.2	3	✓
Residents saying Bellevue is headed in the right direction	78%	79%	78%	80%	✓
Percent of Mobility Management Areas achieving concurrency	100%	100%	100%	100%	✓

Source: City of Bellevue, WA, "2004 Annual Performance Report," http://www.cityofbellevue.org/page.asp?view=38708.

- Are they disseminated to all those who need and can use the information? Often missing is dissemination to people who are most involved and can do something about the data—the front-line staff!

A program will likely find it useful to track a large number of outcome indicators for internal use. However, for external reporting, a considerably shorter list is appropriate. The department's highest officials, its budget office, and the relevant legislative body may want a relatively short list of indicators.

Some Examples of Formats

The first six formats use tables. The intent of each is to illustrate the presentation of comparisons—a key way to make performance data useful and more interesting to readers.

These tabular formats (which use hypothetical data) can be used for reporting both internally and externally. They are a sample of the many formats that can be constructed based on the special needs of a program.

- *Format 1, exhibit 11-3, compares actual outcomes to targets for the last and current reporting periods.* It does this for each of four outcome indicators. This format is likely to be a key one for most programs. Exhibit 11-2 provides an example from the city of Bellevue, Washington.
- *Format 2, exhibit 11-4, is similar to format 1 but shows report period and cumulative values for the year.* This format is useful for outcome measurement systems that provide data more frequently than once a year (as is usually desirable).
- *Format 3, exhibit 11-5, compares the latest outcomes for various geographical locations. This format is useful for making comparisons across breakout categories identified by the program.* For example, a program may want to illustrate comparisons across managerial units, individual projects, or particular customer characteristics. To do this, the program would change the column labels in exhibit 11-5 to correspond to the relevant breakouts. (Refer to exhibit 8-3 for a breakout by family services unit.)
- *Format 4, exhibit 11-6, displays outcome data for one indicator by organizational unit and workload (customer) difficulty.* This format, similar to exhibit 8-3, is likely to be useful for internal reports because it shows how each organizational unit has performed relative to the others. In this case, the client characteristic examined was client difficulty. Displaying by difficulty of the incoming workload will make the comparisons considerably fairer and more informative.

EXHIBIT 11-3

Reporting Format 1: Actual Outcomes versus Targets

Outcome indicator	Last Period			This Period		
	Target	Actual	Difference	Target	Actual	Difference
Percent of children returned to home within 12 months	35	25	−10	35	30	−5
Percent of children who had over two placements within the past 12 months	20	20	0	15	12	+3
Percent of children whose adjustment level improved during the past 12 months	50	30	−20	50	35	−15
Percent of clients reporting satisfaction with their living arrangements	80	70	−10	80	85	+5

Note: This format compares actual outcomes to targets for both the last and current periods. Plus (+) indicates improvement; minus (−) indicates worsening.

EXHIBIT 11-4

Reporting Format 2: Actual Values versus Targets

Outcome indicator	Current Period		Cumulative for Year		Year's target
	Target	Actual	Target	Actual	
Percentage of parents reporting knowledge or awareness of local parental resource center activities	75	70	70	65	70
Percentage of parents reporting that parental resource centers led to their taking a more active role in their child's development or education	50	65	50	60	50

Note: This format shows cumulative values for a year rather than for previous reporting periods. It will only be useful for outcome measurement systems that provide data more than once a year.

EXHIBIT 11-5

Reporting Format 3: Outcomes by Geographical Location

Outcome indicator	Geographical Location				United States
	Eastern	Central	Mountain	Pacific	
Percentage of K–12 schools participating in the Star Schools Program	30%	15%	20%	35%	29%
Number of students enrolled in Star Schools high school credit, college preparatory, or AP courses that had not been available previously	1,500,000	600,000	850,000	1,950,000	4,900,000
Percentage of students reporting increased interest in school because of distance-learning activities in their classes	65%	90%	85%	75%	77%

Note: This format makes comparisons across any breakout categories identified by the program, such as managerial units, individual projects, schools, school districts, or particular student characteristics.

EXHIBIT 11-6

Reporting Format 4: Outcomes by Organizational Unit and Difficulty

Difficulty level	Applications Processed within X Days (%)			
	Unit 1	Unit 2	Unit 3	Total
High	35	30	54	39
Low	52	35	56	47
Medium	58	69	61	63
Total	**48**	**44**	**57**	**60**

Note: This format displays outcome data for one indicator broken out by one demographic or customer difficulty characteristic and displayed for each organizational unit. It shows program staff how each unit has performed relative to others. Displaying this information by key characteristics, such as difficulty of incoming workload, will make the comparisons fairer and more informative.

- *Format 5, exhibit 11-7, displays on a single page responses from a customer survey, broken out by several demographic or program characteristics for a single outcome indicator.* This multiple cross-tabulation is an internal format. It enables program staff to identify which respondent characteristics show unusually positive or negative results for a particular outcome indicator. The format can be used to report on any

EXHIBIT 11-7

Reporting Format 5: Breakouts of Responses to a Customer Survey by Demographic or Program Characteristics

Respondent characteristics	Households Reporting Their Frequency of Use of City Buses in the Past 12 Months (%)				
	Not at all (*N*=50)	A little (*N*=83)	Somewhat (*N*=429)	Considerably (*N*=63)	Total responding (*N*=625)
Sex and race					
White male	7	11	71	10	265
White female	8	13	68	11	284
Nonwhite male	11	30	53	6	36
Nonwhite female	10	17	65	8	40
Age					
18–34	13	16	58	13	272
35–49	6	11	75	8	125
50–64	3	11	80	5	105
65 and over	6	11	74	9	123
Family income					
Less than 20,000	12	22	55	11	150
$20,000–29,999	15	19	55	11	117
$30,000–39,999	4	16	70	10	100
$40,000–49,999	7	5	78	10	69
$50,000–74,999	2	9	78	11	104
$75,000 and over	3	2	88	7	85
Region					
Central	12	17	60	11	150
Northeast	13	16	59	11	174
Northwest	6	12	74	8	76
Southeast	3	9	77	11	113
Southwest	5	9	71	15	112
Total	8	13	69	10	100

Note: This format enables program staff to identify what categories of customer show unusually positive or negative results on a particular outcome indicator.

indicator for which data on a variety of customer (or program) characteristics have been obtained. (See also exhibit 10-4.)

Displaying the findings on a single page eases the task of spotting unusual findings. For example, the data indicate that considerably poorer usage occurred for households with incomes below $30,000, for nonwhite males, for households in the central and northeast regions, and for younger adults. These findings suggest that the program should seek to find out why and consider giving special attention to households with these characteristics. Data obtained in future years will indicate whether any such special attention improved outcomes for those groups.

The previous formats use *tables* to present the data. Other graphic presentations can be considerably more powerful, especially for external consumption. A picture is often worth a thousand words (or numbers)!

Options include the following:

- **Line graphs.** This presentation of individual outcome indicators is especially good for showing trends—the values of the indicator plotted against time, perhaps by quarter or year. Exhibit 11-8 presents an example. As shown, multiple lines can be used to compare breakout groups or jurisdictions (but avoid overcrowding).
- **Bar charts.** These are an excellent way to show comparisons. Exhibit 11-9 compares county high school dropout rates to statewide rates for a num-

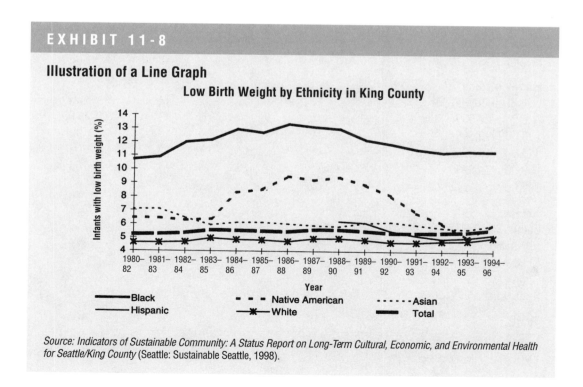

EXHIBIT 11-8

Illustration of a Line Graph

Low Birth Weight by Ethnicity in King County

Source: Indicators of Sustainable Community: A Status Report on Long-Term Cultural, Economic, and Environmental Health for Seattle/King County (Seattle: Sustainable Seattle, 1998).

Performance Measurement: Getting Results

EXHIBIT 11-9

Illustration of a Bar Chart

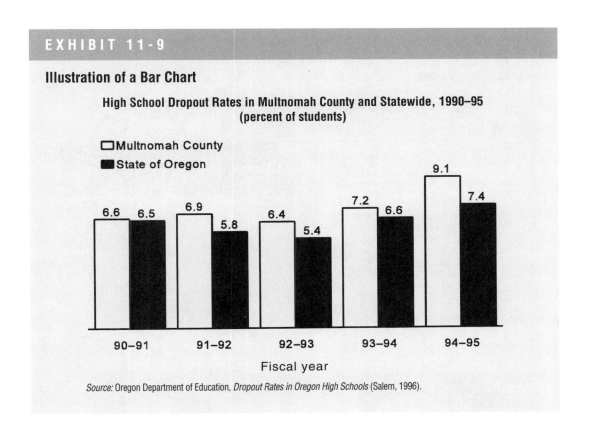

High School Dropout Rates in Multnomah County and Statewide, 1990–95
(percent of students)

☐ Multnomah County
■ State of Oregon

Fiscal year

Source: Oregon Department of Education, *Dropout Rates in Oregon High Schools* (Salem, 1996).

ber of years. Exhibit 11-10 displays a series of bar charts rating a number of outcome indicators on New York City's subway system. Similar ratings were provided for each of the subway system's 19 lines. The published report used color, making the presentation considerably more attractive than this exhibit. (These data were obtained, assembled, and analyzed by a citizens' group, the Straphangers Campaign—see chapter 7).

- **Maps.** Mapping performance information has become very popular as inexpensive mapping software has emerged. Maps are a dramatic way to present geographical data, such as by neighborhoods within cities. The maps might show numbers inserted in each geographical area rated, use shading or colors to distinguish various rating levels, or both. Exhibit 11-11, through the use of map shading, compares youth mortality rates among District of Columbia neighborhoods. Next to each of these maps in the report a table was presented that provided the actual values of the death rates for each neighborhood. For some presentations, if ample room is available, the actual values might be included on the map itself.

The geographical areas might be portions of a county, state, or local jurisdiction, showing the percent of customers who are employed, healthy, satisfied with particular services, have low rates of feeling unsafe

EXHIBIT 11-10

Straphangers Campaign Subway Profile

Straphangers Campaign
C SUBWAY LINE PROFILE

The C line ranks tied for 20th place out of the 22 subway lines rated by the Straphangers Campaign. Our ranking is based on the MTA New York City Transit data below, using a method described at www.straphangers.org.

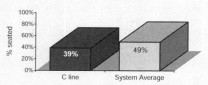

Straphangers Campaign MetroCard Rating 80¢

The C line has less than average daytime service and doesn't run at night.

scheduled minutes between weekday trains
as of January 2006

	AM Rush	Noon	PM Rush	Overnight
C line	9:15	10	10	-
System Average	5:33	8:26	5:48	20

The C arrives with above-average regularity...

% of trains arriving at regular intervals
(without gaps in service or train "bunching")
between 6 a.m. and 9 p.m.

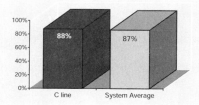

C line: 88% System Average: 87%

but its cars break down more often than those on the average line.

average miles traveled between delays
caused by mechanical failures, 2005

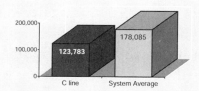

C line: 123,783 System Average: 178,085

You're less likely to get a seat on the C line.

% of passengers with seats at most crowded point
during rush hour

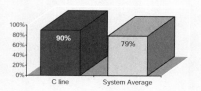

C line: 39% System Average: 49%

The C line is tied for the cleanest line...

% of cars with 'light or no interior dirtiness'
as defined by NYC Transit

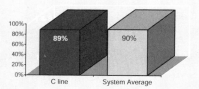

C line: 90% System Average: 79%

but performs below average on in-car announcements.

% of cars with correct announcements
(as defined by NYC Transit)

C line: 89% System Average: 90%

Suggestions? Complaints? Call the C line superintendent at (718) 927-8724.

Source: Straphangers Campaign, *State of the Subways Report Card* (New York: New York Public Interest Research Group Fund, Inc., July 2006).

EXHIBIT 11-11

Mortality Rates for 1- to 19-Year-Olds by Neighborhood Cluster

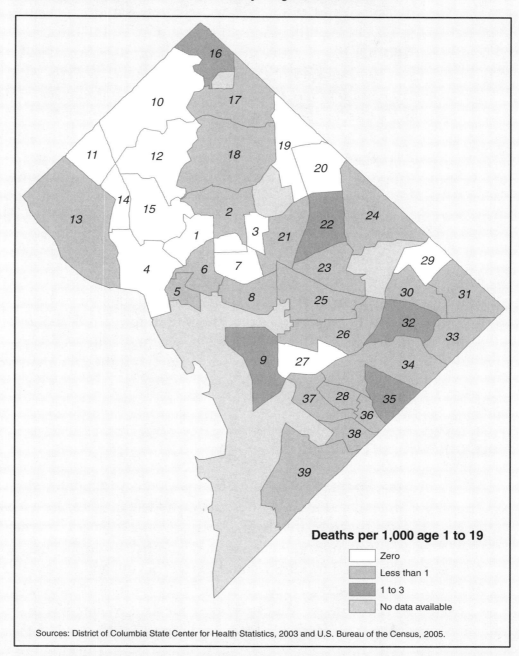

Deaths per 1,000 age 1 to 19

- Zero
- Less than 1
- 1 to 3
- No data available

Sources: District of Columbia State Center for Health Statistics, 2003 and U.S. Bureau of the Census, 2005.

Source: D.C. Kids Count Collaborative for Children and Families, "Every Kid Counts in the Distirict of Columbia" (Washington, DC: D.C. Children's Trust Fund, 2005), map 3.

walking around their neighborhoods during the day or at night, and so on. (See exhibits 7-13, 8-4, and 8-5 for other examples.)

Reminder: When comparing outcomes or expenditures across jurisdictions or programs, it is usually necessary to normalize the data—that is, adjust for differences in size—to make the information meaningful. Another bar chart is shown in exhibit 9-4. Annual library circulation was normalized in two ways. One way was by expressing annual library circulation as *circulation per capita* (i.e., total number of items circulated by the library system divided by the population of the area served). For the second performance indicator, circulation was divided by the number of registered borrowers. For fairer comparisons, exhibit 11-9 shows dropout *rates* (percentages) and not numbers of dropouts.

Some caveats on graphics. Reports frequently tend to overdo graphic presentations, sacrificing clarity for artistic endeavor.[5] For example, pie charts look nice, but they make it difficult for readers to determine size differences. Sometimes performance reports use a three-dimensional option in presenting bar charts. Again, this can make it difficult to judge differences. When using maps, authors tend to include too much information, reducing readability. This may be acceptable if the graphic is intended to merely give an overall impression, but not if the graphic is intended to provide careful comparisons.

Identify the Report Highlights

A considerable danger in performance measurement is overwhelming public officials, both on the executive and legislative side, with indicator data. The staff responsible for the performance report (whether in the agency, in a central management and budget office, or in the legislature—or a contractor) need to identify and extract what they believe are the key findings from the data. This becomes even more important as agencies expand their reporting of indicator breakout data. What are the important issues, problems, successes, failures, and progress indicated by the data and likely to be of concern and interest to the audience of the report? Any important missing outcomes should also be identified.

Thus, performance reports should contain not only the data but also a summary of the report's highlights—emphasizing information that warrants particular attention—to help users focus quickly on the important findings. These highlights should include both "success" and "failure" (problem) stories. The summary should be a balanced account to reduce

Performance Measurement: Getting Results

the likelihood that readers will consider the report self-serving. Explanatory information should be included as part of the report and should be clear, concise, and to the point. Reports, especially those going outside the program, should also identify any actions the program has taken, or plans to take, to correct problems identified in the outcome report. This step, along with explanatory information, can help avert, or at least alleviate, unwarranted criticism.

Highlighting can be done by

- writing out the key findings and issues raised;
- physically highlighting the data, such as by circling or marking in red the data that raise flags (such as illustrated in exhibits 8-3 and 11-7— why are such small percentages of nonwhite males and low-income people using the city bus system?); or
- combinations of these two options.

Preferably, each performance report would contain selected performance comparisons (such as breakouts showing relevant differences in outcomes for various demographic groups) to help identify the key findings. (See chapter 9 for a discussion of comparison options.)

Provide Explanatory Information in Performance Reports

Explanatory information can provide information important for readers' interpretation of the data. It also gives program staff an opportunity to explain unexpected, undesired outcomes, thus potentially alleviating their concern that the data will be misused (and against them).

Explanations can

1. be qualitative (including judgments), quantitative, or a combination.
2. provide context when any of the comparisons show unexpected differences in outcome values, such as when
   — the actual value for an outcome indicator deviates substantially from the target value (better or worse), or
   — the outcome values show major differences among operating units, categories of customers, or among other workload units.
3. consider both internal and external factors. Internal factors affecting outcomes might, for example, include significant unexpected loss of program personnel (or other resources) during the reporting period. External factors might include highly unusual weather conditions or unexpected loss (or gain) of industry within a particular jurisdiction.

4. incorporate the findings from any special evaluations that examine the program and its achievements in depth. Such findings are likely to, in fact, supersede the outcome data collected as part of the routine outcome measurement process. At the very least, findings from recent program evaluations should be given prominence in the presentation of a program's outcomes. Such studies are likely to provide considerably more information about the impacts of the program than outcome data alone can reveal.

Other Necessary Information for Reporting Performance Data

In addition to explanations for unexpected findings, both internal and external performance reports should contain such information as the following, even if only in footnotes:

- Each performance indicator should be clearly defined, such as what the indicator covers. This includes the period covered by the performance data.
- Any important uncertainties or limitations in the data should be identified.
- For indicators based on survey data (whether the surveys are of citizens, of data from agency records, through observations made by trained observers, or of any other source), the following additional information should also be provided:
  — The total number of items surveyed, such as number of respondents—both in total and for each category of respondents for whom data are presented in the report, such as each gender or each racial/ethnic group
  — The response rates (an important indicator of the likelihood of non-sampling error)
  — The dates the survey was conducted
  — How the survey was conducted (e.g., phone, mail, web-based, etc.)
  — Who conducted the survey
- Any substantial changes in the performance indicators and the data collection procedures from previous reporting periods should be identified. (Changing these without giving good reasons can give the appearance of being selective to hide unpleasant findings.)
- Mappings should be used where possible to show outcomes for individual geographical areas in the program's jurisdiction. This is likely to be especially useful for local governments, showing neighborhood or

service district results. States often should report by geographical areas such as counties and major cities, and the federal government should report by state for many of its performance indicators.

- If indices are reported, the individual elements that make up the index should be clearly and fully identified, and the values for each element that make up the index should be readily available.

- Programs may also want to include information on how strongly they can influence the indicator values, as described in chapter 6.

What Happens If the Performance News Is Bad?

Almost certainly, every performance report will include some indicators showing results significantly below expectations (such as compared to the targets for the reporting period). A major function of performance measurement systems is to uncover below-par outcomes so that those who can do something about them are alerted and, after corrective actions are taken, can assess whether the actions have produced the desired results.

Agency and program officials should include with their performance reports explanations for any poor outcomes and the steps taken, or planned, to correct the problem.

As one city police chief told the Urban Institute team in the 1970s, "If the data look good, I will take the credit. If the data look bad, I will ask for more money." This is another approach.

Additional Suggestions for External Reporting

The following are suggestions for reporting outside the agency, such as to the legislature, other funders, and the public. They are based on principles that in the past, unfortunately, have often been violated.

- Be selective about which, and how many, indicators are included. Focus on those indicators most likely to be of interest to the audience (probably not on output or efficiency indicators). Selectivity does *not* mean selecting only those indicators that make the agency look good—reporting needs to be balanced in order to be credible.

- Pay particular attention to making the reports easily understandable. As discussed earlier, use charts and graphs either to supplement tables or as the main focus. Use color if practical.

- Obtain feedback on the reports periodically from major constituencies, such as elected officials, funders, and the public (perhaps obtaining feedback from the public by use of focus groups). Ask about the usefulness and readability of the performance reports. Use the feedback to help tailor future performance reports to the particular audience.

Dissemination of Performance Reports

Performance reports should be disseminated to everyone on the program's staff as soon as possible after the data become available. Program personnel should be given the opportunity to provide any additional relevant explanatory information for the final formal report. This will encourage all program members to feel they are part of a team whose purpose is to produce the best possible outcomes. As will be discussed further in chapter 12, the program manager might hold staff meetings on the outcome data to identify any actions that the performance data indicate are needed.

The performance report—including data, explanatory information, and the highlights or summary—should then be provided to offices outside the program. *A key question to consider is how much detail should be given to those outside the program.* Breakout data also may need to be provided, but selectively, to avoid overwhelming readers with too many numbers. The breakouts should be those considered most important to report users. Outcomes broken out by customer demographic characteristics, such as race or ethnicity, for example, are often important and of considerable interest. More breakout detail can be included in appendixes.

Special news releases, distribution through libraries, special inserts in local newspapers, radio and television, and (increasingly) the Internet are all ways to disseminate the performance material. Here again, the program will need to decide what details will be of interest to these audiences. Inclusion of explanatory information and statements of corrective actions already taken, or planned, can help defuse negative reactions to data that appear to represent poor performance.

External performance measurement reporting is of special concern to agency officials, who can be particularly apprehensive of performance reports provided to the news media. The objective should be to provide media representatives with an understanding of what the data tell and what the data's limitations are.

Avoid choosing just data that make the agency look good, tempting as this may be. Over the long run, the media and special interest groups will catch on, and the reports will lose credibility.

Summary annual performance reports can be an effective way to communicate with citizens and increase public credibility, as long as they are user friendly, timely, and provide a balanced assessment of performance.

References and Notes

1. See for example, James Fountain et al., *Reporting Performance Information: Suggested Criteria for Effective Communication* (October 2003); and Paul Epstein et al., "Government Service Efforts and Accomplishments Performance Reports: A Guide to Understanding" (July 2005), both published by the Governmental Accounting Standards Board, Norwalk, CT.
2. City of San Jose, "2005–2006 Proposed Budget: Budget in Brief" (San Jose, CA, 2005).
3. See the city's biennial "Charlotte Neighborhood Quality of Life Study" reports, such as its 2004 report (Charlotte, NC, September 2004).
4. See the city's "City Service Area Performance Reports," such as its 2003–2004 year-end report (San Jose, September 2004).
5. Two worthwhile discussions of presenting visual data are Gene Zelazny, *Say It with Charts*, 4th ed. (New York: McGraw-Hill, 2001) and Edward R. Tufte, *The Visual Display of Quantitative Information*, 2nd ed. (Cheshire, CO: Graphics Press, 2001) (a classic).

Major Uses of Performance Information and Incentives for Using It

It is one thing to design a good performance measurement process. It's quite another to get the products of that process used effectively. How can and should the information be used? In the past, agencies have most frequently used performance measurement to respond to accountability mandates from higher levels of authority. This is a great waste. Responding to demands for accountability is an important use. Even more important, managers, staff, and other public officials should use performance information to make program improvements that would not have been made in its absence.

This fundamental purpose of performance information has often been neglected. One reason is that such information is new to many managers. Not having received information on outcomes before, managers are unfamiliar with the data and what it can do for them. Another major reason is lack of incentives for managers to use the information for program improvement. Concern (unfortunately, realistic) that the performance data will be used by others primarily to cast blame has led programs to select performance indicators that are easier for them to influence (outputs and a few intermediate outcome indicators, such as response times).

Performance information should be used to learn, not to "shoot the messenger."

Exhibit 12-1 lists 11 major uses of performance information. All but the first (increase accountability) and tenth (improve communications with the public) are intended to make program improvements that lead to improved outcomes. All but the second, budget formulation and justification, are discussed in this chapter. Results-based budgeting is covered in chapter 13.

But first a note on avoiding misuse. Outcome data tell what progress has been made toward objectives, but not why that progress (or lack thereof) occurred. Exhibit 12-2 lists some ways to get this message across and reduce user misunderstanding of what outcome data can and cannot do.

Reminder: If the wrong performance indicators are used, if the data collection procedures are poor, or the data reported are otherwise bad (substantially inaccurate or excessively old), performance information can lead to poorer decisions than if no such information were available.

1. Respond to Elected Officials' and the Public's Demands for Accountability

Traditionally, accountability has been directed at legal and appropriate use of public funds (that is, avoiding waste, fraud, and abuse). When outcome information becomes available, accountability for producing results also becomes a focus.

Because of the limited influence of public (and private) agencies over many outcomes—especially end outcomes—full accountability is rarely possible. *Realistically, accountability for outcomes is usually shared with other agencies, with other levels of government, with private organizations, and with the customers themselves.* This is true today and will inevitably be true in the future, no matter what measurements are used. Some ramifications of this situation are discussed below, in the section on using performance information in monetary incentive systems.

2. Help Formulate and Justify Budget Requests

A major use of performance information, but one surprisingly often neglected, is to help officials determine what resources and activities are likely to produce the best outcomes. That is, past outcome information can be used to help agencies develop their budget requests, rather than first formulating their requests and then including available outcome information as part of their budget submission. The latter process appears the more typical approach.

Similarly, subsequent *reviews* of budget requests should look for evidence on whether the resources (funds and staffing) and activities requested are likely to lead to desired outcome levels.

Tracking outcomes can give potential funders greater confidence that any money they provide will be used beneficially. If a program does not have substantial evidence that it is producing benefits, the program's budget is likely to become more vulnerable to being cut. (See chapter 13 for a discussion of results-based budgeting.)

However, performance information can be a double-edged sword. If a program's measured outcomes are poor or decline over time, funders may decide that the program should be cut or at least changed in some way. This is also a legitimate use of outcome information.

Outcome data can also be used to help secure funds. This applies to both the public and private sectors. In the private, nonprofit sector, local

United Ways have begun using outcome information in their fundraising campaigns. The presumption is that contributors, especially the business sector, will increase or at least sustain their contributions if they are provided evidence that those contributions have led to beneficial outcomes. The same applies to government agencies: evidence of positive outcomes can be used to help obtain continued funding.

3. Help Allocate Resources throughout the Year

The budget is but one part of an agency's resource allocation process. Outcome information should enable program personnel throughout the year to identify where problems do or do not exist, a major step in determining the need to reallocate resources, such as personnel. (If outcomes are extremely low, agencies might choose to reduce program activities or eliminate them altogether.) The following are examples:

- The Occupational Safety and Health Administration (OSHA) uses counts of injuries and illnesses from 80,000 establishments for several purposes; to target work sites for inspections, to identify and encourage employers with moderately high rates to improve their health and safety efforts, and to trigger enforcement actions for serious violations.
- New York City's Police Department used crime data breakouts to identify where crimes were clustering and when they were occurring, between 8:00 p.m. and 2:00 a.m. on Friday and Saturday nights. They found most plainclothes officers worked 9:00 a.m. to 5:00 p.m. The department reallocated these officers' time.
- When the U.S. Coast Guard switched to an outcome focus in its maritime safety program, it examined fatality rates by type of industry. It found that commercial towing had the highest rates. Searching for explanatory information, the Coast Guard found that most casualties were deck hands who fell overboard—a problem that did not lend itself to the Coast Guard's off-the-shelf inspection program for tugboats. The Coast Guard formed a partnership with the towing industry to develop non-regulatory solutions to the problem. After three years, the Coast Guard reported that the commercial towing fatality rate dropped from 77 per 100,000 workers to 27.[1]

The principle illustrated by the above examples is that outcome data can be used to identify elements with poorer outcomes so that additional resources can be focused on them. All three examples also illustrate the

Performance Measurement: Getting Results

importance of disaggregating outcome data by key characteristics (OSHA by establishment, the NYC Police Department by the time crimes occurred, and the Coast Guard by industry).

A variation of this use of performance data is *to help prioritize among options*. This has been done for many years for various infrastructure projects, such as selecting among street repair projects, among water and sewer pipe projects, and among facility repair projects (such as school buildings). In each case, existing conditions and their severity are obtained for each proposed project (often based on trained observer ratings of the infrastructure). Such information is combined with estimates of the cost to bring deficient conditions to some satisfactory condition level, and perhaps data on the number of people affected, for each candidate project. Using the information the projects can be ordered, in part judgmentally, and projects selected based on the funds available.

Exhibit 12-3 presents the criteria for rating large water-pipe projects used by one city's water department. Each pipe's leak history and effect on water quality, along with the condition assessment criteria, are obtained from agency performance data.

Exhibits 12-4 and 12-5 provide two other examples of performance reports that can help operating agencies determine where their scarce resources might best be allocated. Both are based on ratings by trained observers (from a private nonprofit organization, the Fund for the City of New York). The first exhibit, by use of a bar chart, identifies not only the trend in neighborhood conditions but also how long those conditions have existed. The second exhibit displays a map of a section of the city indicating the frequency of problems (sidewalks) at each location in the area. In both cases, public agencies can use this information to help them determine where their maintenance work should go.

Resource allocation decisions, however, can be quite complex. They usually require additional information. This issue is discussed further in the last section of this chapter.

4. Trigger In-Depth Examinations of Why Performance Problems (or Successes) Exist

A key use of performance information is to raise questions. To use performance information to the fullest, program managers need to examine *why* the outcomes are as bad or as good as they are.

Breakout data on outcome indicators, as discussed in chapter 8, can provide partial clues to why problems are occurring. In addition, programs

EXHIBIT 12-3

Criteria for Rating Large Water-Pipe Projects

1. **Visual Inspection**
    - 0 Excellent lining
    - 2 Good lining, no repairs needed
    - 4 Good lining, slight repairs needed
    - 6 Fair lining, some rust, beyond corrective maintenance
    - 8 Loose lining, much rusting and pitting
    - 10 No lining, much rusting and pitting

2. **Necessity of the Water Main for Area Supply**
    - 0 Not needed
    - 1 Long-term shutdown anytime
    - 2 Long-term shutdown except peak draw or special conditions
    - 3 Short-term shutdown anytime
    - 4 Essential during peak draw
    - 5 Essential all the time

3. **Effect on Water Quality**
    - 0 No effect
    - 2 Slight corrosion causing coloration
    - 4 Loose lining
    - 6 Loose lining and slight corrosion
    - 8 Extreme corrosion with no loose lining
    - 10 Extreme corrosion and much loose lining

4. **Percentage of Steel Thickness Removed at Internal Pits**
    - 0 No pitting
    - 2 Surface corrosion only
    - 4 25%
    - 6 50%
    - 8 75%
    - 10 100% (holes from inside corrosion)

5. **History of Leaks over Past Ten Years**
    - 0 No leaks
    - 1 1 to 3 leaks per 10,000 feet
    - 2 4 or 5 leaks per 10,000 feet
    - 3 6 or 7 leaks per 10,000 feet
    - 4 8 or 9 leaks per 10,000 feet
    - 5 10 or more leaks per 10,000 feet

Source: Seattle Water Department, "Steel Pipe Internal Inspection Report."

can undertake or sponsor in-depth studies. Formal, in-depth program evaluations should be undertaken when time and funds permit. However, they are likely to be costly in both time and effort, especially for small programs. More qualitative, less rigorous special studies will likely be appropriate and practical for most programs.

EXHIBIT 12-4

Tracking Conditions Found during Four ComNet Surveys

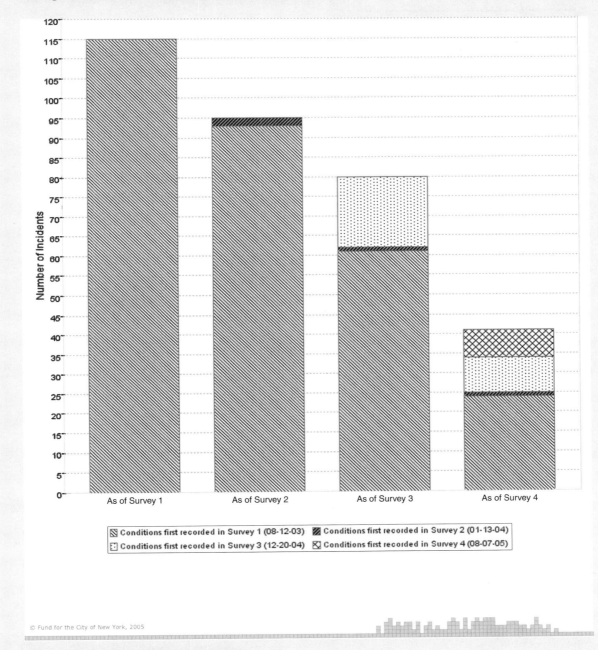

Source: Fund for the City of New York, 2005. Used with permission.

EXHIBIT 12-5

Sidewalk Incidents

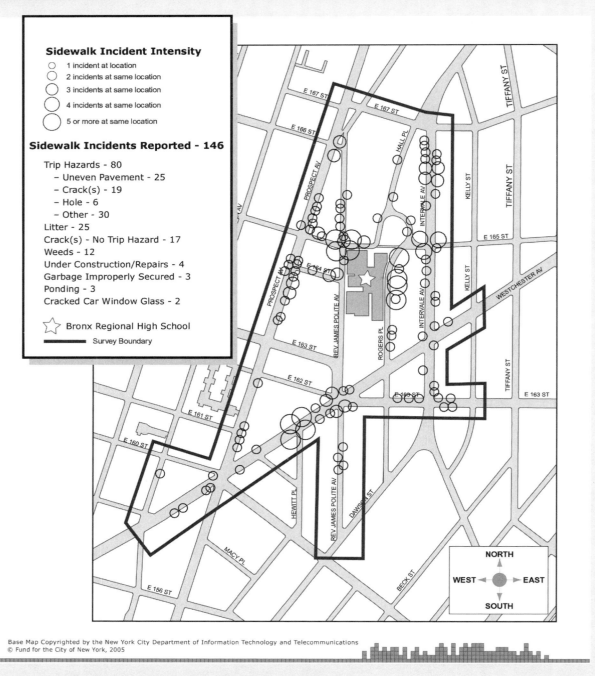

Sidewalk Incident Intensity

○ 1 incident at location
○ 2 incidents at same location
○ 3 incidents at same location
○ 4 incidents at same location
○ 5 or more at same location

Sidewalk Incidents Reported - 146

Trip Hazards - 80
 – Uneven Pavement - 25
 – Crack(s) - 19
 – Hole - 6
 – Other - 30
Litter - 25
Crack(s) - No Trip Hazard - 17
Weeds - 12
Under Construction/Repairs - 4
Garbage Improperly Secured - 3
Ponding - 3
Cracked Car Window Glass - 2

☆ Bronx Regional High School
▬▬▬ Survey Boundary

Base Map Copyrighted by the New York City Department of Information Technology and Telecommunications
© Fund for the City of New York, 2005

Source: Fund for the City of New York, 2005. Used with permission.

A program might form a special team to investigate why outcomes were low and to suggest corrective actions. The program personnel should examine both the outcome and output data, including data breakouts, to help pinpoint where the problems were occurring. Discussions with the service delivery personnel and customers often provide valuable insights. (Such input might be obtained using focus group procedures similar to those described in chapter 5.) Once programs have identified plausible reasons for outcome indicators whose values indicate a problem, they should formulate any necessary corrective actions. The action plans themselves should probably set targets for the future values of each pertinent outcome indicator and when those values should be reached. At those times, the program should again review the outcomes to assess the extent to which the actions taken have led to better outcomes. (Chapters 8, 9, and 10 suggest procedures for comparing alternative service delivery approaches.)

If a program compares its outcomes to those of similar programs in other jurisdictions, it should also attempt to identify the practices that led to particularly good outcomes—practices that might be adapted to the program's own use.

Another variation is to *categorize the outcome indicators by whether their recent values indicate problems* that need to be addressed. For example, the values for each outcome indicator might be assessed using "traffic signals":

- Assign a green light to the indicator if the values are good; no additional attention is needed.
- Assign a yellow light if the values appear to be declining but are not in the danger zone; keep a close eye on the indicator in future reports and/or require more frequent performance reporting.
- Assign a red light if the values appear to be poor; call for a corrective action plan and/or require more frequent monitoring.

Florida's Department of Environmental Protection slotted its programs into similar categories labeled good, watch, or focus. Managers of programs classified as "focus" were required to provide a corrective action plan within 10 days. For example, in the last quarter of fiscal year 1998, compliance rates from random inspections of oyster, clam, and blue crab processing plants decreased from 92 percent to 85 percent. The division responsible submitted a corrective action plan that brought together members of the regulated community and agency staff. Together they developed and implemented an action plan. The department also shifted to more targeted inspections to plants with histories of noncompliance.[2]

5. Help Motivate Personnel to Continue Improving the Program

By focusing on results, performance information can motivate program managers and their staff to identify and implement ways to continually improve services. Many public and private employees are motivated by their desire to produce good results. Regular performance information provided to employees is likely to provide an incentive to improve. Additional encouragement is useful. Exhibit 12-6 lists a variety of incentives to provide such motivation. Each is discussed below.

A major distinction is nonmonetary versus monetary incentives. Monetary incentives in the public and private, nonprofit sectors are quite controversial. Reward schemes, especially monetary awards, have typically relied on supervisors' opinions, a major source of contention. *Performance measurement systems provide more objective data than previously available. The use of more objective data, if the indicators are believed to be appropriate, is likely to increase the acceptance of rewards as motivators by employees, elected officials, and the public.* Some subjectivity is inevitable in establishing winners and losers, but it is diminished to the extent that objectively measured performance information is used as the basis for the awards.

Rewards can be given to individual managers of other employees or to groups of employees (such as of specific offices, facilities, or whole agencies).

EXHIBIT 12-6

Incentives for High Program Performance Derived from Performance Information

Nonmonetary Incentives
- Providing recognition awards
- Disseminating regular performance reports to program personnel
- Setting performance targets and regularly reviewing achievements in relation to those targets
- Providing performance reviews by higher-level managers and elected officials
- Giving managers more flexibility in exchange for more accountability for performance
- Making performance information an explicit part of the agency's individual performance appraisal process
- Establishing performance agreements between central officials and agency heads

Monetary Incentives
- Linking pay to performance
- Allocating discretionary funds to agencies or programs with high performance
- Sanctioning prolonged low performance

Rewards can be based on one or more of several performance criteria:

- *Absolute level* achieved in a period
- *Relative level* achieved in a period compared to that achieved by others in the same period (regardless of the level of performance)
- *Improvement* over a period (an often neglected criterion that encourages performers who did not perform well in the past to strive for improvement)

Rewards can also be based on a variety of periods of performance, such as

- performance in the most recent measurement period or
- performance over longer periods.

Using longer periods as the basis for selecting winners reduces the temptation to focus on quick returns at the expense of longer-term results.

Nonmonetary Incentives

Providing recognition awards. Nonmonetary incentives have the distinct advantage of being inexpensive. They are probably the most common reward in government today, but they are not generally believed to be strong motivators.

Disseminating performance reports to program personnel. Providing the latest information on achievement of outcomes (and efficiency) relative to targeted levels promptly after each reporting period can encourage program personnel to focus on both the data and any apparent shortfalls. For example, *post quarterly or monthly performance reports on entrances or an office bulletin board.* Programs might follow a United Way format for fundraising campaigns—posting regularly updated progress toward the target in the form of a thermometer registering rising temperatures. (If the program does not set targets for the outcomes, it can still post information on the levels achieved. While probably not as effective, it does encourage personnel to focus on performance.) Calling attention to performance provides motivating feedback to all employees who can affect (even if only slightly) the performance of their group.

It seems likely that program personnel will be particularly motivated to seek improvement if the feedback relates to service outcomes, including service quality as perceived by customers. *Regular data on outcomes related to customers may make employees' jobs more interesting and more personally rewarding.*

Regular reports comparing outcomes broken out by organizational units delivering similar services to similar customers can be a particularly powerful motivator for poorly performing units. Such information is likely to encourage employees to identify why they are different and help find ways to improve their outcomes. But care must be taken here. How this competition is handled by the organization's management will be an important determinant of whether it is constructive or destructive, resulting in lower morale and performance.

Setting performance targets and regularly reviewing achievements in relation to those targets. Having program personnel set targets for their performance indicators and relating performance data to them is likely to be particularly effective if

- reporting periods are frequent,
- targets are set for *each* reporting period (even if the overall targets are set annually in the budgeting process), and
- the results are available soon after the end of each reporting period.

Providing performance reviews by higher-level managers and elected officials (or by board members of private, nonprofit organizations). Setting targets, providing regular feedback on performance, and comparing actual performance against the targets are likely to be considerably more effective if the steps are accompanied by higher-level reviews throughout the year. Such reviews indicate the strong, continuing interest of high-level officials in performance. The continued interest, and attention to, the performance information gives strong signals to agency personnel.

Such "How Are We Doing?" sessions (see box) should discuss the latest performance report, identify problem areas indicated there, and discuss what might be done to reduce those problems. As long as these reviews are reasonably frequent, they may be among the most powerful motivational factors for employees of public and private nonprofit agencies.

A Format for "How Are We Doing?" Sessions

One way to motivate personnel is to hold staff meetings shortly after receiving the latest outcome data report. At these sessions, the program manager and staff can address such questions as the following:

- Where have we done well? Why?
- Can we transfer the factors behind our successes to other parts of the program?
- Where have we not done well? Why?
- What can we do to improve these results? Group members can then be asked to develop an action plan to implement these improvements.
- (In later sessions) What has happened since we made changes?

New York City's Police Department kicked off a growing trend in the use of regular, frequent, in-person reviews of performance data. Its Comp-Stat program involves the department's top executives, who meet in rotation with precinct commanders and detective squad commanders from different areas of the city. They review current crime trends, plan tactics, and allocate resources.

That process spread to a number of other New York City agencies, including its Department of Parks and Recreation (ParkStat), the Human Resources Administration (JobStat, along with VendorStat for its vendors), as well as to other local governments. Probably the best know of these others is Baltimore's (MD) CitiStat program. In Baltimore's case, the driving force was the mayor, who set up biweekly reviews with each agency to review each agency's performance data.[3]

Nothing is likely to capture agency attention more than elected officials or board members pushing for accurate outcome information and demanding to see the outcome implications of their appropriations and program policies. A major stimulus to federal agency performance measurement efforts during the early years of the Government Performance and Results Act implementation (1997 and 1998) was Congress's considerable interest in, and its ratings of, agencies' strategic plans and annual performance plans.

Explicit review and questioning of performance *during budget reviews,* and other reviews of suggested changes in program or policy directions, are also likely to be major incentives for agencies and their programs to take performance measurement seriously.[4]

Giving managers more flexibility in exchange for more performance accountability. This is a popular approach for some governments. The national governments of the United States, Australia, and New Zealand, in particular, and some state governments such as Texas, Florida, and Louisiana, used this incentive. Increased flexibility might be granted in

- use of budgeted funds,
- authority to make purchases without going through extensive red tape (such as by raising the dollar level at which a manager has to go through a formal competitive bidding process), or
- authority to hire, remove, compensate, and move personnel to other tasks and positions.

The principle here is granting greater flexibility to an agency or program after evidence that past outcomes or efficiency have been achieved. This approach can be implemented effectively in environments that have basic controls in place to ensure the legal, ethical, and honest use of the added flexibility. Agencies (or countries) without reasonable controls (such as a meaningful internal or external audit process) may not find the granting of much flexibility appropriate.

Making performance information an explicit part of the agency's individual performance appraisal process. Two basic approaches for incorporating performance information into an agency's appraisal process are the following:

- Compare actual to targets for each indicator over which the employee had some control. Achievement of targeted performance might be considered in appraisals for nonmanagement as well as management employees, especially if the focus is on group performance. All people in a group would receive similar ratings on this particular part of the appraisal. (Other parts of the appraisal would address the individual's own contribution.)
- Identify how managers have implemented and used performance information. This approach is much less demanding than the first approach and therefore a weaker motivator.

In the early implementation stages of a performance measurement system, agencies should probably use the second approach until personnel have had sufficient experience with the outcome or service quality data to be responsibly rated on them.

Performance data for the 26 New York City Job Centers, covering job placement, three-month retention, and six-month retention rates (both subsidized and unsubsidized placements), are used at the end of each year as part of each center director's performance review.[5] Each center has its own targets.

Establishing performance agreements between central officials and agency heads. On occasion, performance contracts have been used by governments (such as the government of New Zealand). Under these performance agreements, individual agency heads agree to produce specified amounts of products in return for specified budget levels and more management flexibility (as discussed above). As part of this process, agency heads can receive extra or reduced compensation, or even be dismissed, based on actual performance. (If compensation is a major element of an agency's performance agreement process, then the process becomes more of a monetary than a nonmonetary incentive.)

The government of Costa Rica, for example, has experimented with developing agreements between its president and individual ministries, agencies, and public enterprises.[6] The U.S. government experimented with such agreements in the mid-1990s, but as of this writing has not imposed them. Some state governments, including Florida, have also tried them.

Monetary Incentives

In this motivational approach, compensation for individual employees or groups of employees, or altered funding for the government's agencies, is based at least in part on performance data. Pay-for-performance plans are considered a powerful incentive in private business. They are considerably more controversial in public and private nonprofit environments.

Monetary incentives are fraught with pitfalls and have often been counterproductive in public environments.[7] The problem with many monetary incentive systems in government has been the lack of performance criteria perceived as fair and valid. Almost always, compensation systems linked to pay have ended up relying heavily on the judgments of supervisors. Employee unions usually abhor such a process. Nonunion employees (including managers) who perceive the rewards as unfair can also be upset by them. *If sound performance measurements are used as a major part of the reward criteria and are perceived by employees and public officials (and the public) as reasonably objective, fair, and valid, then the use of performance measurement data in determining monetary awards should reduce their potential negative effects on morale.*

It can also be argued that such awards often go to those who would perform well without them. If such is the case, monetary rewards use up substantial resources and provide little motivational value. To alleviate this problem, awards should also be given for the *degree of improvement,* not just the level.

Three types of monetary incentive programs are described below:

Linking pay to performance. A number of governments, including the U.S. government, have considered or introduced financial incentives tied to individual compensation. The U.S. Postal Service, for example, has provided year-end bonuses to nonunion employees, both managers and nonmanagers (including secretaries). The size of a bonus is based on a formula that includes whether the employees in a cluster of workers met on-time service delivery standards, customer satisfaction targets, and budget targets. The unionized employees decided against bonuses, in part because bonuses are not added to base pay and do not add to retirement benefits.

A major dilemma here is that external factors can play major roles in affecting outcomes, efficiency, and even outputs. *A desirable condition for monetary incentives is that employees, elected officials, and the public all explicitly accept that employees will be rewarded if outcomes improve, regard-less of the extent to which the employees have actually contributed to the improved outcomes.* Conversely, all involved should recognize that employees will not be rewarded if performance levels do not meet expectations, despite what may have been excellent efforts and contributions. (In effect, this is what is done in the private sector, where senior executives receive bonuses based on the performance of their companies, such as sales, profits, and market share.)

Allocating discretionary funds to agencies or programs with high performance. A less-controversial monetary incentive is to reward an agency or individual for good performance with funds that can be used only for organizational purposes, such as for employee training or improving workplace conditions. An example is a teacher incentive system in which high-performing individual teachers receive awards in the form of special equipment or other physical enhancements for their classrooms.

These incentives are likely to be better received by officials and the public, because little additional funding is needed and that funding is used for organization-enhancing purposes. The most common application in the past has been in situations where a group's cost savings (say half) are returned to the group for discretionary use. These are sometimes called shared savings or gain-sharing programs. Usually, the funds are restricted to organizational activities undertaken by the group as a whole.

High performance on outcome indicators does not usually involve monetary savings. Thus, additional funds need to be added to the organization's budget for such rewards. Agencies can propose that an imputed amount be provided, based on estimates of the added expenditures that would have been needed to achieve the added outcomes levels. Such calculations can be difficult.

Any time a public or private agency links monetary incentives to outcome indicator values, the agency should also include indicators that track undesirable negative effects. It is tempting for personnel to focus on outcomes linked to rewards at the expense of other outcomes. For example, if monetary rewards are linked solely to cost per unit of output, employees are likely to focus on producing more output—even at the expense of the quality of that output. Classic examples include focusing on number of arrests, prosecutions, tax collections, or child support payment collections without also including such indicators as the incidence of harassment complaints. The U.S. Internal Revenue Service has periodically come under scrutiny because its tax collection efforts were perceived as encouraging inappropriate activities by IRS agents.

In another example, the *Washington Post* reported in April 1999 that a federal law enacted in 1997 promised, among other things, to pay states $4,000 to $6,000 for every child adopted over a baseline number. This created a substantial financial incentive for the states. The newspaper noted concerns by child advocacy groups that caseworkers would be pressured to seek adoptions before the children or families were ready or to place children with inappropriate families. For example, the family might not be told the extent of the abuse that the adoptive child had suffered, and might subsequently find itself unable to cope with the child.[8] This problem would be considerably alleviated if a performance indicator included a review of the case, say, 12 months after the adoption was finalized.

To reduce this danger, agencies should strive to make their performance measurement system comprehensive. They should ensure the system covers potentially important negative effects linked to program activities, such as number of validated complaints and employee misbehavior.

If incentives, especially monetary incentives, are linked to performance results, be sure to include performance indicators that can identify potential negative side effects.

Monetary incentives for many programs should also depend on whether the outcomes lasted a reasonable amount of time. For example, in the case of the adoption program mentioned above, the monetary inventive should depend on the extent to which the placements were trouble free after a reasonable period of time had elapsed. In such cases, some of the payments would need to be delayed for that period, but the delay would probably ensure that the incentives encouraged successful adoptions.

Sanctioning prolonged low performance. The most dramatic and threatening monetary sanctions for individuals are salary reduction, demotion, and discharge. For organizations, the major sanction of concern is to have substantial cuts in funding. As outcome data become more widespread, the data are also likely to be increasingly used by public officials as a basis for such sanctions. (This issue has been a major one for federal departments with the U.S. Office of Management and Budget's use of the PART process, which rates each major federal program on a number of elements, including results.) Clearly, special care is needed when using outcome data for this "incentive." On one hand, outcome performance presumably will be based on relatively objective findings. On the other hand, outcomes are seldom fully controllable by public managers. *Continued* low performance, rather than performance during one period, should preferably be a major element in such decisions.

As noted above, one form of monetary sanction is to reduce or withhold the funding of agencies or programs that have not met expected performance levels or have not provided adequate information to assess performance. Such sanctions have to be very carefully designed so they do not penalize customers of poorly performing programs or programs struggling with insufficient funding. Again, such sanctions are probably best applied to programs where poor performance has continued over a substantial period. If customers show no signs of deriving significant benefit from the program over time, an agency should consider discontinuing it altogether.

Examples of monetary incentives. The use of financial incentives based on outcome information appears to be growing. The No Child Left Behind Act of 2001 brought major changes to educational system incentive structures, with a variety of "sanctions" to schools that do not meet annual improvement targets. Below are a few examples of older incentive plans.

In 1998, the Maryland Department of Education awarded almost $3 million in cash awards to 83 public elementary and middle schools that showed significant improvement on such measures—an example of a positive incentive. Another 200 schools that did not receive cash bonuses were given recognition awards for significant progress. Awarding on the basis of improvement means that schools with initially high scores and schools with initially low scores both have incentives to improve their performance. Schools received bonuses ranging from $16,000 to $65,000, with the size of the bonus based on the size of the school. Because the awards are one-time grants, schools cannot use them to hire staff. They typically use them to train teachers or to buy computer equipment or classroom supplies.[9]

Similarly, North Carolina's state board of education developed the ABCs of Public Education program in 1996. The program provided monetary awards to individual schools based on student achievement on end-of-course tests in various subjects in a number of grades. It also provided nonmonetary recognition awards to schools with somewhat less improvement but with at least 80 percent of students performing at or above grade level. Schools identified as low-performing (such as those in which a majority of students performed below grade level) were assigned school improvement teams of three to five people full time for a year. In the first year (1997–98), all 15 schools with these assistance teams substantially improved their results.

Virginia once proposed requiring a local school district to pay the cost of any remedial classes that students had to take as college freshmen. This remuneration would have been a strong incentive for local school districts to better prepare students for college-level work, but it might have been a hardship for school districts with high proportions of students with learning disabilities.

A Possible Model for Interagency Motivational Programs

The North Carolina Department of Health and Human Services' Division of Maternal and Child Health worked with the state's Association of Local Health Directors to develop outcome indicators on which each county health department had to provide data annually to the state. The division then generated data comparing the outcomes of the county agencies. The counties were grouped into four categories: urban (the 10 largest), western, central, and eastern. Within each category, counties were ranked annually on each set of indicators. For the family planning program, for example, each county was ranked on four indicators: adolescent (age 10–17) pregnancy rate, percentage of repeat teen pregnancies (age 10–17), percentage of women who had two births within 12 months, and rate of live births to unmarried women.

Counties were ranked on two measures for each indicator: the most recent three-year county rate and the amount of improvement from the previous to the most recent three-year period. The division expected to identify a few counties in each grouping at the top and the bottom of the ratings. It planned to hold meetings with the low-ranking counties to identify needed improvements, perhaps asking the top-ranking counties to help. Counties that received very low program rankings for two consecutive years were subject to increased state involvement. As long as a county made a good-faith effort, the division did not plan to assess any financial penalty. However, if corrections were not made, the division could exercise its option to transfer funds from the county agency to other agencies that could provide the service.

This example illustrates the use of outcome information in motivating lower-level governments constructively. Assistance was made available to offices that were having problems in achieving outcomes that other, similar offices had achieved.

The same approach can be adapted to agencies that have multiple offices within the same level of government, as long as the offices provide essentially the same services to the same types of clients. Similarly, for private, nonprofit service agencies, comparative data can motivate those with lower outcomes to improve, perhaps by seeking ideas from agencies with higher levels of achievement.

Exhibit 12-7 summarizes the components of this model for intergovernmental performance partnerships.

Intergovernment Performance Partnership

1. The central agency and representatives of local agencies jointly select a set of outcome indicators, such as rate of low-weight births.
2. The local agencies provide quarterly information on each data element to the central agency.
3. The central agency tabulates the data for each agency.
4. The central agency provides each local agency with summary data for each outcome indicator and with comparisons among the local agencies.
5. Technical assistance is provided to poorly performing local agencies—perhaps by high-performing agencies.
6. The central agency and representatives of local agencies sponsor an effort to identify exemplary practices and disseminate them to all local agencies.

Source: Adapted from procedures used by human services agencies in North Carolina and Minnesota.

6. Formulate and Monitor the Performance Targets of Contractors and Grantees (Performance Contracting)

If the agency contracts or provides grants to other organizations for services to citizens, it can include outcome-based performance targets in the agreements and then compare outcomes against those targets. This is called performance contracting.

If targets are included in a contract or grant agreement, they need to be carefully developed by the agency and should be compatible with the indicators in the program's performance measurement system. The indicators should be included in requests for proposals (RFPs). In some instances, the targets for each indicator might also be included in the RFP. In other instances, targets are negotiated ahead of time or are part of contract or grant competitions, with organizations that promise higher levels of outcomes given higher ratings.

A combination of rewards and penalties can be included in these agreements, such as

- rewards for meeting or exceeding targets, and
- reduced fees for failing to meet targets.

Most service contracts include termination options for nonperformance, but these options generally apply to extreme circumstances (usually only vaguely defined) and do not appear to provide much incentive for improving performance. An additional motivator for good performance is to *make past performance an explicit criterion for future awards,* as long as this option is legal in the agency's procurement system. For example, a number of United Ways (such as the United Ways of Milwaukee, Twin Cities [Minneapolis and St. Paul], New Orleans, Rochester, and Tucson) consider outcome attainment a significant factor in funding decisions and have required service providers they support to provide outcome data.[10] United Way of Tucson and Southern Arizona and United Way of the Twin Cities have used multiyear contracts with their service providers, at least in part because some end outcomes can take more than one year to achieve. (See chapter 6 for more details on the Tucson effort.)

Outcome-based performance contracting can be attractive to contractors in situations where greater accountability can be exchanged for more flexibility in how the work is performed. Thus, if the contract holds the contractor accountable for results, it probably should contain fewer specifications about implementation.

Many services in the United States have tried performance contracting with incentives, such as payments based on completing road construction on time, the number of vehicles requiring additional work after initial repairs, success in drug treatment, missed garbage collections, the number of persons placed in employment, successful child adoptions, and the amount of child support payments secured.

Example of Performance Contracting

Oklahoma's Department of Rehabilitation Services (DRS) established the Milestone System, an outcome-based payment system for contractors that provided employment services to severely disabled clients of the state's vocational rehabilitation services.[11] At various outcome milestones for each client, contractors were paid a percentage of their "average total cost per successful case closure," as specified in their initial bid. For example, the contractor received a preestablished percentage after the client's initial placement, an additional percentage if the client was still in the job after four weeks, and another installment if the client was still in the job after 10 weeks. The jobs had to meet specific DRS guidelines for employment, such as minimum weekly hours of work and the minimum wage.

United Way of Central Indiana has used a similar arrangement for welfare-to-work projects stressing services for hard-to-place clients. In outcome-based performance contracts, payments are made at the following client milestones: (1) when emergency needs have been met, (2) when an individual employment plan has been developed, (3) when clients are placed in a job, (4) when clients have remained in the job for 90 days, (5) when clients have remained in the job for 180 days, (6) when clients have remained in the job for 360 days, and (7) when clients achieve an advancement in responsibility and/or pay.[12]

The National Science Foundation (NSF) Comprehensive Partnerships for Mathematics and Science Achievement program has used a form of performance contracting in grants aimed at getting more minority students interested in mathematics and science. For example, the program's 1995 five-year, $1.6 million cooperative agreement with the Surry County (Virginia) Public Schools contained a number of performance targets. These included, for each of the five years, the number of minority students (in specified grades) who successfully completed (grade C or better) specific mathematics and science courses. The grantee was required to provide annual reports containing data on its progress in reaching these goals. Moreover, the agreement specified that continued NSF support would depend on an annual review of achievements.

The District of Columbia's 1998 contract to overhaul and maintain 15,000 parking meters specified financial penalties for the contractor if fewer than 97 percent of the meters, on average, were operational.

The U.S. Department of Defense has used various incentives to procure weapon systems, such as airplanes and ships, on time and within cost targets, though with limited success. DOD has had problems with the long-term nature of such procurements. Despite mid-course bonuses, some contractors incur substantial delays and overruns by the time the work is completed.[13]

If you can give them money, why can't you expect results?

Issues in Performance Contracting

When monetary bonuses or penalties are included in contracts or grants, an agency will need to work out incentive provisions that are fair both to the public and to the contractor or grantee. Developing these provisions will require considerable skill and cooperation from the program and contract offices.

To make performance contracting effective, an agency also needs a strong contract oversight function that either collects the performance data itself (e.g., as part of the agency's performance measurement system) or regularly checks the quality of performance data provided by the contractor. In the latter case, if the contractor serves clients that do not come in through the government agency, the funding agency may not be able to follow up clients directly, given the contractor's need to preserve client confidentiality. In such a case, the agency's oversight

Performance Measurement: Getting Results

should probably focus on reviewing the data collection procedures used by the contractor.

The most feasible approach in many cases is to encourage and help grantees and contractors maintain their own outcome measurement processes but require them to allow the funding organization to periodically audit the data systems for quality control. This might include checking a sample of the actual data. (Suggestions for quality control of performance are provided in chapter 14.)

Timing is important in setting performance payment schedules. For some services, important outcomes cannot be assessed for a considerable time after the contractor's services have been completed. In these cases, the performance agreement may need to provide for post-service measurement before final payments are determined. In the Oklahoma rehabilitation service contracts described earlier, the primary service was job placement. The contractor was not paid the final installment until the client had been on the job for 10 weeks. Final payments for such services as drug and alcohol treatment programs and adoptive-services contracts might be based on the client's situation 12 months after completion of treatments. In such cases, final payments will need to be delayed until after the service period.

Incentive provisions among private, nonprofit agencies are less common. However, as some of the above examples indicate, their use in grants to nonprofits seems reasonable for some, if not most, services. Though monetary incentives are likely to be less important to nonprofit organizations than to public agencies, they do seem likely to stimulate motivation.

Exhibit 12-8 lists several issues an agency needs to consider when establishing outcome-based performance contracting.

EXHIBIT 12-8

Outcome-Based Performance Contracting Questions

- To what extent should contractors be involved in the selection of performance indicators?
- What incentives should be included in contracts?
- How should the size of penalties and positive incentives be related to outcomes?
- Should initial performance contracts include a hold-harmless clause?
- What role should the contractor play in data collection?
- How should external factors be considered when determining rewards and sanctions (e.g., escape clauses)?
- How can outcome incentives be used to encourage contractor innovation?
- Should performance on past contracts help determine future contract awards?

7. Provide Data for Special, In-Depth Program Evaluations

An agency's performance measurement system can often provide an excellent starting point for special evaluation efforts. The system can be a source for some of the data the evaluators would otherwise have to collect, saving considerable time. For example, the performance measurement system is likely to be able to provide before-and-after data for at least a preliminary impact estimate of past service changes.

Even when the system does not reduce the amount of data the evaluation needs to collect, the performance measurement information can shed light on the issues addressed by the evaluation and even lead to the framing of new hypotheses. Such information can also provide the basic data needed for *performance audits*, which can be considered a form of program evaluation. Finally, the regularly collected performance measurement information can be very useful in identifying program areas that need explanation and attention. Such information can be very helpful in setting the organization's annual program evaluation agenda.

The usefulness of the performance measurement system to the program evaluators will be considerably enhanced if its regular reports provide breakouts (chapter 8) and explanatory information (chapters 10 and 11).

8. Support Strategic and Other Long-Term Planning Efforts

Strategic planning and other long-run planning efforts are about the future. Thus, they involve many forecasting, projection, and extrapolation tools beyond the scope of performance measurement. Strategic planning can be helped considerably, however, by performance measurement information.

Strategic planning usually requires a mission statement; statements of long-term objectives; and an examination of alternative means of meeting the objectives, including the expected costs, expected impacts, and major implementation hurdles of each alternative. The planning that goes into development of the strategic plan should examine the various trade-offs, including the resulting outcomes that would be expected from each alternative means of meeting the objectives. *The outcome estimates for at least some alternatives probably will need to be based, at least in part, on the past outcome information available.* (The last section of this chapter suggests some steps for analyzing service options, particularly for infrastructure planning, such as for five-year capital improvement programs.)

The plan developed from the planning activity should include *outcome indicators that are explicitly related to the objectives identified in the plan and that can be used to track progress toward meeting these objectives.* The plan should also include *recent values for each outcome indicator* to show where the program stands in regard to key strategic objectives, providing the starting point for the plan. Finally, the plan should select target values for each outcome indicator for the period covered, even if these values are only rough estimates.

Thus, the agency's performance measurement system is needed for three purposes in strategic planning:

- To provide baseline values for each of the plan's performance indicators, and thus establish the extent of action needed
- To provide historical data on each indicator so outcomes can be projected for each option examined
- To provide data on key outcome indicators that can be used in regular reports that track progress toward meeting strategic plan objectives

Agencies might periodically develop "service improvement action plans" for important (perhaps troubled) programs. These plans identify the key outcome indicators, the baseline (recent values) for each indicator, strategies for improvement, their estimated cost, and the expected outcomes from the improvement strategies.

Three distinctions between the numbers contained in the agency's strategic plan and the data yielded by its performance measurement system need to be highlighted. First, *the indicators in the strategic plan will inevitably be only a subset of the indicators an agency needs to track in its performance measurement system.* For example, a strategic plan relating to child health might include a long-term target on infant mortality. The performance measurement system should track infant mortality as one of its outcome indicators, but it should also track indicators covering key intermediate outcomes, such as improving nutrition, avoiding drugs, obtaining adequate prenatal care, and other steps that expectant mothers can take to improve an infant's chances of surviving. The agency's performance measurement system should also break out the outcomes for various demographic groups, such as by mothers' ages and races or ethnicities, and the causes of the infants' deaths. Some of these breakouts might be included in the strategic plan, but others might not.

Second, *strategic plans almost always cover only selected segments of the agency.* For example, the statewide indicators in Oregon's early benchmark plans did not cover the state's road maintenance activities, even though maintenance is a major expenditure. An agency's performance measurement system, on the other hand, should be comprehensive enough to provide regular feedback on results covering all, or all but the very smallest, programs.

Third, *the numbers produced by the performance measurement system are historical. The numbers in the plan are projections.* A major temptation of strategic plans is to set targets at high, politically attractive levels without considering the cost and feasibility of achieving them. Unrealistic targets draw down criticism on the agency when they are not met. Data from the agency's performance measurement system, along with cost data, can be used to help make plausible estimates of what can be achieved, and at what expense. Such information should be provided to agency officials, even if the politics of the situation subsequently mandate setting official outcome targets that are not in line with likely funding or capability.

The performance measurement system and the strategic planning process should be closely related. The strategic planning process may identify indicators that the agency's performance measurement process has neglected, perhaps because some objectives were overlooked. Similarly, the indicators contained in the agency's performance measurement system may suggest objectives and related progress indicators that the strategic plan should include.

Caution: Projecting numbers into the future is something of an art form that requires not only historical data and statistical estimation techniques, but also qualitative judgment formed from experience.

9. Analyze Options and Establish Priorities

A major task for public service organizations is to decide among options and establish priorities among competing claims for scarce resources. No organization can do everything it would like to do. This applies both to operational resource allocation systems (discussed in use 3 above) and to longer-term choices, such as in strategic planning and developing a multi-year capital investment program (discussed in use 8 above).

Information from the organization's performance measurement system can usually provide important information to help make these choices.

Analyzing options and deciding on priorities can be very complex. Chapter 8 provides some suggestions, particularly in the section on break-outs by type and amount of service. The following steps are another approach for such analysis.

Here we illustrate how an agency might address choices involving the construction, repair, and maintenance of physical infrastructure, such as roads, bridges, water supply, sewer systems, and buildings or other facilities (such as parks and other public recreational areas). Repair and maintenance of school buildings will be used to illustrate the steps leading up to final choices.[14]

- Step 1. Assess the condition of each existing element of infrastructure (intermediate outcomes) using information from the agency's performance measurement system.

    In the school example, trained observers rate each subsystem of each school building in the community using a well-defined rating scale, such as "acceptable," "not acceptable," or "hazardous."
- Step 2. Estimate the cost to bring each infrastructure element to an acceptable condition.

    Exhibit 12-9 illustrates the summary table from these two steps. In this example, the cost estimates are to bring the condition levels from "hazardous" or "unacceptable" to "acceptable."
- Step 3. Compare the total cost to the available resources. Inevitably, the total costs will be considerably greater than the need. In the example, which schools and which infrastructure elements should get the repairs? Also consider the various sources of funding and which funds can be used for which activities.

    For example, capital costs often come from a different fund than operation and maintenance (O&M) expenditures. The availability of funding is likely to differ between the two sources. In the school example, some of the large cost repairs are likely to be considered capital expenditures, perhaps with more available funds than funding for repairs that are O&M activities.
- Step 4. Consider other important factors. For example, the *severity* of the unacceptable condition is likely to differ among the infrastructure elements. A natural choice would be to fix hazardous conditions first (which can be called the "worst first" option). This might require much of the available resources, as is the case in the cost numbers in exhibit 12-9 (45 percent of the total need and probably a much larger percent of the total dollars available).
- Step 5. Estimate the number of people (in the school example, the number of students plus school staff) affected adversely by each unacceptable condition. The agency might then calculate the ratio "number of people benefited (by bringing the infrastructure element up to an acceptable condition level) per estimated repair dollar." These ratios provide one useful perspective for prioritization.
- Step 6. If some elements, particularly severe or hazardous ones, have exceptionally large costs, agencies will likely need to identify optional

EXHIBIT 12-9

Cost Estimates for Upgrading Each School Element to "Acceptable" (dollars)

No.	Description	Hazardous conditions	Fire protection	Lighting	Temperature	Water supply	Bathrooms	Sanitation	Communications	Total
1	School A	1,710,000	45,000	16,450	341,000	—	18,000	96,500	27,000	2,253,950
2	School B	25,000	90,000	5,300	457,400	49,000	59,300	20,500	81,000	787,500
3	School C	45,000	45,000	2,600	91,000	28,000	39,000	18,500	27,000	296,100
4	School D	1,000,000	45,000	1,850	80,000	20,000	15,000	11,900	27,000	1,200,750
5	School E	—	45,000	800	37,500	2,250	11,000	8,200	27,000	131,750
6	School F	—	45,000	7,000	150,000	25,000	15,000	10,100	27,000	279,100
7	School G	—	45,000	1,160	8,000	25,000	15,000	8,000	27,000	129,160
8	School H	—	45,000	1,950	134,200	30,000	22,400	20,700	27,000	281,250
9	School I	—	45,000	9,500	199,000	27,160	15,000	6,500	27,000	329,160
10	School J	—	45,000	4,000	123,600	35,000	63,220	11,800	27,000	309,620
11	School K	—	45,000	1,900	79,500	17,000	11,000	8,800	27,000	190,200
	Total	2,780,000	540,000	52,510	1,701,200	258,410	283,920	221,500	351,000	6,188,540

Source: Adapted from Urban Institute work done with one Albanian community.

ways to deal with them. For example, can other sources of funding be tapped? Is there some temporary, partial fix that can be used until more funds become available? If only a few people are affected by particularly costly repairs, are there other ways those people (the students and staff in the example) can be served using less costly means?

Note that the above steps do not take into account "political" considerations, which will often affect resource allocation decisions. The use of such data as that identified above can help reduce such pressures on public officials, including the temptation to spread around the available funding regardless of need.

Note also that performance measurement information provides only a small, though key, part in these resource allocation decisions.

10. Communicate Better with the Public to Build Trust and Support for Public Services

A performance measurement system opens up several new ways to communicate with the public and, over the long run, to increase the public's trust, confidence, and support for public services. The following are three areas in which agencies and elected officials should involve citizens.

1. *Identifying the service outcomes the agency should track.* The use of customer focus groups to provide such input is described in chapter 5. In this case, the agency and its programs should note in performance reports that customers were included in the determination of what outcomes would be tracked.

2. *Obtaining feedback on the outcomes and quality of services.* Chapter 7 points out the importance of, and suggests procedures for, citizen feedback regularly obtained from customer surveys as part of the performance measurement process.

3. *Providing the performance information to citizens.* If performance reports present information that is important to citizens, and the information is presented in a clear, fair, and balanced way, citizens are more likely to support the government and its services. This will also make it more likely that citizen concerns about outcomes will help motivate agency personnel to focus on results.

Summaries of performance should be made available to citizens and interest groups on a regular basis. Those reports should not only contain information that describes the agency's activities and its physical outputs, but also present information on key service outcomes and quality.

A *key is to make the information readily available to citizens.* Primary avenues for getting information to the public include newsletters, radio, TV, libraries, and, increasingly, the Internet. Significant effort should be made to let people know that the information is readily available and how to obtain it. Agencies also need to help citizens understand the performance information, such as what the data tell and do not tell. (Data do not tell, for example, "who is to blame.")

> Government officials, both elected and appointed, have done a terrible job of communicating the value of government services to the public. These officials need to get the message out. Outcome information can be used, but seldom has been, to help public and private service agencies make the case to citizens for needed service improvements.

Exhibit 12-10 provides an example of a newspaper ad that includes a number of output and outcome indicators. The ad was placed in two Tucson newspapers by the United Way of Tucson and Southern Arizona.

Also key to communications with citizens is providing information of interest to them. *Citizens are likely to be considerably more interested in data about their own community or neighborhood.* For some outcomes, citizens will be considerably more interested in the outcome information if it is provided for other demographic groupings (such as age group, gender, and race/ethnicity) than about the nation or jurisdiction as a whole. The latest technologies, such as GIS and more powerful (and inexpensive) computers, have made it considerably more feasible to develop outcome reports by such subgroups.

> "Neighborhood indicators" are becoming more important to public officials as citizens become more involved with local governance. Local governments can develop sets of outcome information for each of its "neighborhoods" covering multiple service areas—and provide reports on, and to, each neighborhood. This process would also provide considerable information to public officials for allocating resources among geographical areas of the jurisdiction. Each agency would be responsible for providing neighborhood data on each outcome for each of its major services. A central office could assemble the information across services for each geographical area.

In all cases, to build trust, performance reports need to be clear and perceived as honest, accurate, and complete—showing the bad as well as the good. Otherwise, performance reporting will damage the organization's reputation.

11. Above All, Help Provide Services More Effectively

Helping to provide better services more effectively, in order to maintain and improve citizens' quality of life, is the goal of performance measurement.

EXHIBIT 12-10

United Way Newspaper Ad Containing Performance Indicators

United Way

**Lasting Changes.
Results that Really Matter.**

▶ **Strong Families**

- **31,866** individuals received emergency aid to avoid being homeless, remain in the workforce, attend school or look for a job.
- **2,400** low-income working families received free tax preparation, resulting in more than $1.2 million in earned income tax credits and $2.4 million in overall federal refunds.
- **1,300** youths received violence prevention training to reduce bullying, family and dating violence.

◀ **Ready to Learn**

- **23,229** local families received books and tips on reading to their children so they can enter school ready to learn and succeed.
- **8,022** youths from racially and ethnically diverse backgrounds participated in nurturing after-school programs five days a week.
- **3,808** children from low-income working families are receiving higher quality child care.

Supporting Seniors ▶

- **161,430** hours of volunteer service were completed by seniors to help them remain active, involved and healthy.
- **6,658** family caregivers received support services to help them care for an elderly loved one.
- **26** neighborhoods or congregations developed formal volunteer programs to support seniors living alone.

Thanks to your support of United Way of Tucson and Southern Arizona, these are just a sample of the results achieved during 2005. With your help, we're creating lasting changes in people's lives and the community. We're getting to the heart of the most serious issues facing families, children and seniors. To learn how you can help, call **903-9000** or visit **unitedwaytucson.org**

This ad supported in part by Tucson's Newspapers and the Tucson Ad Fed.

Source: United Way of Tucson and Southern Arizona.

Here are a few special ways to encourage program improvements:

- Use performance data to identify organizational units with disappointing outcomes.
- Require those units to develop implementation plans.
- Provide them with technical assistance.
- Require more frequent and more intense reporting of the program's outcome indicators to monitor improvement.

- After changes have been implemented and sufficient time has elapsed to expect improved outcomes, use data to help determine whether improvements have indeed occurred.

Florida's Department of Environmental Protection (described in chapter 10) provides an example of this procedure with its shellfish-processing inspection program.[15] After compliance rates deteriorated, the department required the program to submit a corrective action plan. The program administrator drafted a plan after meeting with members of the regulated community to discuss causes and solutions. The department then started using targeted inspections of plants suspected of noncompliance rather than fully random inspections. (This resulted initially in a further decline in compliance, as might be expected since state inspections were targeted primarily at at-risk businesses. To assess long-term results, the department needs to undertake random inspections to compare pre- and post-implementation noncompliance rates.)

All the ways to use performance information discussed in this chapter should help reach this fundamental goal of improving services to the public. If a performance measurement effort does not do this, it will have been largely wasted.

References and Notes

1. Rick Kowalewski, *Using Outcome Information to Redirect Programs: A Case of the Coast Guard's Pilot Project under the Government Performance and Results Act,* Case Study F3 (Washington, DC: American Society for Public Administration, April 1996).
2. Reported in Liner et al., *Making Results-Based State Government Work* (Washington, DC: The Urban Institute, 2001), 54–55.
3. There are a number of written descriptions of these Stats programs. Good descriptions are contained in Dennis C. Smith, "Performance Management in New York City: CompStat and the Revolution in Police Management," in *Quicker, Better, Cheaper? Managing Performance in American Government,* edited by Dall W. Forsythe (Albany, NY: Rockefeller Institute Press, 2001), 453–82; Lenneal J. Henderson, "The Baltimore CitiStat Program: Performance and Accountability" (Washington, DC: IBM Endowment for The Business of Government, May 2003); Paul E. O'Connell, "Using Performance Data for Accountability: The New York City Police Department's Comp-Stat Model of Police Management" (Washington, DC: IBM Endowment for The Business of Government, August 2001); and several sections of a report from a February 2005 conference in New York, "Performance Management in State and Local Government" (Albany, NY: Rockefeller Institute of Government, June 2005).
4. The National Conference of State Legislatures has published a guide to staff outcome-focused program reviews for use by state government legislators: "Asking Key Questions: How to Review Program Results" (Denver, CO, June 2005).

5. "Performance Management in State and Local Government," 45–53.

6. For example, see Government of Costa Rica and the World Bank, *Guidelines for Drafting Compromiso de Resultados* (San Jose, Costa Rica, February 2, 1996).

7. See Harry P. Hatry, John M. Greiner, and Brenda G. Ashford, *Issues and Case Studies in Teacher Incentive Plans,* 2nd edition (Washington, DC: Urban Institute Press, 1994).

8. Barbara Vobejda, "Revamping of Foster Care Brings Surge in Adoptions," *Washington Post,* 13 April 1999, A3.

9. Amy Argetsinger, "Improved Test Scores Pay Off for Maryland Schools," *Washington Post,* 19 November 1998, B6.

10. Telephone interviews, August 21, 1998.

11. See, for example, Daniel O'Brien and Rebecca Cook, "Oklahoma Milestone Payment System," in *Invitation to Change: 1997 Better Government Competition Winners,* edited by Charles D. Chieppo and Kathryn Ciffolillo (Boston, MA: Pioneer Institute for Public Policy Research, 1997).

12. United Way of America, *Workbook from United Way of America's Forum on Outcomes II* (Alexandria, VA, 1997).

13. Renae Merle, "Pentagon Reconsiders Bonus System for Contractors," *Washington Post,* 19 August 2003, E1, E10.

14. This example is adapted from work done by the Urban Institute with several towns in Albania. The local and central governments both participated in this process.

15. Meetings with Department of Environmental Protection officials, March 1999.

Chapter
13

"Look at life through the wind-
shield, not the rearview mirror."

Results-Based Budgeting

Budgeting is the annual (sometimes biennial) process by which organizations estimate their resource needs and allocations for the future. This chapter focuses on how performance measurement information, particularly outcome data, can be used to assist budget formulation and review.

For many governments, making the budget process more results based has been the primary motivation for legislating performance measurement. A budget process should encourage, if not demand, a performance orientation.

Results- or Performance-Based Budgeting: Widely Acclaimed, but Is Anyone Doing It?

Results-based budgeting, more frequently called performance-based budgeting, gives outcomes central attention in the budget process. Presumably, it emphasizes the importance of outcome data in both formulating and justifying proposed budgets. Much lip service has been paid to the topic. Unfortunately, it is not clear how much real attention has been devoted to the actual use of outcome information in budgeting. The suggestions in this chapter identify procedures for incorporating outcomes into a budget process. Individual agencies will need to devote time to refining the process.

Results-oriented performance measurement provides basic information to the staff formulating, and

> Budgeting should be much more than a process for allocating resources. It should also be a process for encouraging improvements in service quality and outcomes.

subsequently justifying, a budget. The information helps locate problems and successes that may need additional or reduced resources. *The key element of results-based budgeting is that it attempts to consider, if only roughly, the future values of performance indicators—the amount of outcomes expected from proposed resources—and projected outputs.*

Agencies preparing performance budgets project values for each performance indicator for the forthcoming year(s). Projections of outputs and outcomes are intended to reflect the estimated consequences of the resources budgeted. These projections represent what the agency is getting for its money. *The data from an agency's performance measurement system should provide basic information for developing budget proposals and subsequently help justify the budget proposals that have already been developed.* This information is likely to have even greater weight if linked to strategic plans.

By focusing systematically on the results sought, results-based budgeting should better enable decisionmakers to achieve the following:

- *Identify poorly performing programs,* thereby signaling the need to make changes and allocate fewer or more funds. (Other information is needed to determine which changes to make.)
- *Identify programs that are performing well* and presumably need no significant changes. (Even here, other information is needed to determine what, if any, changes may be desirable.)
- *Assess new programs* for what they are expected to accomplish, not just their costs or general statements of their expected value. Are the new programs worth their expected costs?
- *Compare different proposed options* on their expected outcomes and costs.
- *Help identify agency activities that have similar outcome indicators* and, thus, are candidates for coordination and perhaps revised funding needs.
- *Justify budget choices more effectively* to agency and elected officials—and the public.
- *Provide the basis for greater agency accountability,* if reasonable performance targets are set for the budget year and achieved values are subsequently compared to targets.

The first three points are discussed at length in chapter 10—primarily in the context of analyzing performance information for changing programs and policies during the budget year. This chapter focuses on using the same information to establish and examine budgets.

Results-based budgeting supports an overall agency focus on outcomes. Here is an example of its use in helping justify budgets:

The Massachusetts Department of Environmental Protection sought to obtain funding from the state legislature to line unlined landfills. It justified the expenditure by reporting the product of the expenditure as *the number of acres expected to be lined.* This did not move the legislature, which turned down the request. The department then switched to a more outcome-based approach and justified the request in terms of *gallons of leachate prevented.* Legislators asked for a definition of leachate. When they found that it referred to potential pollutants leaked into the groundwater and water supply, they approved the funding request.[1]

The U.S. Office of Management and Budget has instituted probably the most extensive use of outcome information as part of its PART process. OMB reviews each major federal program on a number of performance factors, including results achieved. OMB has emphasized that the ratings are not the only factor in decisions and that low (or high) scores do not necessarily mean decreased (or increased) funding. Nevertheless, the ratings appear to have affected, or at least supported, some funding decisions.[2]

In a performance-based budgeting system, agencies need to select targets (make projections) for the budget year for each output, outcome, and efficiency indicator, as well as for expenditures.[3]

A key problem for results-based budgeting, especially at the state and federal levels, is to persuade legislators and legislative staffs to switch from primary dependence on line-item budgeting to an outcomes focus. At the very least, legislators and their staffs need to address outcomes during appropriation hearings. The executive branch is responsible for providing meaningful, reliable, important outcome information to its legislators—in a user-friendly format. When some state governments initiated their results-based budgeting efforts, they loaded legislators with large numbers of indicators and data (sometimes including outputs and outcomes mixed together) presented unattractively, thus discouraging their use.

This book does not cover budgeting in general. Instead, it addresses the new dimension of outcome information. The key issues in results-based budgeting are listed in exhibit 13-1 and discussed later in this chapter—after a bit of history.

A Bit of History

Performance budgeting has been around at least since the 1960s. At that time, it focused primarily on the relationship between inputs and outputs. Some communities (such as Milwaukee, Wisconsin, and Nassau County, New York) produced budgets that contained hundreds of unit-cost

Key Issues in Results-Based Budgeting

1. Need to increase focus on outcomes, not only inputs and outputs
2. Limitations in the usefulness of performance measurement information for results-based budgeting
3. Time frame that should be covered by results-based budgeting, especially considering that outcomes often occur years after the one in which the funds were budgeted
4. Whether proposed inputs can be linked to outputs and outcomes
5. The role of efficiency indicators
6. Setting performance targets in budgets
7. Use of explanatory information
8. Strength of program influence over future outcomes
9. Using performance information in formulating and examining budget requests
10. Applying results-based budgeting to internal support services
11. Using results-based budgeting for capital budgeting
12. "Budgeting-by-objectives" and "budgeting for outcomes"
13. Special analytical techniques for projections
14. The role of qualitative outcome information in results-based budgeting

measurements linking costs or employee-hours to outputs. Sunnyvale (California) has used such measurements since the early 1970s, converting unit costs into productivity indices focusing on outputs. These indices permit comparisons across services and across years. More recently, Sunnyvale has begun focusing on outcomes.

A typical output-based performance indicator would be, for example, "the cost (or number of employee-hours) per ton of asphalt laid." In some cases, these output-based indicator reports were dropped because the number of unit-cost indicators overwhelmed the external users of the information. Nevertheless, such unit-cost information can be useful to managers and supervisors (and elected officials, if they wish) for tracking the technical efficiency of their activities.

The major new dimension is to relate outcomes to budget requests. The term *results-based budgeting* reflects this new focus.[4] At both the federal and state levels, recent legislation has emphasized the concept that budget decisions should be made not based on dollars alone, nor on physical outputs, but in relation to outcomes.

Of the many recent performance measurement systems that have been initiated to provide some form of results-based budgeting, the Government Performance and Results Act (GPRA) of 1993 is a prime example (recently expanded to include the PART process discussed briefly above). This federal budget action was unique in (a) having support from both political parties and both the executive and legislative branches and (b) being explicitly embodied in legislation, unlike earlier approaches such as the Planning-Programming-Budgeting-System (PPBS), Zero-Based Budgeting (ZBB), and Management by Objectives (MBO).

The Texas, Oregon, and Louisiana legislatures were among the first states to legislate a form of results-based budgeting, sometimes including selected outcome indicators with recent and projected data in their appropriations acts.

Key Issues in Results-Based Budgeting

1. Need to Increase Focus on Outcomes, Not Only Inputs and Outputs

Using outcome information for budgeting seems quite sensible on the surface, but in fact, its use in budgeting for agency operations is controversial. It has been, for example, the major subject of debates comparing the New Zealand to the Australian and U.S. approaches to budgeting at the federal level. New Zealand's approach had been to hold its operating departments responsible for outputs but not outcomes—and to use performance agreements with department heads to hold them accountable for outputs. New Zealand's rationale was that agencies control outputs, but too many other factors beyond the control of the operating departments affect outcomes. Only ministers were held responsible for outcomes. New Zealand has recently changed back to including outcomes in department responsibilities.

The counterargument to the view that agencies should be held responsible only for producing outputs is that outcomes are the fundamental reasons for establishing an agency in the first place. The activities of operating agencies clearly contribute to program outcomes, even if no single group of people, whether operating personnel or the policymakers themselves, fully controls results. Take as an example income maintenance and public assistance programs. Primarily policy issues are who is eligible for assistance and what level of payments is to be provided. These decisions are made by the legislature and the upper echelon of the executive branch of government. However, if the policy is not implemented well—if program personnel do not execute the policy properly and get the correct checks to the right people quickly—the desired outcomes will be compromised, and program personnel can be at least partly responsible for the failure.

Encouraging agency personnel to work to improve service outcomes seems a much better way to go. Many, if not most, outcomes are produced by many agencies and sectors of the economy, and responsibility is thus inherently shared. This is the implicit philosophy of the Australian and U.S. governments. As suggested in chapter 10, agencies can note the extent of their influence over individual performance indicators in their performance reports. This alerts users to the inherent limitations of outcome information while retaining a degree of responsibility for each agency.

The controversy over output versus outcome responsibilities has been less an issue at lower levels of government (especially at the local level).

2. Limitations in the Usefulness of Performance Measurement Information for Results-Based Budgeting

Performance measurement looks *backward*. It attempts to provide the best possible data on what happened in the past. Past outcome data provide important information for projections, *but estimating future outcomes differs radically from assessing past performance*. Past trends are only one among many influences on future outcomes. The future effects of those other influences are inevitably a matter of uncertainty, particularly in cases where little is known about the *quantitative* relationship between inputs and outcomes.

Suggestion: For outcome forecasts that are particularly uncertain, provide a range of values instead of a single value. This range is likely to be more realistic and informative.

3. Time Frame to Be Covered by Results-Based Budgeting

Typically, budgets only present data for the current budget year(s). Some central governments, such as those of the United States and Australia, now also include out-year funding estimates (perhaps for three additional years) but not outcome projections, except in separate long-run strategic plans. Including out-year forecasts for outcomes can be important for some programs, particularly at the federal and state levels, for three reasons:

- It reduces the temptation for agencies and their programs to focus all their funding decisions on the short term.
- For some programs, achievement of the hoped-for outcomes will require funds not only from the current year's budget but from future budgets as well.
- When important outcomes will not occur until after the proposed-budget period, the outcome targets for the budget year will not reflect those effects.

Therefore, budget proposals, especially those of the higher levels of government, should include out-year estimates for some outcomes, regardless of whether this information is included in the final appropriation document. For many programs, organizations will be able to better allocate resources when they explicitly consider expected costs and outcomes for out-years. For example, the results of funding a new federal or state program to reduce alcohol abuse might not be apparent for two or more years. (Time will be needed to gain acceptance by localities, train staff members in the program, publicize and run the program, make sure clients receive the program's services, and then measure the outcomes.) Even for intermediate outcome indicators, measurable effects may not be expected until after the budget year. Another example: Road construction can reduce accidents and congestion over several years. Should not estimates of the magnitude of these future improvements be included in the budget justification?

A partial solution is to build into the budget process any important outcomes expected to occur because of the proposed new funding. Programs would be asked to estimate the values for each outcome indicator for each out-year the proposed budget funding is expected to significantly affect. Requiring outcome projections in the budget development process is likely to encourage agencies to consider multiyear effects.

For some programs, this forecasting can be done readily. For example, a federal program to help residential housing might request funds for rehabilitating the homes of a certain number of families. The program can probably predict the years in which those rehabs will occur and the number of families occupying the housing units. A program that provides drug treatment funding will find it more difficult to estimate the number of clients who will become drug free and in which years. Performance measurement data on past success rates will likely help those preparing or reviewing the budget to estimate such outcomes.

A less demanding option is to ask for estimated future outcomes without requiring that they be distributed by year.

The need to consider future outcomes of the current year's budget is less frequent for local than for federal and state programs. But even at the local level, some programs, such as school and health programs, will have long-term outcome goals.

Most governments have not addressed the problem of long-term outcomes. A partial exception is that some state governments separate expansion requests (including new programs) from requests for continuation of current programs. For expansion requests, these governments require out-year projections of future outcomes.

4. Whether Proposed Inputs Can Be Linked to Outputs and Outcomes

In analyzing performance information for budgeting, a critical step is to link information on proposed costs to the projected amount of output and outcomes. Results-based budgeting and similar resource allocation efforts (including strategic planning) enter into this new dimension—*estimating the link between inputs and expected future results.* Such estimates can be subject to considerable uncertainty.

Part of the uncertainty relates to lack of good historical cost, output, and (particularly) outcome information. This problem is potentially curable. More difficult is estimating *future* costs. Even more difficult is estimating the amount of expenditures needed to increase outcomes, especially end outcomes, by specific amounts. Typically, programs do not know with any certainty how much more (or less) funding or staffing is needed to increase (or reduce) an end outcome by a certain amount. As programs gain experience with their outcome data, they should be able to better estimate this relationship, although it will never be as predictable as the relationship between funding or personnel and output indicators.

Estimating the future outcomes that will occur given specific amounts of inputs, even for only one year into the future, is much more difficult than tracking past performance.

Projecting accurately becomes increasingly difficult and uncertain as programs move from linking inputs to outputs, to linking inputs to intermediate outcomes, and, finally, to linking inputs or outputs to end outcomes. The following sections discuss the links between inputs, outputs, intermediate outcomes, and end outcomes. Little past work has examined these latter relationships.

Linking inputs to outputs. The amount of output expected in the budget year can be used to estimate the associated costs and personnel requirements or vice versa. If the amounts of dollars and personnel are the starting point for the budget, the amount of output achievable can be estimated.[5] Many, if not most, programs can estimate somewhat accurately how much workload they are likely to have, and thus the amount of output they can accomplish, given particular amounts of staff and funds. Programs will likely have reasonably accurate counts of past outputs and the direct costs of employee time. If they do not currently record such information, they can obtain it.[6]

If funding needs are developed from estimates of the workload, estimates of future expenditures of employee time and money will be affected by the program's ability to estimate accurately the magnitude and character of the budget year workload and the effects of any new service procedures or technology. For example, school systems try to estimate the next year's school population in order to decide about school buildings, classrooms, teachers, and purchases of books and other teaching materials. Inaccurate projections have been known to embarrass school officials.

Performance measurement information from earlier years normally provides the basis for projecting the relationship between inputs and outputs for the current budget year. However, if the *complexity of the workload* during the forthcoming budget year is likely to differ substantially from that in previous years, this change needs to be considered when developing the budget. For example, the Internal Revenue Service can tabulate the number and complexity of tax returns that come in each year. However, many factors—such as revisions to the tax code—can alter the future mix of tax-return difficulty and thus the amount of time required to review and process returns.

External factors can also affect future workload. For example, at the state and local levels, weather conditions, such as freeze-thaw conditions, can have substantial effects on costs, outputs, and outcomes. Agencies can obtain projections of these for the budget year, affecting such performance indicators as estimates of future roadwork and costs, and accident and injury rates. Similarly, the number and characteristics of incoming clients, such as their need for employment, health, and social service programs, can be highly unpredictable because they are affected by many economic and social factors—and projections based on past data are by no means certain. For some programs, agencies can use reasonably reliable estimates of their client populations, but these are also subject to uncertainties, such as increased immigration from countries in crisis.

Linking inputs to intermediate outcomes. Precise relationships between past input data and past intermediate outcome data can be developed for some outcome indicators. Even so, past relationships between the intermediate outcomes and inputs will usually provide only rough indications of what will happen in the budget year. For example, federal agencies such as the departments of Education, Housing and Urban Development, Health and Human Services, and Labor as well as the Environmental Protection Agency provide much of their assistance to state and local agencies rather than to the ultimate customers. If these state and local agencies undertake promising steps that the federal department has encouraged, the steps can be considered intermediate outcomes for that department. Data on the past relationship between the amounts of federal funds and assistance, on the one hand, and the extent to which the state and local governments undertook promising initiatives, on the other, are likely to be useful. But the past relationship provides only a rough estimate of what state and local agencies will do in the budget year.

Some intermediate outcomes can be estimated relatively accurately. For example, agencies can make fairly accurate estimates of such intermediate outcomes as future response times, given particular amounts of staff and dollar resources.[7] Even here, however, a number of outside factors over which the program has little control can intervene. For example, an unexpectedly large number of requests for service or changes in the proportion of complex requests can have major effects on response times.

Here are some examples of difficult-to-predict intermediate outcomes:

- Number of businesses (or households) that alter their handling of waste to be more environmentally prudent after receiving assistance from state or local programs
- Number and percentage of parents who take special parenting classes and then alter their behavior in ways that encourage their children's learning in school
- Customer satisfaction

All these outcomes are driven not only by agency efforts to seek certain customer behaviors and perceptions but also by many aspects of the behavior and circumstances of the customers themselves, as well as outside factors.

The bottom line is that agencies should expect historical data on costs and intermediate outcomes to be useful in preparing cost and intermediate outcome information for budgets. In many cases, however, agencies will be able to make only rough projections about the future relationship between costs and intermediate outcomes.

Linking inputs to end outcomes. As a rule, agencies should not expect to have solid, known relationships between inputs and end outcomes, no matter how good the historical data are. (In more economic terms, little information is available about the production function that relates the inputs to the end outcomes.) Nevertheless, these relationships are extremely important and need to be considered, *at least qualitatively,* in any budget process.

Some end outcomes are easier to relate to inputs than others. For example, the number and percent of a state or local jurisdiction's roads that are in satisfactory condition can be considered an end outcome indicator for road maintenance services. These numbers relate closely to the funds that the agency applies to road maintenance and repair. Past data on this relationship can be used to estimate the expenditures needed in order to achieve a certain value for this outcome indicator (or conversely, to estimate the percent of road miles in satisfactory condition given a particular funding level). In contrast, how much a client's condition is improved by expenditures of particular amounts of federal, state, local, or private funds to reduce substance abuse or to enhance elementary education is considerably more difficult to estimate.

Projecting how well budgeted resources will achieve *prevention* (whether of crime, disease, family problems, or so on) is extremely difficult. At best, the historical data will provide very rough clues about the relationship between resources and prevention. In-depth studies can provide evidence, but decisionmakers may need to rely more heavily on qualitative information and subjective judgments on the prevention outcomes expected from a particular level of budgeted resources.

In general, the more direct a program's influence over an outcome, the greater the program's ability to develop numerical relationships between inputs and the outcome. Local governments and private agencies generally have more direct influence on end outcomes than state or federal agencies; therefore, the relationships between their inputs and outcomes (both intermediate and end) are likely to be clearer. Nevertheless, for many end outcome indicators, the relationship will inevitably be imprecise. How many more resources would be needed to increase the percentage of customers satisfied with their recreation experiences by 5 percentage points (such as from 65 percent to 70 percent)? The answers to questions like this usually can be estimated only very roughly, at best.

If identifying the quantitative (or even qualitative) relationships between size and type of input, type of intervention, and amount of outcomes achieved is likely to be crucial to future major budget decisions about an existing program, agencies should seek an in-depth program evaluation.

Agencies can systematically track changes in resources to assess the differences on outcomes and then use that information to help make future budget estimates. Agencies and their programs might also be able to intentionally alter the amount of input to certain activities to see how more or fewer resources affect outcomes—and then use such information for future estimates.

Linking outputs to outcomes. Outcomes presumably flow from outputs. For example, the number of calls answered is an output for a service (whether these calls relate to police, fire, sewage backups, travel information, or any other service request). This output leads to outcomes, such as what resulted and whether the requests were fulfilled to the customers' satisfaction. Some outcome indicators explicitly relate outputs to outcomes, such as "the percent of those to whom services were provided [an output] who had successful outcomes."

Staff preparing or reviewing budget proposals should examine the amount of output expected in the budget year and assess what outcomes can be expected from that number—and when. If X customers are expected to be served during the budget year (an output), how many customers (and what percent) can be expected to be helped to achieve the desired outcomes that year and in future years (an outcome)? For example,

- how many persons are expected to find employment after receiving training services, and when?
- what percentage of babies born to low-income women who received appropriate prenatal care will be healthy?

Those preparing the budget request and those subsequently examining it should *ascertain that the outcome numbers make sense relative to the amount of output,* based on past data. For services that have lengthy lag times between outputs and outcomes, the outcome numbers for the budget year need to be compared with output numbers in previous years.

Linking intermediate outcomes to end outcomes. It is likely to be difficult to provide quantitative relationships between intermediate and end outcomes, but it is often easier than directly estimating the relationships between input and end outcomes. For example, a state agency might provide funds or technical assistance to local agencies to undertake an environmental protection regulation designed to lead to cleaner air. The relationship between the local agency's successfully getting businesses to adapt better practices for handling hazardous wastes (an intermediate outcome for both the state and local agencies) and the extent to which cleaner air results (an end outcome for both agencies) is uncertain. Some relationships are clearer, such as the extent to which increased percentages of children vaccinated against a disease can be expected to lead to reduced incidence of the disease among the vaccinated population.

How to make these links? For most programs, knowledge about most of the above links is lacking. Historical data from the performance measurement process, even if it has been implemented for only one or two years, can provide clues. But there will almost always be considerable uncertainty about projections of outcomes, especially end outcomes, for given budget levels. A key is to be able to make *plausible* connections between the amount of budgeted funds and the outcomes projected. *These connections can be based on past performance and modified by information on changes in either internal or external factors expected in the budget year.*

5. The Role of Efficiency Indicators

Efficiency is an important consideration in the budget process. As noted earlier, efficiency is traditionally measured as the *ratio of inputs to outputs.*

The new type of indicator added in results-based budgeting is *ratios of inputs to outcomes*. An example of this is "cost per person served *whose condition improved significantly after receiving the service.*" The more traditional output-based efficiency indicator is "cost per person served."

When reasonably solid numerical relationships exist between outputs or outcomes and the associated inputs, past data can be used to develop historical unit-cost figures, such as the "cost per lane-mile of road maintained" or the "cost per lane-mile rated as in good condition." These figures can then be used to make estimates for the budget year. Likely future factors need to be factored in. For example, road maintenance budget estimates should consider any planned price changes, any new technologies that might be used and their cost, and any indications that repairs will be more extensive or more difficult than in past years.

Some outcomes, such as road condition, can reasonably be numerically related to outputs, such as the number of lane-miles expected to be repaired during the budget year for a given dollar allocation. Budget preparers and reviewers can then examine various levels of the number of lane-miles to be repaired for various levels of expenditures and estimate the number of lane-miles that will be in satisfactory condition for each expenditure option. *These estimates will inform decisionmakers of the trade-offs between costs and outcomes, so they can select their preferred combination.*

In police investigative work, "number of cases cleared per police dollar or per investigation hour" is an outcome-based efficiency indicator. Past data on clearances can be used to make estimates for the forthcoming budget. However, the number and percent of crimes cleared in the budget year will also depend significantly on the number of crimes reported (many more crimes may mean investigators have less time to spend on individual cases), the types of crimes (for example, burglaries have substantially lower clearance rates than robberies), and the amount of evidence available at the scene. Factors largely outside the control of the police department (such as case difficulty) as well as internal factors (such as the amount of investigator turnover and the quality and quantity of investigative effort) can significantly affect clearance rates. Trends in such factors should be considered when projecting clearance rates from past efficiency data.

The use of unit costs in which the units are *outputs* is common in budgeting. However, the use of unit costs in which the units are *outcomes* is rare. One reason for this is that outcome data have not often been part of the budget preparation process. This is changing. In the future, the primary reason for limited use of costs per unit of outcome will be not lack of outcome data but rather lack of solid numerical relationships between inputs and outcomes.

6. Setting Performance Targets in Budgets

The projected values for individual outcome indicators are important numbers in results-based budget submissions. In view of the considerable uncertainty surrounding future conditions and the links between agency resources and indicator values, how should agencies develop these targets? Suggested steps are listed in exhibit 13-2. The specific factors to consider are listed in exhibit 13-3.[8] Additional suggestions are provided in chapter 9.

Two special target-setting options are available to programs that are highly uncertain about the future values of one or more outcome indicators: variable targets and target ranges.

The *variable target option* applies to outcome indicators whose values are believed to be highly dependent on a characteristic of the incoming workload *and* where major uncertainty exists about that characteristic. In this procedure, the expected relationship between the characteristic and outcome is identified first. The final outcome target is determined *after the fact*, depending on the workload characteristics that actually occurred in the budget year.

For example, if an outcome is expected to be highly sensitive to the mix of workload (e.g., customers) coming in, and the mix for the budget year is subject to considerable uncertainty, the program can set targets for *each*

EXHIBIT 13-2

Suggested Steps in Developing Outcome Targets

1. Examine the agency's strategic plan (if one exists). Targets contained in the budget should be compatible with targets in the strategic plan.
2. Analyze the historical relationships between inputs (expenditures and staffing), outputs, and outcomes. Examine any explanatory information that accompanied the historical data. Use that combination of information to provide an initial estimate of targets compatible with the amount of resources being considered for the program's proposed budget.
3. Consider each factor listed in exhibit 13-3 (such as outside resources, environmental factors, changes in legislation or requirements, and expected program delivery changes) and adjust the targets accordingly.
4. Consider the level of outcomes achieved by similar organizations or under various conditions (as discussed in chapter 9). For example, the outcomes achieved by better-performing offices or facilities that provide similar services are benchmarks the program may want to emulate.
5. Review the findings and recommendations from any recent program evaluations to identify past performance levels and past problems. Consider their implications for the coming years.
6. Use program analysis, cost-effectiveness analysis, and/or cost-benefit analysis to estimate the future effects of the program.

Performance Measurement: Getting Results

Factors to Consider When Selecting Specific Outcome Targets

- *Past outcome levels I.* The most recent outcomes and time trends provide a starting point for setting the outcome targets. (For example, recent trends may indicate that the values for a particular outcome indicator have been increasing annually by 10 percent in recent years; this would indicate the next year's number should be increased by a similar percentage.)

- *Past outcome levels II.* If the values for an outcome indicator are already high, only small improvements in the outcome level can reasonably be expected. If the values for an outcome indicator are low, future improvements can be expected to be larger (there is more room for improvement).

- *Amount of dollar and personnel resources expected to be available through the target period.* If staff and funds are being reduced or increased, how will this affect the program's ability to produce desired outcomes?

- *Amount of outside resources expected to supplement the program's resources.* Potential sources include other agencies, foundations, volunteers, and the business community. If such resources can play a significant role in producing the outcomes sought by the program, and the program has indications that these are being significantly increased or decreased, how is this likely to affect the outcomes?

- *Factors likely to be present in the wider environment through the target period.* These include such factors as the economy, population demographics, weather, major changes in industries in the area (such as major new industries scheduled to begin or depart), and major changes in international competition.

- *Recent or pending changes in legislation and other requirements of higher-level governments.* To what extent are they likely to increase or decrease the ability of the program to produce favorable outcomes?

- *Changes planned by the program in policies, procedures, technology, and so on.* It is important to consider lead times to implement such changes.

- *Likely lag times from the time budgets are approved until the outcomes are expected to occur.* This applies both to the effects of past years' expenditures on the outcome values targeted for the budget year and to the likely timing of outcomes produced with the funds allocated in the budget year. (For some outcome indicators, effects will be expected in the budget year, but for others, effects will occur primarily in years after the budget year.)

- *Political concerns.* Politics may at times push for reporting outcome targets that exceed feasible levels. (Even so, the program and budget analysts should provide those selecting the targets with estimates of the likely achievable levels of outcomes.)

category of workload without making assumptions about the workload mix. The *aggregate target* is determined after the budget year closes and the mix is known.

For the indicator "percent of people who leave welfare for work," the program might set separate targets for groups defined by their amount of formal education. Suppose the program estimated that 75 percent of people coming in with at least a high school diploma would find jobs and get off welfare in the budget year, but only 30 percent of those with less than a high school education would do so. These targets would be presented in the budget. The aggregate percent, which might also be included, would be based on the program's estimated mix of clients.

At the end of the year, the aggregate target for the year would be calculated for the actual education mix and compared to the aggregate percent. If 420 people who had not completed high school and 180 people who had completed high school entered the program during the year, the aggregate target would be 44 percent—30 percent of 420 (126) plus 75 percent of 180 (135), equaling 261. Dividing 261 by the total number in the program that year (600) yields the aggregate target for the share expected to go off welfare, 44 percent.

The target might also be linked to the national unemployment rate. For example, the program target might be 15 percent of enrollees off welfare if the national unemployment rate turned out to be over 5.4 percent and 25 percent off welfare if the national unemployment rate turned out to be less than 5.0 percent. The program would not know if it achieved the target until the national figure became available. Another option is to use a formula that relates expected outcome to the value of the external factor—in this example, a formula that relates the expected percentage off welfare to the national unemployment rate.

The *target range option* applies to any outcome indicator with highly uncertain future values. A range of values, rather than one number, is given as the target for the indicator. Many programs might benefit from this approach, especially for their end outcomes. Here are some examples of target ranges:

- The customer satisfaction level is expected to be in the range of 80 percent to 87 percent.
- The percentage of clients who will be off illegal drugs 12 months after program completion is expected to be between 40 and 50 percent.

The danger of gaming and ways to alleviate it. As higher-level administrators and elected officials begin to use targets in budget documents, the temptation to game targets will inevitably grow. Such gaming can occur at any level. Program managers and upper-level officials might set targets so their projected outcomes will look good. (This is an argument for legislators to ask independent audit offices to review and comment on proposed budget targets, especially at the state and federal levels.) Elected officials might manipulate targets for political purposes.

Setting targets that are easy to achieve will be tempting to those whose funding or individual compensation is based significantly on achieving targets. The opposite—setting very optimistic, if not impossible, targets—is tempting to those seeking support for high budgets.

The following are some ways to alleviate gaming:

- Establish a multilevel review process in which executive personnel check targets to identify values that appear overly optimistic or overly conservative.
- Examine the past relationships between inputs, outputs, and outcomes to see if the proposed targets are consistent with those relationships.
- Use one of the special target-setting options noted above to avoid a single-number target. These ranges can still be gamed, but the effects of gaming should be reduced.
- Explicitly identify in performance reports any future outcomes that are particularly difficult to estimate. Budget documents should also identify new outcome indicators, pointing out that setting targets for them is particularly difficult because there is no experience on which to base estimates.
- Ask programs to provide explanations for unusual-looking targets.
- Reduce reliance on major incentives that link funding or salary compensation to target achievement. However, pressure to link compensation to target achievement is likely to increase as agencies switch to outcome-based target-setting procedures. In such cases, an in-depth examination of the reasons for highly successful or highly unsuccessful outcomes should be undertaken before final funding or salary decisions are made.

In some instances, executives and elected officials will prefer unclear, fuzzy goals. For example, school districts have debated whether they should include precise objectives on student test improvement (such as increasing the overall scores by 5 percentage points or reducing the difference in performance between the minority and majority student population by 7 percentage points during the year). These officials might be willing to accept a target range.

Note: Agency personnel sometimes are reluctant to provide targets that are lower than the previous year's targets, even if budget-year resources are lower in real terms (i.e., after allowing for cost increases). They fear this will make them look bad. Even so, it is important that agencies and their individual programs realistically estimate the consequences of reduced resources. Agencies should encourage such reporting if it can be justified. Not being able to do everything they did in the previous year is not a basis for applying blame to programs if resources are cut. Upper

A Special Concern with Targets

Will reporting outcome targets increase liability for not achieving them? In some situations, agencies may be concerned that reporting targets may increase their liability if the targets are not met, particularly when a standard is built into the indicator. Consider, for example, the outcome indicator "percent of time that responses to calls for emergency medical services exceeded X minutes." Does such an indicator increase the responsibility, and thus the liability, of an agency when the standard is not met? Can families successfully sue an agency if the response to their request exceeded the standard and the patient appeared to have added health complications as a result? These are legal questions an agency needs to address.

Nevertheless, for most performance indicators, liability does not seem likely to become an issue. These targets are *projections* based on a variety of conditions and factors that can affect achievement of outcomes. Moreover, the target data in budgets are *grouped data,* not data for specific individuals or households. In any case, even if there is no formal performance measurement system, an agency can be subject to litigation if evidence exists that agency personnel performed irresponsibly in a case where serious damage resulted.

management may believe that productivity improvements can make up for the reduced resources (and this may be true—up to a point). If political pressure requires that a program establish published targets that are higher than the program believes are achievable, the distinction should at least be made clear internally.

Setting performance targets is an excellent management tool for agencies, particularly if the targets are provided and progress is examined periodically during the year, such as monthly or quarterly. Even if an agency does not use outcome targets in its budget process, the agency can choose to retain an internal outcome-targeting process.

7. Use of Explanatory Information

As discussed in chapters 10 and 11, agency programs should be encouraged to provide explanatory information along with their past performance measurement data when developing and submitting budget requests.

Staff preparing budgets should examine such information for insights into why the program performed well or poorly and for any suggestions about what is needed to improve it. This information can also help identify program changes likely to affect cost and outcome estimates.

As already noted, the results of any relevant program evaluations should be part of budget preparation and review. The findings on outcomes and the extent to which the program has been instrumental in producing the outcomes are important for judging the value of the current program. Persons who review the program's proposed budget can use later performance data to assess whether the proposed budget reflects the changes suggested by the evaluation. *Program evaluation findings should typically take precedence over findings from the agency's performance measurement system.*[9]

For target values that deviate substantially from past results, agency programs should be encouraged to provide explanations for those targets, especially on key outcome indicators. Such information should identify the basic assumptions used to develop the outcome projections and any important external factors expected to make the outcome value deviate from past performance levels.

Explanatory information on past performance, including any available findings from recent program evaluations, can help identify the reasons for success or lack of it—that is, program strengths and weaknesses. Budget preparers and reviewers can then assess the extent to which steps have been taken, or are needed, to correct problems.

8. *Strength of Program Influence over Future Outcomes*

Agency managers are usually quite apprehensive about including outcome indicators as a part of their performance measurements. As discussed in previous chapters, managers often have only partial control over outcomes, especially end outcomes.

To alleviate this concern in budget preparation, and to give budget reviewers a better perspective on the projected outcome data, agencies *should consider categorizing each outcome indicator by the extent of the agency's influence over it* (see chapter 6). This will identify the extent to which the agency can affect each indicator relative to outside factors likely to affect the program's outcomes.[10] Note, however, that *agencies and their programs may have more influence than they think*. In many instances, innovative approaches to their missions might influence outcomes in meaningful ways, including making recommendations for legislative changes.

Indicators can be slotted into a small number of broad categories, such as considerable influence, some influence, or little influence. (If the program has no influence over the value of a performance indicator, then it should not be considered a performance indicator. For budget examination purposes, however, programs should be asked to identify the reasons they think they have no influence.)

Lack of influence may indicate that the program is not doing the right things, perhaps requiring major program changes.

9. *Using Performance Information in Formulating and Examining Budget Requests*

The budget preparation and review process is intended to help ensure that needed resources are budgeted for the most cost-effective purpose. The availability of data on past inputs, outputs, outcomes, and efficiency, as well as explanatory information, allows analysts to formulate and examine program budget proposals much more comprehensively and meaningfully than in the past. Outcome information, even if relatively crude and partial, enables analysts to consider both resource needs and likely outcomes from those resources—and under what conditions results have been good or bad. This adds much more substance to a budget process. Chapter 10 described how to analyze *past* performance. Similar approaches are useful in results-based budgeting. A later section of this chapter lists and discusses 18 steps for using performance information to examine budget requests—whether inside an operating agency, by a central office such as a budget office, or by elected officials.

10. Applying Results-Based Budgeting to Internal Support Services

Governments at all levels and private agencies support a variety of administrative functions, such as building maintenance, facilities maintenance, information technology, human resources, risk management, purchasing, and accounting. The link between the products of such activities and public service outcomes is distant and usually extremely difficult or impossible to determine, even roughly.[11]

These activities are nonetheless important in providing needed support for operating programs. Good management requires that administrative services track their own internal intermediate outcomes (such as the quality of their services to other agency offices). The principles and procedures described in earlier chapters can be readily adapted to administrative services. For example, the types of data collection described in chapter 7—agency records, customer surveys, and trained observer ratings—can be used to obtain data on service quality.[12]

11. Using Results-Based Budgeting for Capital Budgeting

Many state and local governments prepare separate capital budgets, sometimes in the form of multiyear capital improvement programs. Capital budgets typically list proposed projects and the estimated capital funds required for each project in the budget year. Multiyear plans usually contain such information for each out-year. These plans may include general statements about the purposes of the expenditures, *but they seldom contain information about their expected effects on outcomes.*

There is no reason results-based budgeting should not apply to capital budgets. The agency should gain experience with results-based budgeting and then call for the explicit estimation of the effects of major capital expenditures on outcomes. For example, planned capital expenditures for road rehabilitation might be justified in terms of their expected effects on future road conditions, such as added rideability and safety, compared with the conditions that would occur without the capital expenditures. Similarly, funds for water and sewer purposes should be related to projected improvements in water quality and health protection. For capital projects that primarily benefit particular segments of the community, estimates should be provided on which, and how many, citizens are expected to benefit.

Many agencies are also faced periodically with the need to invest in information technology. These investments should be assessed not only on their costs but also on their expected benefits. For example, how does the proposed technology reduce response times to customers or change the accuracy of service delivery?

Some capital expenditures, such as those for administrative services, do not link well with end outcomes. New construction of office buildings is a good example. For this construction, a performance measurement system might track such internal outcomes as work completed on time, work completed within budget, ratings of the quality of the facilities built, and any added efficiencies or improved working conditions for employees.

Decisionmakers and the public should not be expected to make capital investment decisions without information on the benefits expected from these expenditures.

12. "Budgeting-by-Objectives" and "Budgeting for Outcomes"

Conceptually, it makes sense for a department to submit budgets with proposed funding grouped by major objectives.[13] For example, child abuse prevention, alcohol abuse reduction, unemployment assistance, and traffic accident reduction might be major objectives. All activities related to the particular objective would be included, regardless of which program or agency is involved. Budgeting-by-objectives was a characteristic of the original program budgeting and PPBS (Planning-Programming-Budgeting-System) in the late 1960s and 1970s. However, this approach has rarely been used.

The major question that confronts organizations that try this approach is how to sort out objectives and programs. Most programs have multiple objectives, and their personnel and other resources simultaneously affect more than one objective. The crosswalk between objectives and programs or agencies can be cumbersome. If some activities simultaneously affect more than one objective, how should costs be split between them, or should they be split at all? For example, transportation programs can influence multiple objectives across a wide range of the policy spectrum, including making transportation quick and convenient, enhancing health and safety, and protecting the environment.

A recent variation of budgeting-by-objectives is "budgeting for outcomes." Here, service organizations estimate how much outcome they will provide and at what cost. The focus is not on programs but on the results the organization says it will achieve. Budgeting for outcomes encourages innovation in the way outcomes will be produced, and can even encourage providers outside the government to "bid." The government might also preselect the major outcomes it wants and establish a total expenditure level for each outcome.[14] The State of Washington has experimented with this approach, but it is too early to assess its long-term success. The approach has some major hurdles, including the need to have good outcome information and be able to judge the claims of bidders. In addition, most government organizations seek many outcomes, and sorting them all out and determining allocations for each outcome (and what to do about outcomes that are not considered "major") present major difficulties.

At this point, it is by no means clear whether budgeting by objectives or budgeting for outcomes can be made practical. *Providing crosswalks linking activities to each outcome, however, does seem a reasonable approach* for modern information technology (as has been done by the states of North Carolina and Oregon and by Multnomah County, Oregon). Agency programs that contribute to several outcomes can be coded to identify which programs contribute to which outcomes.[15] Such crosswalks can at least trigger the need for coordination and cooperation among programs, and they will help budget examiners detect the need for across-program budget reviews.

13. *Special Analytical Techniques for Projections*

Budgeting, like strategic planning (and unlike performance measurement), involves projecting costs and outcomes into the future. Estimating future costs, and especially future outcomes, can be very difficult, as already emphasized. Program analysis (sometimes called cost-effectiveness analysis) and cost-benefit analysis can help agencies select service delivery variations. The findings should help the agency select the service option that should be budgeted, help estimate the outcomes, and then help justify the budget proposal. These techniques have been around for many years, but their use in budget preparation and review is rare.

This book does not detail these techniques, but the following review briefly identifies the major features of each that can help in results-based budgeting.

Program (cost-effectiveness) analysis. This term applies to special quantitative analyses used to estimate the future costs and effectiveness of alternative ways to deliver a service. While program evaluation is retrospective, program analysis is prospective. The Department of Defense is one of the few agencies in the country that has designated personnel to undertake regular program analysis. Otherwise, systematic program analysis has not taken hold in the public sector or in nongovernmental organizations. The Department of Health, Education, and Welfare (now the Department of Health and Human Services) and the state of Pennsylvania had special offices with such expertise in the 1960s, when these were fashionable as part of PPBS efforts, but later discontinued them. While some agencies have policy analysis shops, these are usually heavily qualitative. Program evaluation offices, which primarily examine past performance, may sometimes take on this role, since some of the same technical skills are involved. Information from program evaluations is valuable when the past data can be used to help decide about the future.

For results-based budgeting, program analysis is particularly helpful when an agency proposes to introduce a new service delivery approach or a significant variation of an existing approach. Unless the delivery approach proposed closely resembles an approach for which relevant past data are available, projecting costs and outcomes from past data may not be very useful.

Agencies can consider doing pilot tests or experiments (as discussed in chapter 9), using the performance measurement system for data on the old and the new service approaches and then using that information as the basis for estimating outcomes and costs. These procedures are worthwhile if the agencies can wait to make their final decision until the test has been completed and the findings have become available. Agencies should use the findings from such analyses and experiments to help formulate and subsequently justify budget proposals.

As the use of performance measurement, and particularly results-based budgeting, grows, the need to project outcomes systematically will also grow. The field of program analysis may then stage a comeback.

Cost-benefit analysis. Cost-benefit analysis goes one step further than program analysis. It provides a *monetary estimate of the value of a program.* (Cost-benefit analysis can also help evaluate the value of a program's past performance.) Its key characteristic is that it translates nonmonetary outcomes into monetary ones. The costs are compared to the estimated dollar benefits to produce cost-benefit ratios and estimated differences in the monetary values of the costs and benefits. Before the calculations into monetary values can be performed, the basic outcome values, usually measured in nonmonetary units, are needed. That is, program analysis needs to be done first. Cost-benefit analysis adds an additional, usually difficult, step to the process.

The monetary value of the outcomes has to be *imputed* in some way. For example, an estimate that X number of traffic accidents could be avoided by a particular activity might be converted into monetary estimates of the costs of those accidents, including damage repair, hospital and other health care, time lost from work, and the economic value of any lives lost. The costs of the activity being considered would then be compared to these dollar valuations and a cost-benefit ratio calculated.

Sound cost-benefit analysis, whether of past program accomplishments or projected program value, can provide major backup information for program budget requests. Such calculations can also appeal to public and private officials, because most outcomes are converted into dollars and summarized in one number (the cost-benefit ratio), which can be interpreted as the value of the program. One summary number is much easier for decisionmakers to handle. The usual application of this approach is to compare options within a single service area, but it could also be used to compare programs across services.

Cost-benefit analysis has a number of drawbacks. The calculations of monetary value usually require numerous assumptions that can be quite controversial. For example, how should the value of lost work time or of deaths be determined? (The value of lives lost has sometimes been estimated based on the economic potential of human beings at particular ages. This approach sounds reasonable, but giving older people little or no value in the calculations implies that it is all right to "knock off" the elderly.) Another problem is that the monetary values often accrue to different populations from the populations that pay the costs. For example, revenues for most government expenditures are raised by taxes from the public and businesses, but the benefits often accrue primarily to particular groups.

If performed and used carefully, cost-benefit calculations can provide insights into the expected value of the proposed budget for a program. However, cost-benefit analysis reports should *always* spell out the value assumptions used so readers can better understand the basis for the findings.

Cost-benefit analysis tends to be time-consuming and expensive. As a result, it has been used very selectively, primarily by the federal government. The Army Corps of Engineers has undertaken many such studies when selecting major water and other construction projects. Cost-benefit analysis has also been used, and sometimes mandated, for federal regulatory programs.

14. The Role of Qualitative Outcome Information in Results-Based Budgeting

As discussed in chapter 6, not all outcomes can be adequately measured in quantitative terms. An agency's budget process should at least *qualitatively* consider the implications of the budget for desired (and undesired) outcomes. Even if outcomes can only be expressed qualitatively, explicitly including them in the budget, and in the political debate over amounts and allocations, can help improve decisions on expenditures.

Steps for Examining Performance Information in Budget Reviews

Some basic steps for developing and examining budget requests are listed in exhibit 13-4 and discussed below.[16] Together, these steps represent a heavy workload for those reviewing or developing budget requests. However, these steps can be used selectively. They are also likely to be appropriate at any time during the year when a program seeks additional resources.

1. Examine the budget submission to ascertain that it provides the latest information and targets on workload, output, intermediate outcomes, and end outcomes—as well as the funds and personnel resources requested. The budget submission should include past data on each indicator, the latest available outcome data for the current budget year, and the targets for the fiscal year(s) for which the budget is being submitted. If an indicator is too new for data or targets to be available, the submission should note this and indicate when data will be available (both actual data and targets).

If the program does not believe it can obtain numerical values for important indicators, then it should explain why and provide qualitative information on past and expected future progress.

2. Assess whether the outcome indicators and targets are consistent with the mission of, and strategies proposed by, the program and adequately cover that mission. If the agency's programs do not have explicit mission statements that adequately define their major objectives (such as those included in strategic plans) or descriptions of the strategies the programs propose to use to achieve the objectives, the reviewers will need to ask the program to construct these or construct these themselves—discussing them with program personnel as necessary.

For example, federal, state, or local litigation offices may have emphasized deterrence of future criminal behavior in their formal mission statements. Litigation programs, however, do not usually include indicators that explicitly address deterrence. The outcome indicators tracked will

EXHIBIT 13-4

Steps for Examining Performance Information in Budget Requests

1. Examine the budget submission to ascertain that it provides the latest information and targets on the workload, output, intermediate outcomes, and end outcomes—as well as the funds and personnel resources requested.

2. Assess whether the outcome indicators and targets are consistent with the mission of, and strategies proposed by, the program and adequately cover that mission.

3. If the program is seeking increased resources, assess whether it has provided adequate information on the amount each output and outcome indicator is expected to change over recent levels.

4. Examine the program's projected workload, outputs, intermediate outcomes, and end outcomes, as well as the amounts of funds and personnel. Make sure these numbers are consistent with one another (e.g., that the amount of output is consistent with the projected workload). Determine whether the program has included data on the results expected from the outputs it has identified.

5. Compare *past data* on workload, output, intermediate outcomes, and end outcomes with the proposed budget targets. Identify unusually high or low projected outputs or outcomes.

6. Examine the explanatory information, especially for outcome indicators whose past values fell significantly below expectations and for any performance targets that appear unusually high or low.

7. For programs likely to have delays or backlogs that might complicate program services, be sure the data adequately cover the extent of delays, backlogs, and lack of coverage.

8. For regulatory programs, be sure that adequate coverage is provided for compliance outcomes (not merely number of inspections).

9. Ascertain that program has sufficiently considered possible changes in workload that are likely to affect outcomes (such as higher or lower proportions of difficult workload).

10. If recent outcomes for a program have been substantially worse than expected, make sure the program has included in its budget proposal the steps, and resources, it plans to take toward improvement.

11. Examine findings from any program evaluations or other special studies completed during the reporting period. Assess whether these findings have been adequately incorporated into the budget proposals.

12. Determine whether the program has developed and used information on the relationship between resource requirements, outputs, and outcomes (e.g., the added money estimated to increase the number of successfully completed cases by a specified amount).

13. Identify indicators with significantly reduced outputs or outcomes projected for the budget year (compared to recent performance data) and no decrease in funding (adjusted for projected price increases) or staffing. Identify and assess the program's rationale for these reductions.

14. Identify outcome indicators with significantly improved outcomes projected by the program for the budget year (compared to recent performance data) and no increase in staffing, funding (adjusted for projected price increases), or output. Identify and assess the program's reasons for these increases.

15. Identify what, if any, significant outcomes from the budgeted funds are expected to occur in years beyond the budget year. Assess whether they are adequately identified and support the budget request.

16. Identify any external factors not considered in the budget request that might significantly affect the funds needed or the outcomes projected. Make needed adjustments.

17. Compare the latest program performance data to those from any other programs with similar objectives for which similar past performance data are available. Assess whether projected performance is compatible with that achieved by similar programs.

18. Identify any overarching outcome indicators that can provide a more meaningful and comprehensive perspective on results. Recommend coordinating with other programs, other agencies, and other levels of government.

probably focus on bringing offenders to justice. From the program's viewpoint this focus is reasonable, but reviewers should consider whether it is feasible to track deterrence using counts of nondeterrence as a surrogate (i.e., the amount of reported criminal behavior) or be content to seek qualitative information. (Note: Measuring deterrence directly is usually best done, if done at all, through in-depth studies and not through a performance measurement process.) Reviewers might also decide that the litigation program does not in fact have the responsibility or the capacity for estimating prevention. They might determine that the mission statement was overstated and that the program's focus on number of offenders brought to justice is appropriate.

3. If the program is seeking increased resources, assess whether it has provided adequate information on the amount each output and outcome indicator is expected to change over recent levels. The changes might be expressed as a special table showing pluses or minuses for each affected indicator. Programs need to make clear what effects their special proposals are expected to have on outputs and outcomes—not merely on funding and personnel resources.

4. Examine the program's projected workload, outputs, intermediate outcomes, and end outcomes, as well as the amount of funds and personnel. Make sure these numbers are consistent with each other (e.g., that the amount of output is consistent with the projected workload). Determine whether the program has included data on the results expected from the outputs it has identified. Use steps such as those listed in exhibits 13-2 and 13-3 to develop and examine the targets. Output indicators normally should be included in the budget submission for each major category of workload. (Note: outputs represent completed work. Workload includes work in progress and items that are pending.) Intermediate outcomes should be consistent with outputs and end outcomes consistent with intermediate outcomes. If such information has not been included, the program can be asked to provide the needed data.

The data on outputs and outcomes should be checked for consistency with each other. For example, do the number of successes for a reporting period exceed the number of cases completed during that period?

Note, however, that substantial time lags can occur between the time a customer comes in for service and the outcomes. For example, the outcome indicator "percent of cases that were successful" should be derived by dividing the number of cases expected to be successfully completed during the budget year by the number of cases completed during the year, regardless of the year the case was initiated, not by the number of cases worked on or started during the budget year. Another example: A budget-year estimate for the outcome indicator "percent of child adoption cases in which the child was placed with adoptive parents within 24 months of the child's entry into the system" would need to be based on the number of children that came into the child welfare system two years before the budget year. Where appropriate outcome indicators and/or outcome data have not been provided, ask the program to provide them.

Two reminders:

- Outcomes can result from activities undertaken before the budget year. Also, some outcomes intended to result from the proposed budget might not occur until after the budget year. The budget submission should identify such situations.
- In the initial years of the performance measurement system, programs may not be able to provide data on some outcome indicators.

5. Compare past data *on workload, output, intermediate outcomes, and end outcomes with the proposed budget targets. Identify unusually high or low projected outputs or outcomes.* This can be done in at least two ways:

- Compare the latest data on actual performance to those for previous reporting periods and to the proposed budget targets.
- Compare historical data on individual outcome indicators to the past targets set for those indicators *to assess the program's accuracy in setting targets.* In light of this past experience, assess the program's proposed targets. Some agencies may have a pattern of being highly optimistic about their ability to achieve outcomes; others may have a pattern of overly conservative targets. Budget analysts should take this into account as they interpret target achievement. Ideally, targets should be set at a level that encourages high, but achievable, performance. (The budget analysis office should attempt to track the proclivities of individual program managers to set their targets overly high or low.)

Where projected performance values differ considerably from past values, or appear otherwise unusual, seek explanations. Has the program provided any other information that explains this? If not, ask for explanations. For example, if a program has the same targets it had last year, and it fell far short of those targets, ask what has changed to make the targets more achievable this year. If the program is requesting a considerable increase in funds without increasing outcome targets over previous years' actual results, ask why the added funds are needed. If a program projects lower values for outputs or outcomes, find out why. The program might report, for example, that the reason was reduced workload (check the related workload indicators), reduced resources (check the related expenditure and staffing amounts), unusually difficult or complex workload (check any evidence provided by the program), or reduced efficiency or effectiveness in delivering the service (not likely to be reported by the program).

6. Examine the explanatory information, especially for outcome indicators whose past values fell significantly below expectations and for any performance targets that appear unusually high or low. This step should be given special attention when any of the earlier steps indicate that the performance levels projected need further examination. Explanatory information should be examined before any conclusions are drawn about the performance of the program and its resource implications.

Explanations can be substantive or be merely rationalizations or excuses. To assess the value of the explanations, the analysts may need to follow up with the program to clarify and/or obtain more information.

7. For programs likely to have delays or backlogs that might complicate program services, be sure the data adequately cover the extent of delays, backlogs, and lack of coverage. Buildups of such problems can be a major justification for added resources. The size of any delays or backlogs, and how these may be growing, can be important customer-focused, quality-of-service performance indicators for social, health, welfare, licensing, and many other programs. For legal prosecutions and court cases, "justice delayed is justice denied."

Conversely, if a program's indicators show no evidence of significant delays, then existing resource levels appear adequate for the future— unless the program provides evidence that a significant buildup of its future workload is likely. Programs, where possible, should systematically categorize their incoming caseloads by level of difficulty or complexity (see chapter 8). Programs should also project the size of their caseload by difficulty or complexity as a factor in determining their proposed budget. Is there any evidence that the program is now getting or expects to get more complex and/or more difficult cases? Such changes would offer justification for additional (or fewer) resources.

Indicators that programs can be asked to provide include the following:

- Counts of the number of cases pending and projected at the end of each year (tracked over time, this will indicate buildups)
- Indicators of the time it has taken and is expected to take, given proposed budget resources, to complete various activities
- Estimates of the number of cases that will have to be turned away (for programs that have the discretion to turn them away)

8. For regulatory programs, be sure that adequate coverage is provided for compliance outcomes (not merely numbers of inspections). Examples include environmental regulation programs, work-safety programs, civil rights programs, and regulatory boards. The analysts should ascertain that the outputs and intermediate and end outcomes of compliance-monitoring activities are identified. For example, does the budget proposal report on expected outputs (such as the number of needed inspections that are expected), and the intervals at which they are projected to be done? Do the indicators provide past data on such outcomes as the number of organizations found in previous years not in compliance and then the number and percent that subsequently were found to have fully corrected the problems? Do the indicators include the incidence of problems that occurred despite the regulation activities? Do the budget-year projections include such estimates for the budget period? Do the monitoring resources proposed in the budget appear too little or too large compared to the expected outcomes?

9. Ascertain that the program has sufficiently considered possible changes in workload that are likely to affect outcomes (such as higher or lower proportions of difficult workload). Programs may not report such breakouts in their budget submissions, but they are often able to supply such information. (Programs should be encouraged, for their own data analyses, to break out their outcome data by various work and customer characteristics, such as type of case, its difficulty, and different locations or facilities.) For example, federal and state correctional facilities will probably have internal reports on individual facilities and facility categories, such as security level and type of prisoner. Health and human services programs can probably provide some service data on individual facilities or offices and on various demographic groupings of clients.

Examine whether the outcomes differ substantially for some service characteristics (such as for some facilities or regions) over others. If so, examine why. This information can be very helpful in interpreting a program's projected outcome data. For example, certain types of locations or cases may be considerably more difficult to handle than others, suggesting that lower-than-desired projected performance is the result of an increase in the proportion of difficult cases and thus providing a supportable case for lower outcomes. Budget reviewers should look for evidence that substantially more cases that are difficult (or easy) are likely to come in during the budget year.

Comparing outcomes among demographic groups is also important in assessing equity and fairness. Are some groups underserved? Should additional resources be applied to those groups? Even though identifying who loses and who gains can be a political hazard, the information is basic to resource allocation.

10. If recent outcomes for a program have been substantially worse than expected, make sure the program has included in its budget proposal the steps, and resources, it plans to take toward improvement. If the program projects improved performance, are the resources and planned steps commensurate? If not, why not? (For example, substantial time may be needed between the time that funding is approved, implementation, and the consequences of the funded activities for achievement of certain outcomes.)

11. Examine findings from any program evaluations or other special studies completed during the reporting period. Assess whether these findings have been adequately incorporated into the budget proposals. This includes studies produced by other organizations. Such information may provide added support for the activities and budget proposed by the program, or it may contradict the findings produced by the program to support its proposed activities and budget.

12. Determine whether the program has developed and used information on the relationship between resource requirements, outputs, and outcomes (e.g., the added money estimated to increase the number of successfully completed cases by a specified amount). Assess that information for plausibility. Few programs are likely to have undertaken much systematic analysis of this relationship. Programs should be encouraged to do so to help substantiate future budget requests.

Relating expenditures and resources to outcomes (both intermediate and end outcomes) is usually difficult and uncertain. However, to the extent that additional dollars and staff enable the program to take on more work (more customers, more investigations, more road repairs, more inspections, etc.), the program can probably estimate roughly how much additional work it can handle based on past performance information. For example, a program may be able to estimate the percent of cases or incidents it might not be able to handle (such as identifying illegal immigrants) without the added funding requested.

Many, if not most, programs will be unlikely to have investigated the cost-to-output and cost-to-outcome relationships that underlie their budget requests. However, these relationships are at the heart of resource allocation decisions, implicitly if not explicitly, and the program should be pushed to be as explicit as possible about them. After all, *the projected targets the program sets each year based on its outcome indicators by definition imply such relationships, however rough the estimates may be.*

A program seeking additional resources will tend to be overly optimistic about the outcomes that will result. Budget analysts should look for supportable estimates of the relationships between resource requirements (dollars and personnel) and at least approximate values for each outcome indicator.

Over the long run, programs should be encouraged to develop information about these relationships. The analysis needed for such studies usually requires special background, however, which is not likely to be in place in most programs. Analytical staff, whether attached to each program or to a central analysis office, should be helpful for this purpose.

13. Identify indicators with significantly reduced outputs or outcomes projected for the budget year (compared to recent performance data) and no decrease in funding (adjusted for projected price increases) or staffing. Identify and assess the program's rationale. Reduced funding or staffing projections are obviously plausible rationales for reduced outcome projections, as is a more difficult or complex workload in the new year. If the program has been systematically categorizing its incoming caseload by level of difficulty or complexity, it should be able to provide evidence supporting a reduction. The program might already have in its pipeline many especially difficult cases. For example, litigation or investigation programs may be working on several cases that are highly complex and require additional program resources.

Other possible reasons for lower outcome targets include (a) an unexpected jump in workload during the budget year without an accompanying increase in resources, leading to reductions in the percent of cases for which the program can produce successful outcomes; (b) new legislative or agency policies that add complications or restrictions, reducing the probability of successful outcomes in certain categories of cases; and (c) external events that would impair outcomes, such as the expected departure of key industries from a community, affecting local employment and income.

14. Identify outcome indicators with significantly improved outcomes projected by the program for the budget year (compared to recent performance data) and no increase in staffing, funding (adjusted for projected price increases), or output. Identify and assess the program's reasons for these increases. Budget reviewers should ask the program how it expects to achieve the improved performance—to check the plausibility of the higher targets. Such improvements might occur if the program plans to improve the efficiency of its operations. Another reasonable rationale is that the program expects its workload to be easier or less complex. The program may already have in its pipeline cases that it expects to be successful in the budget year.

15. Identify what, if any, significant outcomes from the budgeted funds are expected to occur in years beyond the budget year. Assess whether they are adequately identified and support the budget request. As noted earlier, many programs and their activities affect outcomes in years beyond the budget year (particularly federal and state programs that work through other levels of government and any investment funding). To justify expenditures for such activities, programs should project these expenditures' effects on the various outcomes for years beyond the budget year. The program should also provide rationales for such projections. Budget analysts should review these rationales for plausibility.

16. *Identify any external factors not considered in the budget request that might significantly affect the funds needed or the outcomes projected. Make needed adjustments.* The persons examining the budget request may be privy to information not available to those preparing it. For example, newly proposed or passed legislation or recently released economic forecasts can have major effects on the outcome projections.

17. *Compare the latest program performance data to those from any other programs with similar objectives for which similar past performance data are available. Assess whether projected performance is compatible with that achieved by similar programs.* This point and the next are resource-allocation issues that cross program lines. Agency budget analysts should consider the performance experience of other, similar programs even if the programs are in another agency. Are the program's past accomplishments poor relative to similar programs? If so, work with program personnel to determine why and identify what can be done to improve future performance. Make any resource judgments that such future actions might entail. Does the program complement or overlap other programs' efforts? If they are complementary, check whether the data are consistent among the programs. If they overlap, consider whether altered resource allocations are appropriate to reduce the overlap.

18. *Identify any overarching outcome indicators that can provide a more meaningful and comprehensive perspective on results. Recommend coordinating with other programs, other agencies, and other levels of government.* Few programs produce outcomes alone, especially end outcomes. This is a core concern in performance measurement. Programs related to employment, youth development, substance abuse, crime, and so on generally involve scores of other programs that also influence the desired ends. For example, crime control involves investigation, apprehension, adjudication, punishment, and probably a variety of social services. Each component is critical to final success, and each is handled by different programs and agencies.

Look for, and examine, consolidated outcome indicators that apply to all such programs. The budget examiners should make recommendations for any needed coordination and collaboration among programs and agencies. This would include the use of common cross-cutting outcome indicators and determining the roles and responsibilities of each program in achieving jointly targeted outcomes.

For example, reduced drug and alcohol abuse involves many different programs, agencies, and sectors. Each agency with a substantial role in helping reduce substance abuse should track the overall incidence and prevalence (but one agency would normally be responsible for data collection)—recognizing that their responsibility is shared. Each program will likely have its own intermediate outcome indicators and focus on one part of the overall problem (such as on reducing drug abuse by one age group).[17]

Summary of the Relationship between Performance Measurement and Results-Based Budgeting

The primary uses of performance data in budgeting are to help formulate the budget and to make a more convincing case for the budget recommendations. Performance information, especially if it includes credible outcome data, should lead to better choices and more convincing choices than are possible in its absence. Outcome targets for the budget year also establish a baseline for accountability (encouraging reviews of actual accomplishments throughout the year and at year's end).

Performance measurement of outputs, outcomes, and efficiency for past years is important for budget allocation decisions. First, the performance information provides baseline data on outcomes, which is fundamental for making decisions. *If you do not know where you are, you will have difficulty determining where you need to go.* Second, historical data are usually a primary *basis* for budget projections of future accomplishments.

Making projections for the budget year and beyond is considerably more difficult and is subject to *much* more uncertainty than measuring past performance. The future is very hard to predict, even if for only one or two years, because of the many external factors that can affect results. This problem becomes particularly troublesome if the program is suggesting significant new program variations or new programs to tackle its mission. Then past data will be a much less adequate guide to the future.

However uncertain the data, addressing the relationship of inputs to outcomes should be a major issue in making resource allocation decisions and budget justifications in any budgeting system. *Even if such discussions are heavily qualitative and judgmental, they are far better than nothing, because they encourage those making budget decisions to focus on what is most important to achieve.*

The budget review effort should be viewed as an opportunity for both the program and the agency's budget review staff to develop the best possible budget, to make the best possible case for budget requests, and to focus on maximizing outcomes for a given amount of resources. The inherent tension between budget analysts who perceive their primary job as keeping costs to a minimum and program personnel who want to obtain as many resources as they can will inevitably pose problems. The two groups will find the process much less difficult and less contentious if they work to make it as much of a partnership as possible. The interests of both groups are best served if the final resource-allocation decisions forwarded to higher levels are presented as effectively as possible. These days, that means proposals need to be justified, at least in part, based on outcomes—the potential benefits to the public.

References and Notes

1. Personal communication with Commissioner of Massachusetts Department of Environmental Protection, December 4, 1997.
2. The OMB web site fully describes the PART process. The web site also presents the detailed ratings for each federal program. See, for example, a PowerPoint summary of the process, "Program Assessment Rating Tool (PART): Improving Performance," March 2005.
3. The word *target* is not always used in this context. The Government Performance and Results Act of 1993 uses the term *annual goals*. Another terminology problem arises for programs, such as law enforcement, in which the word *targets* for some outputs or intermediate outcomes might be interpreted as establishing quotas, such as on the number of arrests, prosecutions, or collections. For this reason, programs whose missions are investigative, such as criminal investigation activities, might use another, more neutral, label, such as *projections*.
4. The terms *performance-based budgeting* and *budgeting-for-results* are also used.
5. This book does not address the many issues involved in developing comprehensive cost estimates for particular programs, such as how to handle indirect or capital costs. For many public and private agencies, cost accounting is deficient. Efforts such as activity-based costing may help, but they still have substantial limitations for projecting future costs. More important for budget formulation is for agencies to have good cost *analysis* capability—that is, to be able to estimate the likely *additional* expenditures that will be incurred to produce particular outcome levels. One approach to cost analysis is contained in David H. Greenberg and Ute Appenzeller, *Cost Analysis Step by Step: A How-to Guide for Planners and Providers of Welfare-to-Work and Other Employment Training Programs* (New York: Manpower Demonstration Research Corporation, October 1998).
6. This, however, can be a major problem for developing countries that have not yet established reasonably accurate procedures for tracking expenditures and outputs.

7. Those readers who do not believe that response times to requests for services should be labeled an outcome might prefer a label such as *quality-of-output* indicator.

8. For the application of performance targeting in other countries, see Sylvie Trosa, "Public Sector Reform Strategy: A Giant Leap or a Small Step?" in *Monitoring Performance in the Public Sector: Future Directions from International Experience*, edited by John Mayne and Eduardo Zapico-Goni (New Brunswick, NJ: Translation Publishers, 1997).

9. Preferably, an agency would sponsor in-depth program evaluations for each of its major programs, say, once every few years. New programs might be required to provide an evaluation strategy. Unfortunately, in-depth evaluations are expensive and time-consuming. Agencies and programs with highly limited resources might instead schedule periodic, but less comprehensive, reviews of each of their programs to learn more about how well they are working and why.

10. Degree of influence does not refer to the ability of an agency or program to *manipulate* the data to its own advantage. That is a quality control issue, discussed in chapter 14.

11. The costs of support services, however, need to be considered when analyzing the total costs of a program and comparing its costs to its benefits.

12. Note that activities relating to collecting revenues, such as taxes and fees, are *not* included here as "internal" activities. Performance indicators indicating the extent of success, such as "percent of owed taxes that were collected," can be considered major outcome indicators for governments.

13. This approach is discussed in Mark Friedman, *A Guide to Developing and Using Performance Measures in Results-Based Budgeting* (Washington, DC: The Finance Project, May 1997).

14. This approach is presented in *The Price of Government* by David Osborne and Peter Hutchinson (New York: Basic Books, 2004), especially chapter 3.

15. An example of this is the crosswalk developed by the Oregon Progress Board and the Department of Administrative Services, *1999 Benchmark Blue Books: Linking Oregon Benchmarks and State Government Programs* (Salem, May 1999).

16. Few publications are available that suggest specific steps for reviewing budget proposals that include examining the outcome consequences of the proposed budget levels. A recent document prepared for state legislative analysts nevertheless appears also applicable to budget examinations for any level or branch of government: "Asking Key Questions: How to Review Program Results" (Denver, CO: National Conference of State Legislatures, 2005). However, it primarily focuses on past results, rather than also including an examination of the proposed outcomes.

17. The U.S. Office of Drug Control Policy has been a leading agency in attempting to work out such cooperative efforts among federal, state, local, and foreign governments. See, for example, "National Drug Control Strategy: FY 2007 Budget Summary" (Washington, DC: The White House, 2006).

Part

IV

Other Performance Measurement Issues

Joseph S. Wholey

Quality Control: Assessing the Accuracy and Usefulness of Performance Measurement Systems

As more performance measurement systems have been implemented, policymakers, managers, auditors, and evaluators have begun to focus on quality control issues—those related to assessing the accuracy and usefulness of performance measurement systems. Quality control usually does not get much attention in the early stages of developing and implementing a performance measurement system. Typically, potential users question the information's accuracy and usefulness only after they begin using it. When the stakes for bad or good performance become high (as in, for example, the federal government's No Child Left Behind program), the temptation to juggle data can become considerable. *It is preferable to consider ways to ensure reasonable quality of the performance measurement process from the beginning—* to help build accuracy and usefulness into the design of the measurement system and into the training of personnel.

This chapter addresses performance measurement quality broadly, considering not only the *technical* quality of the data but also the quality of the indicators and the *usefulness* of the information generated. It presents criteria for judging the quality of a performance measurement system and suggest ways they can be applied and by whom.

One approach to judge quality is to focus mainly on technical quality—how clearly and accurately performance data portray agency and program performance. Another approach is to focus on agency use of performance information in management and reporting. The assumption underlying reliance on the second approach is that, if agencies are really *using* performance measures, most of the other criteria will be met.

Both perspectives are legitimate. Clearly, the technical quality of performance measurement systems is important, but its usefulness is at least as important. Performance information is intended to be used by managers, policymakers, and others affected by or interested in agency or program activities to improve agency and program management and performance, increase accountability to key stakeholders and the public, and support resource allocation and other policy decisionmaking. If performance information is inaccurate (invalid or unreliable), reliance on performance data can be expected to lead to poor decisions. Therefore, program managers, higher-level officials, and legislators should encourage agencies to be concerned about data quality.

Note on system cost: The cost of performance measurement is always a significant issue. Whether the primary purpose of a performance measurement system is improvement of performance, accountability, or support for decisionmaking, agencies must balance the cost of performance data against the value added. Finding the appropriate balance is the key. Costs of performance measurement systems include management, staff, and other stakeholders' time used in designing the measurement systems; management and staff time to collect, analyze, and use performance data; the cost of any contracts for data collection and analysis; the burden imposed on reporting entities; and the cost of checking data quality. In assessing performance measurement systems, therefore, the ultimate questions are: Are the performance data sufficiently accurate and useful to justify the cost of the performance measurement system? Would changes in the performance measurement system make the performance data less costly, more accurate, or more useful?

Concern with the cost of performance measurement is a subsidiary theme in this chapter. The central focus is the criteria and processes that managers, auditors, evaluators, and others can use to assess the accuracy and usefulness of performance measurement systems. *It is appropriate to ask periodically about individual parts of the performance measurement system, and performance measurement system as a whole, "Are we getting enough value from the information generated by the performance measurement to justify its cost?"*

Exhibit 14-1 presents basic criteria for assessing performance measurement systems. These criteria are drawn from the Government Performance and Results Act, technical quality standards, expert opinion, and the experiences of leading public-sector organizations. In this exhibit and the discussion that follows, the criteria are grouped under two overarching questions: (a) Are the prerequisites for useful performance measurement ("technical" quality) in place (criteria 1–3)? (b) Is the performance information used (criteria 4–7)? The technical quality of performance information is discussed in

---

EXHIBIT 14-1

Criteria for Assessing Performance Measurement Systems

A. Are the Prerequisites for Useful Performance Measurement in Place?

Criterion 1: A reasonable level of agreement exists on goals and strategies. Senior officials, managers, staff, and other key stakeholders more or less agree on agency or program goals (including outcome-related goals) and on the resources, activities, and processes required to achieve the goals.

Criterion 2: The performance measurement system is of sufficient technical quality to assess and report on performance in terms of the agreed-on goals. The system provides data that are complete, accurate, and consistent enough to document performance and support decision-making (see exhibit 14-2).

Criterion 3: The performance information presented is clear, understandable, and meaningful. The performance indicators are understandable without extra effort, they are fully labeled, and the areas they cover (such as periods of time) are clear.

B. Is the Performance Information Used?

Criterion 4: Performance information is used to manage the agency or program to achieve performance goals: for example, by creating intangible or tangible incentives for improved program performance, reallocating resources to improve performance, or redirecting program activities to improve performance (see exhibit 14-4).

Criterion 5: A reasonable degree of accountability is provided. Performance information is used to document progress toward agency or program goals. Performance information is used to communicate the value of agency or program activities to key stakeholders and the public.

Criterion 6: Performance has improved or become more effective, indicating that agreed-on goals have been met or that current performance exceeds prior performance—or the reverse. The information is used to help identify successful, and unsuccessful, practices so future practices are improved.

Criterion 7: Performance information supports resource allocation or other policy decision-making. Policymakers within or above the agency use performance information in resource allocation; development of legislation, regulations, or guidelines; and other policy decisions.

---

detail in a later section. *A performance measurement process cannot be high quality unless technical quality and use of the information are both present.*

Are the Prerequisites for Useful Performance Measurement in Place?

Three prerequisites are needed for useful performance measurement systems: (a) the agency and other stakeholders have reached a reasonable level of agreement on goals and strategies for achieving the goals; (b) the measurement system is technically capable of documenting performance in a way that supports decisionmaking; and (c) the resulting performance information is clear, understandable, and meaningful.

Criterion 1: A reasonable level of agreement exists on goals and strategies. To assess the quality and usefulness of a performance measurement system, one must first understand what is to be assessed. An acceptable level of agreement must exist among senior officials, managers, staff, and other key stakeholders on strategic or performance goals (performance targets) and on the resources, activities, and processes required to meet those goals. As discussed in chapter 4, though differences will always exist, agencies can often achieve a satisfactory level of agreement on goals and strategies through broad consultation with (a) managers and staff, (b) those who influence the allocation of needed resources, (c) those who make other policy decisions affecting the agency or program, and (d) other key stakeholders affected by, or interested in, agency or program activities.

Agencies should define performance broadly enough to cover the dimensions that are important to the various intended users of performance information. To meet concerns raised by Radin and others,[1] the definition should be extended to include minimizing, or controlling, important unintended outcomes of agency or program activities, such as corruption, creaming, other failures to provide fair treatment, or costs incurred by individuals or organizations as they respond to agency or program activities. Managers and staff can use logic models to ensure that they have identified relevant elements of the program design: key program inputs, activities, outputs, intermediate outcomes, end outcomes, assumed causal links, and key external factors that could significantly affect performance (see chapter 5). If agency or program managers have not developed appropriate logic models, auditors or evaluators can develop such models for, or with, them.

Rarely will a single performance indicator meet the information needs of all key stakeholders. Different performance indicators often pull managers and staff in different directions. *Performance measurement becomes more useful as the measurement system reflects and relates to a coherent set of goals and strategies covering any single program and collections of agency pro-*

Performance Measurement: Getting Results

grams and activities. Those reviewing performance measurement systems for quality control need to assess whether the agency has achieved reasonable agreement on defining performance. As the U.S. General Accounting Office (GAO) put it, results-oriented organizations

- involve their stakeholders,
- assess their internal and external environments, and
- align their activities, core processes, and resources to support mission-related outcomes.[2]

Criterion 2: The performance measurement system is of sufficient technical quality. As agencies implement performance measurement systems, they should balance the cost of data collection against the need to ensure that the data are sufficiently complete, accurate, and consistent to document performance and support decisionmaking at various organizational levels. In particular, the data must be sufficiently free of bias and other significant errors that would affect conclusions about whether program goals have been achieved.

One particular source of potential bias is the incentive for employees to game the system by manipulating indicator values to make their performance look good. A classic example of such ingenuity in circumventing quality control procedures took place several years ago in West Virginia. The Postal Service has for many years funded a contractor to mail letters quarterly from various locations to assess delivery times. (This is a form of the trained observer rating procedures discussed in chapter 7.) A window clerk in a West Virginia post office somehow became alerted that a particular batch of letters was part of this test mailing and notified other post offices around the state about the addresses involved. Post offices in the state gave special attention to those letters to ensure quick delivery times.[3]

To meet criterion 2, the technical quality of the system and the data it produces must be assessed along a number of dimensions (exhibit 14-2). Tension among the various quality dimensions and between quality dimensions and cost is inevitable. If performance measurement systems focus on results or outcomes (dimension A), for example, performance measurement will tend to be more costly, and it may be more difficult to ensure that performance data are sufficiently accurate (dimension E). Similarly, dimension B encourages limiting performance measurement systems to a small number of key performance indicators for each goal at upper organizational levels, whereas dimension C encourages greater comprehensiveness and tends to increase the cost of performance measurement.

Dimensions of Technical Quality in Performance Measurement Systems

A. Demonstrate results: Performance indicators should tell each organizational level how well it is achieving its goals, such as those related to intermediate outcomes, end outcomes, or productivity.

B. Cover the major goals: Performance indicators should be provided for each major goal. For upper organizational levels, the number should be limited to the vital few. These indicators should cover the key performance dimensions that will enable an organization to assess accomplishments, make decisions, realign processes, and assign accountability.

C. Cover multiple perspectives: Performance measurement systems at each organizational level should provide information that covers, to the extent feasible, the perspectives of various interest groups (such as individual families, businesses, and various citizen demographic groups), taking into account such factors as quality, cost, and customer satisfaction. The performance indicators should create incentives for managers to strike the difficult balance among competing demands. These systems should cover the performance dimensions—the outputs and outcomes that are important to the various primary expected users of the performance information.

D. Link to responsible programs: Performance indicators should be linked to program offices that have responsibility for making programs work. This will likely require disaggregating at least some of the performance data by managerial units (as discussed in chapter 8).

E. Be sufficiently timely, accurate, and consistent: Performance data should meet reasonable tests of validity, reliability, and timeliness. As agencies implement performance measurement systems, they should balance the costs of data collection against the need to ensure that data meet these tests. Agencies should periodically review data collection procedures and the completeness, accuracy, and consistency of at least a sample of the data.

Whatever the data source on which a performance measurement system is based—agency or program records, records of other agencies, surveys, or ratings by experts or trained observers—technical quality issues can arise. Exhibit 14-3 lists questions for evaluating a system's technical quality.

Though managers typically have more ongoing contextual information than policymakers, both groups need formal assurance that agencies and programs have in place reasonable quality control processes that review data collection procedures and test the validity and reliability of at least a sample of data periodically.

Criterion 3: The performance information presented is clear, understandable, and meaningful. Clear, user-friendly presentation of performance information is vital, but it has been overlooked too often. Even the highest quality technical performance information can be neglected if potential users are discouraged or turned off by the presentation. Performance indicators and the data provided should be understandable without extra effort and be fully and clearly labeled. The coverage of the data also needs to be clear, such as the time period the data cover.

Questions for Assessing the Technical Quality of Performance Measurement Systems

I. Validity

1. *Completeness:* Do the performance indicators cover the performance dimensions that are important to the intended users of the information? Are the data timely?
2. *Accuracy:* Do the performance indicators measure what they purport to measure? Are samples representative? Are response rates sufficiently large? Could managers or staff be manipulating performance data to serve their own interests?

II. Reliability

3. *Consistency:* Are samples large enough to yield reliable data? Do repeated measurements yield the same results? Do measurements by different staff members yield the same results? Are data from different offices, projects, or organizations based on similar definitions of data elements and data collection procedures?

III. Validity and Reliability

4. *Data collection procedures:* Are there flaws or errors in collecting, recording, or transcribing data? Are performance data analyzed for inconsistencies or unusually high or low values?
5. *Data maintenance procedures:* Are there adequate procedures for maintaining data? Could records be altered, lost, or incorrectly transferred?
6. *Data analysis procedures:* Are data analyzed correctly? Are correct formulas used to analyze and summarize information?

IV. Other

7. Do staff have the training required to collect sufficiently complete, consistent, and accurate data?
8. Does the agency have procedures for ensuring that performance data are free of significant error and that bias is not introduced?
9. Do the agency's procedures provide for periodic review of data collection, maintenance, and processing procedures to ensure that they are consistently applied? Is there appropriate documentation to permit similar data collection and analysis in the future?
10. Do the agency's procedures provide for periodic sampling and review of performance data to ensure that they are sufficiently complete, accurate, and consistent?
11. Do the agency's procedures call for formal assessments of performance data by external parties?
12. Do the agency's procedures address known problems in data quality?
13. Does the agency certify the accuracy and completeness of its data and identify any limitations?

Sources: Adapted from Harry P. Hatry et al., *Customer Surveys for Agency Managers: What Managers Need to Know* (Washington, DC: Urban Institute Press, 1998) and U.S. General Accounting Office, *The Results Act: An Evaluator's Guide to Assessing Agency Annual Performance Plans* (Washington, DC: GAO, 1998).

Is the Performance Information Used?

Performance measurement systems are intended to be useful to managers, policymakers, and other key stakeholders affected by or interested in the program. If the information generated by the system is not used, the time, effort, and cost of performance measurement will be wasted. Thus, when the quality control reviewers are satisfied about the technical quality of the performance measurement system, they still need to explore how, and the extent to which, the information the system produces is actually used.

Criterion 4: Performance information is used to manage the agency or program. Use in managing agencies and programs is a major, perhaps the major, use of performance information. This criterion addresses the use of internal reporting in performance-based management. As discussed in chapter 12 (and listed in exhibit 14-4), performance-based management practices include delegating authority and flexibility in return for accountability for results, creating incentives for improved program performance, redesigning management systems to focus on performance, reallocating resources or redirecting program activities to improve performance, and developing partnerships designed to improve performance. To help assess the quality and extent of use of performance measurement systems, determine how often uses such as those listed in exhibit 14-4 (and discussed further in chapter 12) have occurred during, say, the past year.

Criterion 5: A reasonable degree of accountability is provided. This criterion focuses on reporting outside the agency. Those assessing perfor-

---

EXHIBIT 14-4

Managing for Results: Internal Uses of Performance Information

1. To delegate greater authority and flexibility in return for greater accountability for results—for example, by simplifying the rules for budgeting, human resource management, or financial management.
2. To create nonfinancial incentives for improved program performance—for example, through performance agreements that set challenging but realistic performance goals for agencies or programs, through quarterly or more frequent performance measurement and reporting, through meetings focusing on performance issues, through recognition rewards or publicity about relative performance levels or changes in performance, or by delegating greater authority and flexibility in human resource management or financial management to high-performing organizations.
3. To create financial incentives for effective organizational performance—for example, by introducing competition among service providers, reallocating resources to higher-performing or most-improved service providers, or giving bonuses to managers and staff of high-performing or most-improved organizations.
4. To provide training and technical assistance where performance information indicates such help is needed; to build expertise in strategic planning, performance measurement, and management use of performance information.
5. To redesign central management systems (budgeting, human resource management, information management, procurement, grants management, financial management) to focus on performance.
6. To incorporate goals, performance indicators, and performance incentives into contracts and grant programs.
7. To reallocate resources to improve performance.
8. To redirect program activities to improve performance.
9. To develop partnerships designed to improve performance—for example, among public agencies, among nonprofit organizations, or between public sector agencies and nonprofit organizations or private firms.

mance measurement systems will need to examine how well the performance data included in outside reports to the chief executive, the legislative body (or board of directors), other key stakeholders, and the public cover the agency's mission and goals. Do agency reports provide accurate perspectives on agency or program performance?

Criterion 6: Performance has improved. Do performance reports provide credible information demonstrating that performance targets have been met or that current performance represents improvement over past performance?

Criterion 7: Performance information supports resource allocation or other policy decisionmaking. What evidence is there that higher-level managers, budget analysts, or legislators have been using performance information in their resource allocation or other policy decisions? Have policymakers made appropriate use of performance information? To obtain such information, those assessing the quality of a performance measurement system will probably need to interview a sample of relevant personnel and other stakeholders.

Specific Technical Data Quality Issues

Following are a number of typical "technical" problems that arise in performance data. These problems, listed in exhibit 14-5, should be identified when

---

EXHIBIT 14-5

Potential Technical Quality Problems That Should Be Assessed

1. Progress toward identified program (or agency) goals is not adequately measured by the performance indicators.
2. Poor, invalid indicators are used.
3. Each indicator is not defined clearly and completely.
4. No written procedures are available describing how the data are to be collected.
5. People do not collect or record the data the same way, the way specified in the documentation.
6. The report containing the performance indicator values does not provide sufficient information for users to understand the data.
7. Data sources are not adequately identified when reporting data.
8. Limitations in the data are not clearly identified.
9. The period covered by the data is not clearly identified.
10. The data are too old.
11. The performance indicators change excessively from one year to the next.
12. The files, whether electronic or not, are not protected from tampering.
13. Staff responsible for data collection and processing are inadequately trained.
14. Who is responsible for data quality is unclear. Are there formal, recognized policies about data quality procedures?
15. The program or agency has no process for periodically checking the data quality.

---

reviewing the technical quality of data. (This material has been considerably aided by material drawn from a 2003 audit of the Georgia Department of Education's performance data.[4] The examples given below are also primarily drawn from that work.)

1. *Progress toward identified program (or agency) goals is not adequately measured by the performance indicators.* The Georgia Audit Office in its review of the Department of Education's 2004 budget found that 24 percent of the indicators had no actual results reported (for various reasons).

   These omissions can occur if, for example, an agency or program excludes important performance indicators on the grounds that it has little control over the outcome. Most end outcomes are affected by external factors, often significantly affected. As long as the agency or program has some say over the outcome and the outcome is important to the government and citizens, it should be measured.

2. *Poor, invalid indicators are used.* The problem can occur in the inherent subject of the indicator or in the way it is defined and collected. Here are two examples.

   The indicator "percent of targets met" is a dubious indicator, at least when used as the major way to assess an agency's or program's performance. The performance indicators included are likely to vary considerably in importance. The agency or program could easily manipulate the overall indicator by including more easy-to-achieve (probably considerably less important) indicators. Even if the agency or program does not intend to manipulate the indicator, outsiders can be put off by these possibilities. (This indicator was a major part of the U.S. Department of Education's FY 2004 Performance and Accountability Report.)

   Some human resources agencies have reported for a given 12-month period the "percent of clients whose condition had improved significantly," using as the denominator the total number of clients served during that period. The total would inevitably include new clients (who began service perhaps quite late in the year) who had not had enough time to have been helped or to have completed service. A considerably more valid indicator would be "percent of clients whose condition had improved significantly *as of a prespecified period, such as 12 months, after starting (or completing) service.*" The denominator would then include all those who had begun (or completed) service X months ago. (If the indicator focuses on those who had completed, rather than started, service, the indicator would not consider dropouts. Such a limitation should be noted in the performance report.)

Performance Measurement: Getting Results

3. *Each indicator is not defined clearly and completely.* Both the program collecting the data and the later users of the data need to be clear about what is being measured. A classic example is that of response times. Many, if not most, programs will likely include such information in their performance indicators. But response times can usually be defined in many ways. When should the clock start—when the request is first phoned in, when the appropriate person in the agency has received the request, or what? When should the clock stop—when a formal written response has been mailed to the customer, when some appropriate action has been started, or at some other time?

4. *No written procedures are available describing how the data are to be collected.* We suspect that this is the case for the majority of performance indicators used by any government or nongovernment agency. Documenting data collection procedures can be cumbersome. However, it clearly is good practice to write down the procedures. This will help ensure that different (perhaps new) staff will use the same procedures that other staff have used, thus helping ensure inter-rater reliability.

5. *People do not collect or record the data the same way, the way specified in the documentation.* A classic example is police officers reporting which category of crime was committed. Officers have discretion in labeling certain crimes depending on estimates of the amount of property stolen or other factors. Another example: the Georgia audit cited earlier found that one county school system had been understating discipline problems by as much as 85 percent.

6. *The report containing the performance indicator values does not provide sufficient information for users to understand the data.* A performance indicator used by Georgia's Department of Education was "percent of students scoring 3 or above on Advanced Placement exams." What is the significance of a score of "3"? If the reader was notified that scoring a 3 on the exam allows the student to obtain college credit for the class, the reader could understand that such a score is indicative of being prepared for college.

7. *Data sources are not adequately identified when reporting data.* The source needs to be spelled out clearly and completely. Many federal government reports that provide data tables identify the source at the bottom of each table or in extensive description of data sources in an appendix. This is good practice. Still, public agencies do not consistently identify data sources in their reports.

8. *Limitations in the data are not clearly identified.* This is a chronic problem. Limitations can come in many forms. The agency may still want

to report the data but should make clear the limitations of the data. For example, when performance information is based on surveys whose findings are based on only a small number of responses, users should be alerted to this limitation. This is often done by providing confidence intervals. However, even such reporting often neglects another potential source of error: the possible effect of nonresponse bias. How many of those people the agency attempted to reach were not reached? Response rates should also be provided.

The Georgia Agricultural Education program reported results from the National Assessment of Educational Progress (NAEP) Math and Science. However, because the NAEP test is administered to only a sample of schools and students in each state, less than 400 students in Georgia had taken the test in the year, raising questions about the representativeness of the program's achievement. In this instance, the agency noted the number taking the test in the reported results.

Many federal and state agencies depend on data from lower-level governments, the quality of which is not clear. For example, state-level agencies may not be auditing performance data of local agencies or school districts. Data coming from nongovernmental organizations, such as program completion and post-service outcome rates, may not be readily accessible to reviewers. And review costs can become quite large. (Public agencies that *contract out for services,* however, are more likely to check, and be explicitly responsible for checking, the quality of performance information coming from contractors.)

9. *The period covered by the data is not clearly identified.* Individual performance indicators may have differing time periods. For example, agencies that survey their customers may do so at various times of the year. The period when the survey was administered should be identified.

10. *The data are too old.* This is sometimes a special limitation of data that are provided. Often, especially at the state and federal levels, government agencies report data that are two or more years old and thus say little about recent program results. This probably usually occurs because of time lags before the data become available. However, agencies should attempt to speed up the process so timely data can be provided. Similarly, web sites available to the public often provide old data—a problem common to local government web sites as well.

One way to reduce this problem is to encourage agencies to obtain and report *preliminary* data, identifying the data as such and indicating when the final version will be coming.

11. *The performance indicators change excessively from one year to the next.* Some changes can be expected—and are justified—because of improve-

ments in measurement. Changes in indicators can be in the form of new ones, deleted ones, or ones in which the data collection procedure has changed so much that current measurements no longer can be compared with previous ones. However, too much change means that comparisons over time cannot be made. And, users will become suspicious that the changes are intended to assure that indicators with favorable outcomes will be measured in a given year.

The Georgia auditors found that only 16 (23 percent) of the 70 key measurements remained the same between the education department's FY 2004 and FY 2000 performance reports. Between 2002 and 2003, many were deleted or replaced.

12. *The files, whether electronic or not, are not protected from tampering.* Accidental or intentional breaches of confidentiality or security need to be guarded against, especially with data that are likely to have major implications for the agency, program, or staff.

13. *Staff responsible for data collection and processing are inadequately trained.* Reviewers of a performance measurement system should assess whether people collecting, entering, or otherwise involved in processing the data are doing so correctly. If the program has documented its data collection procedures, it can compare the documented procedures with those being implemented.

A typical concern is staff turnover. New staff need training in proper data collection and recording. For trained observer ratings, as discussed in chapter 7, the agency should periodically recheck samples of ratings to assess whether the observers have "telescoped" their ratings over time or have otherwise begun deviating from the rating standards. For surveys of citizens or customers, if done in house, the performance measurement system reviewers should carefully check the procedures being used, including checking the work of the persons responsible for sample selection, for administering the survey, and for processing completed questionnaires when returned.

14. *Who is responsible for data quality is unclear. Are there formal, recognized policies about data quality procedures?* Some agencies use an "outcome indicator specification" form that identifies who is responsible for the indicator. The form might identify the person responsible by name or the responsible office. (Such a form, illustrated in the next chapter, also is likely to contain information on the specific data collection procedure being used.)

The Georgia audit report cited earlier found that only 2 of 15 subprograms in the Department of Education's results-based budget submission identified a contact person.

Each government, each agency (public or private) needs a formal policy clearly identifying the importance of data quality and the respective responsibilities of managers and staff. These responsibilities include overseeing all aspects of the data collected, such as

— training others in data collection,
— implementing procedures for double-checking data entries,
— examining the reasonableness of the data (are they in an appropriate range?),
— checking on data outliers, and
— sampling a subset of the data for accuracy.

15. *The program or agency has no process for periodically checking the data quality.* Agencies should establish some procedure for periodically checking completeness and accuracy. For trained observer ratings, a supervisor should check a sample of ratings to assess whether they are reasonably complete and accurate. For citizen surveys, some supervisor of the organization administering the survey should check that interviewers, data entry staff, and computer programmers have been thorough and accurate in their work. For agency record data, entries made by human beings should be periodically sampled to assess their completeness and accuracy. Computer checks can often be included that look for certain types of mistakes such as out-of-the-range numbers, unusual patterns in the recorded data (such checks have been used with school test score data to help detect cheating), and missing data.

An earlier audit (2002) of the Georgia Bureau of Investigation's Drug Enforcement and Prevention program reported that the Bureau did not check the data for accuracy or completeness.[5]

Who Should Assess Performance Measurement Systems?

Program managers are the first line of defense against poor quality data. They should be accountable for data quality. However, the performance measurement system should also be subject to periodic assessment by other, more independent offices or organizations.

Agency and program managers bear the primary responsibility both for collecting performance data and for controlling the quality of the performance measurement process. Thus, managers should be responsible for periodically reviewing their performance measurement systems to ensure that the data are sufficiently complete, accurate, and consistent for use in documenting performance and supporting decisionmaking. Assessment of data quality will also be less costly if agency or program managers and their

Performance Measurement: Getting Results

staffs do their part. Managers might be asked to attest formally to the quality of the data they provide. As a practical matter, such attestation should be allowed to identify any reservations about particular data elements. (For example, higher levels of government that have to obtain key data from lower levels may not have full confidence in at least some of that data.)

Central program and budget review office staffs are an important second protection from poor quality data. These people need to use their knowledge and judgments about programs to look out for unusual, unexpected data—and to question programs about such data.

Independent organization, such as audit offices, provide a third level of quality control. Such organizations can systematically examine the performance information for quality. When performance measurement systems are used for accountability to higher levels or to the public, public officials may fear that the data might be manipulated or otherwise misleading. This is why independent efforts are also needed periodically to ensure the accuracy and credibility of the performance data. Independent assessment of the quality of the performance data or the measurement process can be requested from internal or external auditors, evaluators, statistical agencies, or others with the required expertise.

In Texas, the State Audit Office (SAO) provides such an independent review. It annually examines a sample of agency performance indicators. SAO determines whether each indicator should be classified as "certified" (if reported performance is accurate within 5 percent and it appears that controls are in place), "certified with qualification" (when performance data appear accurate but controls over data collection and reporting are not adequate), "inaccurate" (when the actual performance is not within 5 percent of reported performance), or "factors prevented certification" (if documentation is unavailable and controls are not adequate to ensure accuracy).[6]

Such independent organizations might examine all the key performance information or systematically choose a random sample of the performance indicators to review. They might examine only the soundness of the data procedures used or the accuracy of the actual data reported, or both.

An Overall Process to Assess the Accuracy and Usefulness of Performance Measurement Systems

Exhibit 14-6 outlines five steps that an agency or independent office might use to assess the accuracy and usefulness of a performance measurement system. The first three steps are preliminary activities before examining technical quality and usefulness.

Suggested Process for Assessing Performance Measurement Systems

Step 1. Assess the extent of agreement on goals and strategies for achieving them.

Step 2. Clarify how each goal is to be achieved. Use logic models to identify relevant inputs, activities, processes, outputs, intermediate outcomes, intended results, important unintended outcomes, assumed causal links, and key external factors that could significantly affect achievement of the goals.

Step 3. Identify the performance indicators and data collection procedures in use in the agency or program.

Step 4. Assess the technical quality of the performance measurement systems (see exhibit 14-1, criteria 1–3).

Step 5. Assess how widely the performance information is used in systems for managing the agency or program to achieve performance goals, in accountability to key stakeholders and the public, in demonstrating effective or improved performance, and in resource allocation or other policy decisionmaking (see exhibit 14-1, criteria 4–7).

Step 1. Assess the extent of agreement on goals and strategies for achieving them. Agency missions, multiyear goals, and strategies for achieving the goals will typically be presented in agency strategic plans or business plans. Annual performance targets for agency programs will typically be presented in performance plans, performance reports, grant applications, or budget requests. Targets may also appear in strategic plans, business plans, and similar documents. Information on the extent of agreement or disagreement on agency goals and strategies is often found in legislation, hearings, committee reports, and audit and evaluation reports—but may have to be acquired through interviews, focus groups, or surveys of managers, staff members, and other key stakeholders.

Step 2. Clarify how each goal is to be achieved. This involves identifying the chain of inputs, program activities, processes, outputs, and intermediate outcomes needed to achieve agency or program goals and the key external factors that could significantly affect achievement of the intended results. Some information on strategies for achieving goals may be found in agency plans and other documents. Additional information may have to be acquired through interviews with managers and other key stakeholders. As noted earlier, logic models can be a very useful way to help identify relevant performance indicators by highlighting inputs, activities, outputs, intermediate outcomes, end outcomes, important unintended outcomes, assumed causal links, and key external factors that could significantly affect achievement of intended results (see chapter 5).

Step 3. Identify the performance indicators and data collection procedures in use. An agency is likely to have many performance measurement systems, including measurement systems for individual programs and sub-programs. Information about these systems can be extracted from agency plans, management systems, audits, evaluations, and performance reports.

Step 4. Assess the technical quality of the agency's performance measurement systems. This should be done in terms of the quality dimensions listed in exhibits 14-2 and 14-5. Such reviews preferably would examine

- whether the agency has quality control systems in place;
- the soundness of the data collection procedures used; and
- the completeness, accuracy, and consistency of the data collected—for at least a sample of performance indicators.

The Federal Occupational Safety and Health Administration, for example, periodically compares reported workplace injuries and illnesses with employers' records.[7]

It may also be useful to compare the agency's systems with those of other agencies. The U.S. Department of Transportation (DOT), for example, produces an online compendium that provides source and accuracy statements for the data used to compute each of its performance measures.[8] The DOT annual performance plan for FY 2004 discussed the sources of its performance data, data quality, and efforts to improve data quality.[9] The U.S. Department of Education is working with state educational agencies to improve the quality and timeliness of educational information by creating an electronic data exchange system for performance information on federal K–12 education programs, a central database for the K–12 data, and a data analysis and reporting system that will be available to the department and the state agencies.[10]

No performance measurement system is—or ever will be—perfect. The most important question is whether the performance data are sufficiently complete, accurate, and consistent to document performance and support decisionmaking at various organizational levels. If the answer to this question is yes, the system can be considered adequate on technical quality.

Step 5. Assess how widely the performance information is used. The final step is to identify how, and the extent to which, the performance measurement system is used. Potential uses, discussed in chapter 12, include supporting resource allocation or other policy decisionmaking and providing accountability information to key stakeholders and the public. The assessment process should respect the reality that many factors other than performance measurement data influence management, agency and program performance, and policy decisionmaking. Assessors will need to judge whether the performance information has been sufficiently used.

Several information sources can be used to examine *internal* use of performance data. Sources include agency documents, audit reports, evaluation reports, interviews, focus groups, and surveys of managers and staff.

The U.S. Government Accountability Office (formerly the General Accounting Office) is assessing the status of implementation of the Government Performance and Results Act and identifying significant challenges confronting agencies in their efforts to become more results-oriented. GAO has been surveying representative samples of mid- and upper-level managers in 24 federal agencies about every two years. The survey asks managers about their perceptions on such topics as the use of performance information, hindrances to measuring and using performance information, and improvements seen or expected as a result of implementation of the act.[11]

For examining *external* use (by key external stakeholders and the public), such sources as the following are likely to be appropriate: budget justifications, other agency documents, audit and evaluation reports, hearings, interviews and focus groups with interest group representatives, surveys of key stakeholders, and observations of the decisionmaking process.

Exhibit 14-7 lists the information sources likely to be relevant in assessing agency progress in terms of each of the criteria proposed in exhibit 14-1.

Implications for Managers, Auditors, and Evaluators

Assessment of the quality and usefulness of performance measurement systems is an important, emerging issue. Such assessments will be increasingly important as public and nonprofit organizations start regularly reporting performance information and using such information to allocate resources.

Policymakers, managers, auditors, and evaluators are all moving toward closer involvement in performance measurement. For the foreseeable future, a wide variety of performance-based management initiatives is likely to affect public management, the intergovernmental system, and the nonprofit sector. In coming years, there will be a premium on managers, auditors, and evaluators with the knowledge, skills, and abilities to assess the quality of performance measurement systems and help ensure that performance information is sufficiently complete, accurate, and consistent to document performance and reliably support decisionmaking.

This chapter has proposed criteria for assessing performance measurement systems and suggests how to approach the task of assessing the quality and usefulness of performance measurement systems. The suggested process explores whether an agency has achieved agreement on defining

EXHIBIT 14-7

Sources of Information for Assessing Performance Measurement Systems

For criterion 1: Agreed-on goals and strategies

- Agency strategic plans, business plans, performance plans, and performance reports; grant applications, budget requests, and appropriations justifications; and other agency documents
- Agency management systems
- Audit and evaluation reports
- Legislation, hearings, and committee reports
- The opinions of key stakeholders on the extent of agreement—or lack of any strong disagreement—on performance goals, including outcome-oriented goals[a]

For criterion 2: Sufficient technical quality

- Systems for assessing and reporting on agency and program performance
- Strategic plans, business plans, performance plans, performance reports, and other agency and bureau documents related to systems for assessing and reporting on agency and program performance
- Grant applications, budget requests, and appropriations justifications
- The performance measurement, evaluation, and reporting systems of other agencies and programs
- Audit and evaluation reports
- The professional literature

For criterion 3: Presentation is clear and meaningful

- Reports and budget materials

For criterion 4: Performance information used to manage the agency or program

- Agency plans; agency management systems, including informal or formal incentive systems designed to stimulate effective performance in terms of performance goals; audits, evaluations, and other performance reports
- Memoranda proposing or approving program changes
- Use of performance information in the management systems of other agencies and programs
- The opinions of key stakeholders on the existence of systems for managing the agency or program to achieve performance goals[a]

For criterion 5: Outside accountability

- Information from performance measurement and reporting systems, statistical programs, audits, evaluations, and other analyses related to performance in terms of agreed-on goals and performance indicators
- Budget documents, annual reports, and other publications describing the program
- Speeches, press releases, and press coverage
- The opinions of key stakeholders on how well performance information has been used to communicate agency or program performance or changes in performance to key stakeholders or the public[a]

For criterion 6: More effective or improved performance demonstrated

- Information from performance measurement and reporting systems, statistical programs, audits, evaluations, and other analyses related to performance in terms of agreed-on goals and performance indicators
- Budget documents and annual reports
- The opinions of key stakeholders on whether the program has demonstrated effective or improved performance[a]
- The professional literature

For criterion 7: Performance information used for resource or policy decisionmaking

- Budget documents
- Documents related to use of performance information in decisionmaking by agency policymakers, those who influence the allocation of needed resources, and other key stakeholders interested in agency activities[a]
- Committee reports and other documents related to legislative use of performance information
- The opinions of key stakeholders on the types and extent of use of performance information in resource allocation and other policy decisionmaking[a]
- The professional literature

[a] Key stakeholders include program managers and staff; senior agency officials; elected officials; authorizing, appropriations, and oversight committee staff; budget examiners; auditors and evaluators; and persons served by the agency or program.

performance in terms of agency or program goals and strategies for achieving those goals; whether the performance measurement system is of sufficient technical quality to document performance and support decisionmaking; and how widely performance information is used in managing the agency or program, in accountability to key stakeholders and the public, and in supporting policy decisionmaking.

Undertaking periodic, but regular, assessments of the quality of the performance measurement process can take considerable effort. Assessing usefulness probably can be done quickly and inexpensively in many cases when it is clear that the performance data are being used for important purposes. However, even then, the examination might reveal substantial blocks of data that have little or no use and can be deleted.

The proposed assessment criteria and assessment process in this chapter are still somewhat rudimentary. Procedures for quality control of public service performance data is still a new, and difficult, topic. Improvements are needed in this emerging public management arena.

References and Notes

1. Beryl A. Radin, "Performance-Based Management and Its Training Implications" (paper prepared for the International Symposium on Performance-Based Management and Its Training Implications, Caserta, Italy, September 24–26, 1997).
2. U.S. General Accounting Office (GAO), *Executive Guide: Effectively Implementing the Government Performance and Results Act* (Washington, DC, 1996), 13.
3. *Washington Post,* 10 January 1998, A7.
4. "Program Evaluation: Department of Education's Results-Based Budgeting Data" (Atlanta: Georgia State Auditor's Office, August 2003).
5. "Program Evaluation: An Assessment of the Georgia Bureau of Investigation Drug Enforcement & Prevention Results-Based Budget Goals and Desired Results" (Atlanta: Georgia State Auditor's Office, August 2002), 9.
6. An example of one of these reviews is Texas State Auditor's Office, *An Audit Report on Performance Measures at Five State Agencies,* Report No. 05-030, March 2005.
7. U.S. General Accounting Office, *Program Evaluation: Studies Helped Agencies Measure or Explain Program Performance* (Washington, DC, 2000), 9.
8. Bureau of Transportation Statistics, "Source and Accuracy Compendium," http://www.bts.gov/programs/statistical_policy_and_research/source_and_accuracy_compendium/.
9. U.S. General Accounting Office, *Results-Oriented Government: GPRA Has Established a Solid Foundation for Achieving Greater Results* (Washington, DC, GAO-04-38), 186.
10. U.S. Department of Education, *FY 2004 Performance and Accountability Report* (Washington, DC, 2004), 240.
11. U.S. General Accounting Office, *Results-Oriented Government.*

Other Performance Measurement Issues

Agency and program managers should expect to face numerous problems as they attempt to implement and sustain an outcome measurement process. This chapter alerts managers to the types of problems they are likely to run into and suggests ways to deal with them. Problem areas include the following:

- Personnel training needs
- Overall system cost and feasibility
- Changes in legislative and agency priorities
- Maintaining indicator stability over time
- Documentation of the outcome measurement process
- Fear and resistance from program managers
- Role of other levels of government and the private sector in results
- Aggregation of outcomes across projects, programs, or sites
- Community-wide versus program-specific outcomes
- Legislative support
- Overexpectations
- Politics
- Sustainability

Personnel Training Needs

Many managers and staff are likely to have had only limited exposure to, or training in, outcome measurement. However, program personnel at all levels need some training. Managers do not need much technical detail, but they do need to understand what the performance information can and cannot tell them and how such information can be appropriately used. Those who will be responsible for data collection need some technical detail. Agencies should consider including at least a small module on managing-for-results in each of their management courses and in most specialized training courses. (For example, staff training on new program procedures should include a discussion of the procedures' effects on service quality and outcomes.) Non-management personnel need to be informed of their program's objectives, how progress is measured, and their own roles in helping meet those objectives.

Escalating this need for training is the inevitable turnover of personnel in any organization and the introduction of new measurement techniques. Training needs to be continual, not done merely when an agency first implements a performance measurement process.

Small programs in particular may have trouble finding funds and/or persons who can provide the necessary training. Agencies will probably need to obtain assistance, whether from analytical offices within the organization or from outside consultants or universities.

Overall System Cost and Feasibility

To the extent that new data collection procedures are needed (customer surveys, trained observer procedures, and the like), implementing and sustaining data collection is likely to require resources for these activities. Initial development and startup costs, in particular, can be quite time-consuming. However, once the procedures become routine, the annual time and cost requirements should shrink.

It certainly can be argued that tracking results-focused performance information is just a basic requirement of good management and that resources for it should be budgeted as part of normal agency operations. But special data collection activities, such as customer surveys and trained observer rating procedures, are quite visible, and their costs will inevitably be particularly vulnerable to budget cuts when funds are very tight. (Chapter 7 includes a number of cost reduction options for customer surveys, some of which also apply to trained observer rating procedures.)

As important a concern as monetary cost is feasibility. Organizations that do not have and cannot afford to obtain personnel with the specialized technical skills needed for some data collection procedures face a major impediment to implementing regular in-house data collection.

Many agencies, especially small ones, have problems administering surveys, whether by mail, telephone, or in person. The key then is likely to be to find inexpensive technical assistance from outside the organization—such as consultants, local colleges or universities, and volunteers—to help set up the procedures (including data collection instruments), undertake any needed training of personnel in the procedures, and subsequently periodically examine the quality of implementation. Some tasks, such as jurisdiction-wide household surveys, may need to be done primarily by an outside survey organization.

Private, nonprofit organizations agencies may be able to obtain considerable volunteer assistance to help their programs with the special technical requirements of surveys, trained observer ratings, and associated data processing.

Changes in Legislative and Agency Priorities

Periodic changes in priorities (perhaps driven by changes in elected or appointed officials), including funding uncertainties, are inevitable but need not discourage development of a stable performance measurement process. Priorities often do not substantially change the mission (and the associated end outcomes) of a program but rather focus on *how* to accomplish the mission. A well-constructed outcome measurement process should be able to provide much, if not most, of the information required by such changes as part of its regular tracking function. Changes are most likely to be needed in intermediate outcome indicators, since these are most directly affected by changes in service approach. However, if decisions about an agency's mission change, outcomes and outcome indicators may need to be modified.

Maintaining Indicator Stability over Time

Since a major use of performance information is to examine changes over time, performance indicators need to be reasonably stable to avoid, as the saying goes, comparing apples to oranges. As discussed in chapter 9, comparing current performance with the previous period's performance is common and usually given considerable attention. Examination of outcome data over several years is also useful to programs for examining what is happening, such as whether actions taken are having the desired effects.

The stability concern is not so much with adding new indicators as with dropping or substantially modifying old ones. Changing either performance indicators or the data collection procedures associated with them can destroy, or at least reduce, comparability with previous reporting periods. Continuing improvement of the performance measurement process is obviously desirable. The trick is to keep such changes small. From an external perspective, a program that makes frequent changes may even be looked on with suspicion: Is the program manipulating the performance indicators so only those with favorable outcomes that year are reported?

Obviously, for good government and good management, indicators should not be deleted because they bring bad news. This tactic may be advantageous in the short term, but it will hurt long-term credibility. Equally obviously, past data collection procedures that turn out to be invalid should be changed. A pragmatic solution for the comparability problem is to retain the older, less satisfactory indicators and data collection procedures, introduce the new approach, and then phase out the less satisfactory procedures.

Documentation of the Outcome Measurement Process

The outcome measurement process should be documented so the people responsible for data collection, and the users of the data, know what is supposed to be done. Documentation is particularly helpful in alleviating problems due to staff turnover. The program may find it useful to *prepare outcome indicator specification sheets for each outcome indicator* so program personnel and any other users have a description of each indicator. Exhibit 15-1 illustrates a basic format for such documentation.

Fear and Resistance from Program Managers

Program managers are usually less than enthusiastic about imposed requirements to identify, collect, and report outcome data. Since such mandates from higher levels seek more accountability and justification of budget proposals, the requirements will more often than not, understandably, be perceived as a threat to the managers and to the program's budgets. Managers will worry that they will be blamed for less-than-expected results over which they have only limited control.

Outcome Indicator Specification Sheet

Program: _____ Date: _____

1. Outcome

2. Outcome indicator

3. Category of indicator (e.g., intermediate or end outcome)

4. Data source and collection procedures

5. Breakouts of the outcome indicator that are needed

6. Frequency of collection and reporting

7. Who is responsible for data collection and its quality

This concern is a legitimate one, as we have noted in previous chapters, but agencies can alleviate managers' fear and resistance in several ways:

- Make sure that program managers have a major role in selecting the performance indicators. (See chapter 3.)
- Provide adequate training and technical assistance to program managers (as discussed above), so they fully understand the performance measurement process and how *they* can use the performance information (such as the internal uses discussed in chapter 12).
- Make explicit provision for, and encourage the use of, *explanatory information* in performance measurement reports so program managers have an opportunity to account for less-than-expected results. (See chapters 11 and 13 for a more detailed discussion.) This step provides managers with a formal way to provide their perspectives in situations when performance was not as good as expected.
- Make sure that program managers see the performance measurement results *before* they are sent to higher levels (or outside the agency) to give them an opportunity to provide explanations where needed.
- Use the performance measurement report information constructively and nonpunitively, at least until it becomes fully clear that punitive action is appropriate.

Even if all these steps are taken, the fears of program managers may be justified when performance measurement information is transmitted to higher administrative or policy levels and to the media. Opponents of a program, and the media, will inevitably use unpleasant performance information in unpleasant ways. *No matter what the program does, with or with-*

out performance measurement, opponents will find reasons to criticize. Because of the major benefits it can confer in the context of managing for results, performance measurement should not be made the scapegoat.

Role of Other Levels of Government and the Private Sector in Results

Many program services, especially at the federal and state levels, are ultimately delivered or otherwise affected by agencies of other levels of government or by the private sector. Thus, much of the data for outcome measurement may need to be obtained from, or at least with the cooperation of, these other agencies. One problem that arises is that the amount of detail needed by different levels is likely to be different. For example, local governments and private, nonprofit service agencies are likely to need data on outcomes broken out by neighborhood—information state or federal agencies likely do not need. State agencies are likely to need data broken out by county or municipality. Federal agencies may need data broken out only by state or region of the country.

Data might be collected by the lower-level agencies and then aggregated by the higher-level agency. Alternatively, the higher-level organization can choose to collect the outcome information itself (such as by contracting with a consulting firm to survey samples of customers from lower-level service agencies). This has the considerable advantage of ensuring that the data collection procedures are the same across sites, thus making the data more comparable. A disadvantage is that the data will not be as useful to the lower-level agencies because not enough of their own customers will have been included in the samples. (It is usually desirable that the lower-level service agencies be encouraged to track the outcomes of their own services so they can use that information to improve their programs.)

If the data are to be collected by the upper-level organization, the upper-level organization will need the cooperation of the lower-level agencies in providing information on customers, such as names, addresses, and/or telephone numbers, so they can be surveyed. A classic example occurs in county human services agencies. A county may want outcome data from its contractors and grantees, which are likely to be numerous. It is much easier for the county to ask each contractor or grantee to collect outcome data than to collect this information itself. This procedure has the added advantages of encouraging each contractor or grantee to build outcome information into its own management system and, at least on the surface, of saving the county government money. The drawback is that the upper-level organization will have to work out procedures to assure that each agency providing data collects it correctly and in approximately the same way.

Organizations with such outcome relationships should consider ways to develop data collection partnerships with other organizations, including agreement (to the extent possible) on common data collection procedures. Performance partnerships should be considered. Such partnerships can substantially increase the logistics and time required for outcome measurement development (to ensure that all interests are met). However, this joint effort is likely to pay off in the long run by yielding a smoothly running and more useful outcome measurement process.[1]

Aggregation of Outcomes across Projects, Programs, or Sites

Aggregating outcomes is important to organizations that support a number of projects or programs from different sites that focus on similar objectives. Such organizations will likely want to assess the combined effects of groups of these projects, programs, or sites on key outcome indicators. For example, a local, state, federal, or private agency may be supporting a number of projects aimed at reducing juvenile delinquency. It would like to add up the outcomes of each project to assess what total outcomes the total resources have achieved.

Aggregation can be messy. As a first step, the agency may need to separate its programs into groupings with similar objectives. For example, Ramsey County's (Minnesota) Department of Community Human Services and United Way of Minneapolis Area (UWMA) have each experimented with identifying clusters of services and synthesizing outcome findings across projects within each cluster. In 1998, UWMA had 14 clusters. Its Strengthening Families cluster included about 19 service agencies, its Youth Development cluster included 21, and its Parenting/Teen Pregnancy cluster included about 23.

Even when programs have similar objectives, aggregating performance information can be much tougher than it looks, particularly if the data collection procedures are not standardized. If possible, an organization should identify a set of key outcome indicators and compatible data collection procedures that all, or at least most, projects and programs in the group would agree (or be required) to use and report. This would enable the organization to aggregate the outcomes from all the reporting projects and programs.

One example is the Department of Education, which needs to aggregate data from individual states on indicators of learning achievement, such as test scores. But each state, and sometimes each school district, uses somewhat different tests, and each tests different subject matter and children in different grades. For some purposes, the federal government can use aggregate data from the National Assessment of Educational Progress (NAEP). However, the NAEP covers only samples of schools and students. Such data are not adequate for many programs. This problem faces not only Department of Education programs but also those of other agencies that want to use learning indicators, such as educational programs of the National Science Foundation. Another example is the Environmental Protection Agency's National Estuary Program, which wants to aggregate progress in improving water quality across all the estuaries in its program. However, each estuary uses its own indicators of water quality.

An option in all these cases is to *aggregate the percent improvements* from each project or organizational unit, with or without some system of weighting. For the estuary program, for example, an estimate of percent improvement might be used for particular bodies of water and particular types of pollution. Each estuary might be weighted equally. Or the estuaries might be weighted by the size of the body of water, funding, population, and so on. For test scores, the Department of Education might aggregate percent improvement weighted by number of students represented by each project or organizational unit.

The alternative to collecting data from each project, program, or site is for the agency to undertake its own data collection, using common procedures for all projects and organizational units. While this approach may seem desirable, its feasibility depends on the quality of the data collection by each contributing unit. Even if feasible, cost considerations may necessitate the use of sampling. This may be adequate for some uses of the data but not for all, especially if more detailed breakouts are sought.

This dilemma has not been really resolved. It is likely to become increasingly challenging for organizations that need aggregate performance information. For organizations with mandating power, uniform reporting procedures can be required from lower levels. In other cases, one option for encouraging individual projects, programs, or sites to provide standardized performance data themselves is to offer incentives, such as partial subsidies for the added data collection effort.

Community-wide versus Program-Specific Outcomes

As discussed in chapter 6, a concern related to aggregation is the relationship of agency program outcomes to community-wide outcomes. Individual agencies, particularly nonprofit agencies, are likely to have severely limited resources and be able to help only a small number of people in the community. Thus, no matter how good they are at achieving desired outcomes for their customers, they may not be able to significantly affect community-wide outcomes. For example, if a program only has resources to serve 100 people in a community with 10,000 in need of help, even if it succeeded in helping all 100, it would still affect only 1 percent of the total population in need.

A program's scale needs to be considered when assessing its performance. If an organization has resources that enable it to serve only a small portion of the potential customers, it should be held accountable for only those customers its resources permit it to serve. An exception here is a particular government's and its agencies' responsibility to their whole jurisdiction. Even though the responsible public agency may only have sufficient resources to meet the needs of a portion of those in the jurisdiction, it should track, and be considered responsible for, the magnitude of unmet need as an overall performance indicator for the government as a whole. Government does, after all, have some responsibility for seeking to meet the full need.

Nevertheless, government officials and the public should distinguish between two public responsibilities: (1) the outcomes for those customers the program is able to serve; and (2) the extent to which the program is able to meet the overall need in the jurisdiction. Clearly, the program's influence over this first outcome is considerably greater than its influence over the second, which is likely to be constrained by the program's resources. As discussed in previous chapters, we recommend that agencies categorize each outcome indicator by the level of influence the agency and its programs have over the outcome, and that they provide this information to users of their performance reports. This will enable users to interpret program performance more fairly.

Nongovernmental community organizations, such as local United Ways and community foundations, may also want to track and work to improve at least some community-wide outcomes. Usually, their resources will be too limited to have significant effects alone. However, such organizations can join in performance partnerships with other organizations in the community to undertake actions that can lead to significant community-wide effects.

Legislative Support

As discussed in chapter 12, a major incentive for agencies to produce sound, supportable performance information is the interest taken by the legislature in outcomes related to budget submissions and agency proposals for program and policy changes. A number of concerns surround the role of legislatures, however, in helping or impeding the achievement of a successful performance measurement process:

1. The legislature's support for the performance measurement process is vital. While many performance measurement efforts in the United States have been solely executive branch efforts, legislatures can clearly undermine a particular effort if they express little or negative interest, including deleting funding for data collection.
2. Legislators and their staffs need to be adequately educated about what outcome information can tell them and what it cannot tell them. A crucial need is for legislators to understand that outcomes only tell *what* progress is being made, *not why*. This reduces the potential for legislators to use the performance information inappropriately and unfairly against agencies and their programs. Preferably, the legislature would provide its own training programs for its personnel. The executive branch should help provide such education informally whenever it briefs legislators or their staffs on executive branch proposals.
3. Legislators have an important role in ensuring the validity of performance data. Inevitably, legislators will be concerned about the quality of the data they are given. As discussed in chapter 14, data quality control is an important legislative concern. In judging the merits of the system, it is legitimate for the legislature to call for its own audits of the data and place requirements on the executive branch for quality control efforts.

For a legislature to perform these roles constructively, *the executive branch must provide data on important outcomes of interest to the legislature in a clear, easily accessible form.* Too often, legislatures have been blamed for not being interested in or not using performance information when in fact they were given great volumes of data that were difficult to interpret and heavily weighted with process and output information—with the important outcome data buried in backup volumes (if there at all).

Similarly, legislative bodies and their committees are likely to need some help in screening the large amounts of performance information increasingly coming to them. Congress and state legislatures, and some large city and county legislatures, may have their own staffs that they trust and that can review and screen program performance data to extract what is important for the elected officials' needs and interests. Most local legislatures will likely need to rely on staff support from the administration.[2]

One of the most pernicious problems that performance measurement faces is overexpectations by those examining results-based performance reports (such as upper-level managers, elected officials, the media, and citizens). As emphasized throughout this book, performance measurement information can tell what the outcomes, the results, of a service or program have been. But by itself it will *not* tell the extent to which the service or program has caused the outcomes. Nor will past information tell what the results will be in the future.

With the great push for accountability throughout the world in recent years has come the considerably danger that performance information will be misunderstood and be given too much influence. Too many external factors outside the control of public and private organizations also affect the outcomes. *Public and private service organizations are inherently unable to have full accountability for outcomes.* These organizations should be responsible for measuring outcomes and for continually working to improve them, but they have only partial accountability for the results.

Politics

Political concerns will sometimes have considerable effects on the results-based information that is developed, reported, and used. This applies to annual performance reporting, to strategic plans, and to information provided as justification for budgets, including projected performance targets.

Some public officials have been worried that performance measurement might be an attempt to replace political decisionmaking. The information would hamper officials' abilities to use their own judgment—equating performance measurement to running the city by computer. Some elected officials may feel that getting information at open hearings and through complaints they receive from constituents is adequate. The counterargument is that *having performance information before elected officials make decisions can help them improve their decisions to the benefit of their citizens and their own reputations.*

Problems can arise even after elected officials have given reasonable support, particularly if the support has been primarily passive:

- Political officials in both the executive and legislative branches may believe that spelling out the expected consequences—negative as well as positive—in budget proposals will cause resistance to the proposals from groups that feel they will not benefit sufficiently. This may lead to the suppression of particular performance indicators and particular break-out information on outcomes.

- Political officials may insist in some situations on more optimistic targets than analysis has found feasible given the budgeted resources.
- Political officials may fear that targets will be perceived by some groups as quotas that will lead to harassment of their constituents. Politicians may therefore discourage agencies from including important performance information in their systems. Such harassment is of particular concern in police (arrests and traffic citations), litigation, child support enforcement, and tax collection programs. As noted in earlier chapters, a way to alleviate this problem is to also include performance indicators reflecting undesirable unintended consequences of excessive zeal, such as counts of complaints of harassment.
- Political officials may believe that being very explicit about objectives in strategic plans and annual performance plans will raise the resistance of groups that do not agree with the way the program purposes are specified in those plans.

These are all real-life situations. Inevitably, the people implementing results-based performance measurement will need to compromise. Preferably, those compromises will be made after everyone has fully considered the possible consequences of not being as clear and accurate as possible.

Educating elected officials on the benefits of results-based measurement should help to overcome their doubts. Results-based performance measurement cannot, and should not, replace political decisionmaking—but it should help to better inform the decisionmaking process.

Sustainability

Public officials, managers, and even line staff, come and go. Organization funding goes up and down. Interest in performance information ebbs and flows. What can be done to increase the likelihood that performance measurement and performance management will continue to provide a steady flow of reliable performance information? Following are some of the keys to sustainability:

- Agency managers and/or public officials find the information understandable and useful. (More detailed suggestions for achieving this goal are presented in chapters 8–13.)

- The data are perceived as reasonably accurate. (More detailed suggestions for achieving accuracy are presented in chapter 14 on quality control.)
- The details of the process (such as thorough definitions of the individual indicators) are documented so new personnel can readily grasp what is needed.
- The organization and its agencies have adequate performance measurement technical capacity, such as knowledgeable personnel to ensure the integrity of the process.
- Legislation or regulation requires that organizations measure performance.

Notes

1. Ideally, private-sector *customers* should be included in these performance partnerships. Private citizens and businesses that receive services from agencies almost always have important responsibilities that contribute significantly to service outcomes. For example, citizens need to put their garbage out in the right containers, at the right locations, at the right times, and, where required, with the right waste sorting. Parents are responsible for encouraging students to attend classes and complete their homework. Patients are responsible for showing up on time to appointments and following instructions. Such responsibilities might be spelled out along with the responsibilities of the various public and private agencies.

2. As noted in a previous chapter, a guide to such reviews has been published by the National Conference of State Legislatures for state legislators. Much of that material also appears applicable to other levels of government. See "Asking Key Questions: How to Review Program Results" (Denver, CO: NCSL, June 2005). In additional, NCSL's 2003 report "Legislating for Results" suggests actions legislatures can take to obtain better outcome information and to make effective use of it.

Part

V

Summary

Chapter 16

As Bluebeard said to his wives, "I won't keep you much longer."

Wrap-up of Key Performance Measurement Elements

T his chapter highlights key elements of an ongoing, results-based performance measurement system.

Key Elements

1. **Public services are for the benefit of the public,** the customers of those services—not for the benefit of the service providers (though providers need to be treated fairly).
2. **There are four prerequisites for a successful performance measurement system:**
   — *Upper-level support.* As with any ongoing process, support from upper management and legislators is crucial to providing needed resources and using the information generated.
   — *Data processing support.* Data processing personnel should be brought into the planning stages early.
   — *Analytic support.* Persons who know data and how to analyze it are needed to ensure reasonably reliable data collection procedures and proper interpretation of trade-offs.
   — *Patience and time.* Implementing a full performance measurement process is probably impossible in less than a year and will take several years for most programs. Agencies should expect many iterations before a stable set of performance indications is implemented.

3. **Outcomes and outcome indicators to be tracked should be developed primarily by the program.** However, upper-level management should provide input to make sure the indicators are appropriate for the agency. The program should also seek input from citizens to make sure its performance indicators cover the concerns of the affected "customer" groups—for example, by using focus groups of its customers, as discussed in chapter 5. Input from the legislature (or the board of private nonprofit organizations) is also highly desirable to reduce problems later. Outcomes tracked should include negative side effects. Citizen input should be obtained to be sure that the indicators include elements important to citizens (see chapters 3–5).

4. **Agencies and their programs need to track, and distinguish between, outputs and outcomes and between intermediate and end outcomes.** Ultimately, organizations need to link inputs (e.g., costs and personnel resources) to outputs, intermediate outcomes, and end outcomes (as discussed in chapter 13 on results-based budgeting). Outputs are products and services delivered by the program. Outcomes are events, actions, or behaviors that occur outside the program and in ways that the program is attempting to affect. Customer satisfaction with the helpfulness and quality of services should be considered an important outcome, but it is usually an intermediate rather than an end outcome. Considerable effort should be made to ensure that agency personnel understand the distinctions among these indicator categories. End outcomes should be tracked even though the program does not completely control them. Intermediate outcomes usually occur earlier, and programs usually have greater influence over them than end outcomes, providing program managers with important, timely information on which to act. Managers should be able to take credit for successful intermediate outcomes but should recognize that achieving end outcomes is the ultimate goal (see chapter 2).

5. **The limitations of performance measurement information should be made clear to all personnel and users of the information.** Everyone involved with preparing and using performance measurement information should recognize that outcomes only tell what happened, not why. Thus, outcome data should not be used to blame or praise a program in isolation from additional material explaining those outcomes. Considerable misunderstanding can occur on this point. Agencies should consider including in performance reports flags that indicate the extent to which the outcome values can be influenced by the agency (a simple scale such as *little influence, some influence,* and *considerable influence* may be sufficient).

6. **To track new outcomes, many agency programs need to go beyond their currently available data,** using such major data collection procedures as customer surveys and trained observer ratings. Customer surveys, in particular, can be a very important tool for performance measurement. They can provide not only customer satisfaction information, but often—and usually more important—a variety of factual information on outcomes. Examples include changes in employment and earning status, household use of different services (such as recreation, park, and library services), and changes in behavior (such as fewer risky behaviors by clients).

   A major gap in performance measurement systems has been the lack of follow-up of events *after* the service has been provided. Major outcomes of human services, education, health, environmental protection, economic development, and international relations programs cannot be assessed until some time has elapsed since the service was provided, such as one or two years. At that time, important indicators of success should be measurable. (Longer-term follow-up can become quite difficult and expensive. Special studies, not performance measurement systems, are needed to seek such longer-term information, as well as more in-depth examination of programs.)

   New procedures require additional funds and efforts. Bargain basement procedures are often available for programs that do not require much precision in measured values. Organizations that are serious about results-based performance measurement, however, will probably need some added resources to collect the new data. It can be argued that feedback on results is a basic element of program management. Any added expenditures should pay off in improved outcomes over the long run. If it becomes clear that the new data collection procedures are not useful, they should be dropped (see chapter 7).

7. **For budgeting purposes, reporting data only once a year may be sufficient; for management purposes, performance data need to be available more frequently.** Data should be collected, analyzed, and reported internally at least quarterly. The frequency of useful reporting on individual performance indicators can vary considerably.

8. **Performance information, particularly outcomes, will be considerably more useful to all users if the data are broken out by key characteristics.** Breakouts—by geography, by citizen/customer demographic characteristics, by individual organizational units providing the same service, by difficulty of the incoming workload, and by type and magnitude of service—enable users to identify where and under what conditions outcomes appear more or less successful. Such breakouts can

provide major clues to program personnel about where problems exist and can even indicate particular actions that might be taken. Breakouts by customer characteristics also provide basic information on service equity—often extremely important for service agencies. Breakouts add considerably to the amount of data generated by the outcome measurement process. Transmitting all the data to higher levels can overload users' capacity (and willingness) to examine the information. Therefore, program reports should highlight key breakout findings. Such findings can be of considerable interest to even the highest levels of government (see chapter 8).

9. **To provide a sense of whether the performance information is good or bad, and to help guide adjustments, outcome information needs to be compared with other data.** Traditionally, the primary benchmark has been previous year's performance. Other benchmarks should also be used. Comparisons can be made among breakout categories, for example. A government agency or a professional organization might establish a relevant standard, such as on air and water quality, that can be used by other agencies.

   In addition, comparisons can sometimes be made to similar organizations, such as other agencies in other jurisdictions delivering the same service, or, in some cases, private business organizations. However, comparisons with other organizations are fraught with problems and need to be carefully made to ensure reasonable comparability.

   The regular availability of performance information can encourage staff to try out new procedures, by enabling them to obtain information comparing the outcomes of old versus new program approaches.

   A major, and increasingly frequent, option is to compare actual performance against targets (goals) set by the program at the beginning of each year. Keep in mind, however, that selecting such targets is often more of an art than a science and that interpreting comparisons between targets and actual performance takes judgment (see chapter 9).

10. **Programs should be asked to provide appropriate explanatory information along with the performance data.** Explanations should be provided when performance on an indicator fell significantly short of, or far exceeded, a program's expectation. Explanations can be quantitative or qualitative. Elements affecting a program's performance level might be external (for instance, national economic changes or unusual weather conditions) or internal (such as major cutbacks in funding and staff that were not expected at the time targets were established). A classic example of internal factors is adding more responsibilities to a program without providing needed additional

resources. Such situations can be alleviated somewhat if the performance measurement process allows programs to adjust their projections of outcomes as well as to provide explanations. Providing a formal process by which managers can provide their explanations for poorer than expected performance can reduce the natural fear of managers of performance reporting and being unfairly blamed for conditions out of their control (see chapters 10, 11, and 13).

11. **Performance information can be of substantial use for budget formulation and justification and for strategic planning,** as well as for ongoing program and policy analysis. Performance measurement information provides baseline information and can be used, up to a point, to help project future performance. However, projecting into the future involves a number of quite difficult analytical issues that make it more difficult and uncertain than measuring past performance (see chapters 12 and 13).

12. **A results-based orientation should penetrate to all levels of agency personnel, not just upper-level officials and managers.** Performance measurement data can and should play a major role in many key management activities, such as employee motivation and performance contracting. Incentives for managers and groups of employees can be based, at least in part, on performance, as measured by efficiency and outcome indicators. In addition, contractors and grantees that provide services to customers can receive incentives based at least to some extent on the outcomes they achieve. Outcome indicators and target values can be included in various ways in performance (incentive) agreements and contracts.

    Basing incentives, especially monetary incentives, on outcome measurement needs to be done with caution. Agencies should recognize that employees will be highly sensitive about the fairness of judging who receives rewards. Pay for performance, if used, should be linked at least in part to objective outcomes. Also, as highlighted above, achievement of outcomes should not be used alone to place blame (or credit) on a manager or group. The reasons for good or poor outcomes must also be explored. Employees and public officials need to accept the fact that such compensation schemes will yield rewards that are affected by external factors. If external factors are favorable, employees will receive windfall gains; if external developments are adverse, they will receive windfall losses (see chapter 12).

13. **Program managers should consider using performance reports as a basis for regular "How Are We Doing?" sessions with their personnel.** Such sessions seek to identify where things are going well and

should be continued (and possibly expanded elsewhere) and where the program is doing not so well, so the group can identify actions that might improve outcomes. Any actions taken can be followed up in later reporting periods in such sessions by an assessment of whether outcomes have improved (see chapter 12).

14. **In-depth program evaluation and performance measurement should be considered complementary activities.** Program evaluations can likely use data from the performance measurement system as part of formal evaluations. Performance measurement data are useful in selecting the future program evaluation agenda because they identify areas with outcome problems. Relevant information from completed program evaluations should be included in performance measurement reports. In some instances, such information will supersede that obtained from the performance measurement system (see chapter 12).

15. **Few outcomes are affected by only one program, or even by only a single agency.** Federal, state, and local governments and private non-profit agencies often have joint influence over outcomes and joint roles in service delivery. Each shares responsibility for the outcomes. Some form of performance partnership is highly desirable to determine what performance information should be collected by whom, how it should be analyzed and reported, and who needs to do what to improve the service. Such performance partnerships, while usually difficult and time-consuming, are likely to be a major future direction for public administration.

16. **Training is needed for all involved—managers, their personnel, and users at all levels, including legislators.** Some training will need to be technical, but most should focus on providing an overall understanding of performance information, its limitations, and its uses. Refresher training and training for new employees should be routine. Training need not be lengthy. Technical assistance is likely to be needed in the early stages of performance measurement system development and in implementing later modifications (see chapter 15).

17. **It is incumbent on the agency and its programs to ensure that the data are of reasonable quality.** Information is power. The right type of information, reasonably accurate, needs to be provided. To ensure that the performance indicators, procedures, and data are reasonably valid and useful, agencies need to establish quality control steps, including periodic audits of the performance measurement system. Periodic audits should also be made of the usefulness of the performance measurement process. If not found useful, the process should be modified or dropped (see chapter 14).

EXHIBIT 16-1

Steps to Promote the Use of Performance Information

- Require that outcome information be included as part of *budget proposal justifications.*
- Require *new* programs to identify their objectives, outcomes, indicators, data collection procedures, and breakouts before full implementation.
- Use in training programs. Require each training program to contain at least a brief module on outcomes—not only management training but also training on specific operational topics.
- Require that *contracts* for services include outcome indicators and that appropriate procedures for data collection be established.
- Include a component related to progress on organizational outcomes in annual *performance appraisals of managers.*
- Give managers the positive incentive of more flexibility in the use of funds, contracting authority, and/or personnel authority if they achieve or exceed desired outcomes. Adjust flexibility periodically, based on recent performance (say, over the past two years).
- Use performance measurement findings to help establish the organization's annual program evaluation plan.
- Identify key outcomes and outcome indicators in strategic planning. Provide long-range targets for the key indicators. Use annual performance data to provide the baseline for plans and to assess progress on meeting the targets.
- Translate the performance findings, especially on outcomes, into attractive, readable, and substantive annual reports for the public—the customers of the services provided.

18. **Agencies need to pay full attention to their performance report presentations.** Presentation can be half the battle! Performance reports are needed at all levels of a service organization as well as by elected officials and the public. Attractive, clear, user-friendly reports, tailored to user needs, are a necessity for agencies and their programs wanting to encourage interest in, and use of, performance data. Poorly presented information, no matter how good its quality, will lose much of its power. Do not overwhelm readers with voluminous data. Be selective but in a balanced way. Highlight findings that deviate substantially from expectations. (see chapter 11).

19. **Public agencies should work with the news media to help them understand the data—and what the data tell and do not tell.**

20. **A performance measurement system can be said to be fully implemented when it is taken for granted and its data are used regularly to help make program and policy changes—and to help improve the quality and outcomes of services.** Exhibit 16-1 summarizes a number of key steps to promote the *use* of results-based performance measurement information. Exhibit 16-2 lists a few "tips and traps." As the last tip says, don't give up if the difficulties of implementation seem large at first.

EXHIBIT 16-2

Tips and Traps for Measuring Performance

Tips	Traps
Focus on results that matter.	Measure what is available.
Keep it simple.	Dazzle them with statistics.
Focus on the critical few.	Try to measure everything.
Link performance measurement to decisions.	View performance measurement as an end, not a means.
Success is not instant.	Change course at will.
Ask customers what they want.	This is a job for professionals.
Report results widely.	Use performance measures to blame people.
Data are a necessary expense.	Expect measures to report on themselves.
Don't give up.	Inaction: It is easy to avoid the hard work of focusing on results.

Source: National Academy of Public Administration, "Powering the Future: High-Performance Partnerships. Summary Report" (Washington, DC: National Academy of Public Administration, 2003), 13.

21. **Finally, it cannot be emphasized enough that the performance measurement process is only one source of information for government managers,** though it is a very important one. All performance information will have uncertainties, in some cases considerable uncertainties. Bad data are worse than no data. However, it is better to be roughly right than precisely ignorant.

Final Words

When you get right down to it, much of performance measurement is just good old common sense. Its basic principles are hardly rocket science. Doing it right, however, can be a major challenge.

A millionaire threw a lavish party in a hotel for his business associates and friends. After dinner he took them out to the hotel's swimming pool. Inside the pool was an enormous crocodile. The millionaire said, "I will give $1 million to anyone who jumps into this pool and swims to the other end." No one moved. They started walking back into the hotel dining room. They heard a splash. They turned around. There was Joe in the pool, swimming like crazy to the other side. They pulled him out. He was battered and bleeding but in surprisingly good shape. The millionaire ran up to Joe and gave him a check for $1 million. The mil-

lionaire said to Joe, "That was the bravest act I have ever seen. Is there anything else I can do for you?" Joe thought for a moment and then said, "Yes, tell me who pushed me."

Don't blame the author for pushing you into performance measurement. The route to successful measurement is strewn with perils. However, for those who get to the other side with implementation of a good results-based measurement system, the rewards for the organization and the public should be great.

Appendix

Selected Readings

Ammons, David N. 2001. *Municipal Benchmarks: Assessing Local Performance and Establishing Community Standards*. 2nd ed. Thousand Oaks, CA: SAGE Publications.

———. 2002. *Tools for Decision Making: A Practical Guide for Local Government*. Washington, DC: CQ Press.

Annie E. Casey Foundation. Various years. *Kids Count Data Book: State Profiles of Child Well-Being*. Baltimore, MD: Annie E. Casey Foundation.

Aristigueta, Maria Pilar. 1998. *Managing for Results in State Government*. Westport, CT: Quorum Books.

Berman, Barbara J. Cohn. 2006. *Listening to the Public*. New York: Fund for the City of New York.

de Bruijn, Hans. 2002. *Managing Performance in the Public Sector*. London: Routledge.

Epstein, Paul D., Paul M. Coates, and Lyle D. Wray, with David Swain. 2006. *Results That Matter: Improving Communities by Engaging Citizens, Measuring Performance, and Getting Things Done*. San Francisco, CA: Jossey-Bass.

Fink, Arlene, ed. 2002. *The Survey Kit*. 2nd ed. Thousand Oaks, CA: SAGE Publications.

Forsythe, Dall W., ed. 2001. *Quicker, Better, Cheaper? Managing Performance in American Government*. Albany, NY: Rockefeller Institute Press.

Fountain, James, Wilson Campbell, Terry Patton, Paul Epstein, and Mandi Cohn. 2003. *Reporting Performance Information: Suggested Criteria for Effective Communication*. Research Report GRPI. Norwalk, CT: Governmental Accounting Standards Board.

Friedman, Mark. 2005. *Trying Hard Is Not Good Enough: How to Produce Measurable Improvements for Customers and Communities*. Victoria, British Columbia, Canada: Trafford Publishing.

Fund for the City of New York, Center on Municipal Government Performance. 1998. *How Smooth Are New York City's Streets?* New York: Fund for the City of New York, Center on Municipal Government Performance.

Gormley, William T., Jr., and David L. Weimer. 1999. *Organizational Report Cards*. Cambridge, MA, and London: Harvard University Press.

Guajardo, Salomon A., and Rosemary McDonnell. 2000. *An Elected Official's Guide to Performance Measurement*. Chicago, IL: Government Finance Officers Association.

Halachmi, Arie, ed. 1999. *Performance and Quality Measurement in Government: Issues and Experience*. Burke, VA: Chatelaine Press.

Halachmi, Arie, and Geert Bouckaert, eds. 1996. *Organizational Performance and Measurement in the Public Sector: Toward Service, Effort, and Accomplishment Reporting*. Westport, CT: Quorum Books.

Hatry, Harry P., and Linda M. Lampkin, eds. 2004. Series on outcome management for nonprofit organizations. Washington, DC: The Urban Institute.
Reports in the series:
Analyzing Outcome Information: Getting the Most from Data
Developing Community-wide Outcome Indicators
Key Steps in Outcome Management
Finding Out What Happens to Former Clients
Surveying Clients about Outcomes
Using Outcome Information: Making Data Pay Off

Hatry, Harry P., Elaine Morley, Shelli B. Rossman, and Joseph S. Wholey. 2003. *How Federal Programs Use Outcome Information: Opportunities for Federal Managers*. Washington, DC: IBM Endowment for The Business of Government.

Hatry, Harry P., Louis Blair, Donald M. Fisk, John M. Greiner, John R. Hall, Jr., and Philip S. Schaenman. 2006. *How Effective Are Your Community Services? Procedures for Measuring Their Quality*. 3rd ed. Washington, DC: International City/Council Management Association and the Urban Institute.

Henderson, Lenneal J. 2003. *The Baltimore CitiStat Program: Performance and Accountability*. Research report. Washington, DC: IBM Endowment for The Business of Government.

International City/County Management Association (ICMA). Various years. *Comparative Performance Measurement*. Annual data reports. Washington, DC: ICMA.

Kamensky, John M., and Albert Morales. 2005. *Managing for Results 2005*. Lanham, MD: Rowman & Littlefield Publishers, Inc.

Kusek, Jody Zall, and Ray C. Rist. 2004. *Ten Steps to a Results-Based Monitoring and Evaluation System: A Handbook for Development Practitioners*. Washington, DC: The World Bank.

Leithe, Joni L. 1997. *Implementing Performance Measurement in Government: Illustrations and Resources*. Chicago, IL: Government Finance Officers Association.

Liner, Blaine, Harry P. Hatry, Elisa Vinson, Ryan Allen, Pat Dusenbury, Scott Bryant, and Ron Snell. 2001. *Making Results-Based State Government Work*. Washington, DC: The Urban Institute.

Mackay, Keith. 2006. "Evaluation Capacity Development: Institutionalization of Monitoring and Evaluation Systems to Improve Public Sector Management." Washington, DC: The World Bank.

Martin, Lawrence L., and Peter M. Kettner. 1996. *Measuring the Performance of Human Service Programs*. Thousand Oaks, CA: SAGE Publications.

Mayne, John, and Eduardo Zapico-Goni, eds. 1997. *Monitoring Performance in the Public Sector: Future Directions from International Experience*. News Brunswick, NJ: Transaction Publishers.

Appendix

Metzenbaum, Shelley H. 2006. *Performance Accountability: The Five Building Blocks and Six Essential Practices*. Washington, DC: IBM Center for The Business of Government.

Miller, Thomas I., and Michelle Miller Kobayashi. 2000. *Citizen Surveys: How to Do Them, How to Use Them, What They Mean*. 2nd ed. Washington, DC: ICMA.

Mullen, Edward J., and Jennifer L. Magnabosco, eds. 1997. *Outcomes Measurement in the Human Services*. Washington, DC: National Association of Social Workers.

National Conference of State Legislatures. 2003. *Legislating for Results*. Denver, CO: National Conference of State Legislatures.

————. 2005. *Asking Key Questions: How to Review Program Results*. Denver, CO: National Conference of State Legislatures.

Nelson A. Rockefeller Institute of Government, The. 2005. *Performance Management in State and Local Government*. Albany, NY: The Nelson A. Rockefeller Institute of Government.

New York, City of. Various fiscal years. Office of Operations *Mayor's Management Report*.

Norquist, John O. 1998. *The Wealth of Cities: Revitalizing the Centers of American Life*. Reading, MA: Addison-Wesley.

O'Connell, Paul E. 2001. *Using Performance Data for Accountability: The New York City Police Department's CompStat Model of Police Management*. Washington, DC: The PricewaterhouseCoopers Endowment for The Business of Government.

Osborne, David, and Peter Hutchinson. 2004. *The Price of Government*. New York: Basic Books.

Patton, Carl, and David Sawicki. 1993. *Basic Methods of Policy Analysis and Planning*. 2nd ed. Englewood Cliffs, NJ: Prentice-Hall.

Paul, Samuel. 2002. *Holding the State to Account: Citizen Monitoring in Action*. Bangalore, India: Books for Change.

Penna, Robert M., and William J. Phillips. 2004. *Outcome Frameworks: An Overview for Practitioners*. Rensselaerville, NY: The Rensselaerville Institute.

Phillips, William R., Bonnie L. Brown, C. Morgan Kinghorn, and Andrew C. West. 1997. *Public Dollars, Common Sense: New Roles for Financial Managers*. Washington, DC: Coopers and Lybrand.

Rossi, Peter H., Mark W. Lipsey, and Howard E. Freeman. 2003. *Evaluation: A Systematic Approach*. 7th ed. Newbury Park, CA: SAGE Publications, Inc.

Shah, Anwar, ed. 2005. *Public Services Delivery*. Public Sector Governance and Accountability Series. Washington, DC: The World Bank.

Stokey, Edith, and Richard Zeckhauser. 1978. *A Primer for Policy Analysis*. New York: W.W. Norton.

U.S. General Accounting Office (GAO). 2004. *Results-Oriented Government: GPRA Has Established a Solid Foundation for Achieving Greater Results*. GAO-04-38. Washington, DC: U.S. General Accounting Office.

U.S. Government Accountability Office (GAO). 2005. *Managing for Results: Enhancing Agency Use of Performance Information for Management Decision Making*. GAO-05-927. Washington, DC: U.S. Government Accountability Office.

United Nations Development Programme Evaluation Office. 2002. *Handbook on Monitoring and Evaluating for Results*. New York: United Nations Development Programme.

United Way of America. 1996. *Measuring Program Outcomes: A Practical Approach*. Alexandria, VA: United Way of America.

Walters, Jonathan. 1998. *Measuring Up: Governing's Guide to Performance Measurement for Geniuses and Other Public Managers*. Washington, DC: Governing Books.

White, Barry, and Kathryn E. Newcomer, eds. 2005. "Getting Result: A Guide for Federal Leaders and Managers." Vienna, VA: Management Concepts, Inc.

Wholey, Joseph S., Harry P. Hatry, and Kathryn Newcomer, eds. 2004. *Handbook of Practical Program Evaluation*. 2nd ed. San Francisco, CA: Jossey-Bass.

World Bank. 2004. *Monitoring and Evaluation: Some Tools, Methods & Approaches*. 2nd ed. Operations Evaluation Department. Washington, DC: The World Bank.

Wye, Chris. 2002. *Performance Management: A "Start Where You Are, Use What You Have" Guide*. Arlington, VA: The IBM Endowment for The Business of Government.

Index

benchmarks/comparisons, types of (*continued*)

    performance of other jurisdictions, 146–47, 148

    performance of private sector, 147, 148

    performance of similar organizational units or geographical areas, 141

    recognized general standard, 145–46

    targets established at start of performance period, 149–50

bias, 271

breakout characteristics, special, 135–36

breakout data, reporting, 188, 189

breakouts/disaggregation, 305–306

    by individual staff members, 135

    need for, 121–22

    procedures for choosing, 136–37

    types/categories of, 123–36

        by difficulty of workload, 129–32, 158–63

        by geographical location, 127–29

        by organizational unit or project, 123–24, 158–59, 162

        by reason for outcome or rating, 134–35

        by type and amount of service, 132–34

        by workload or customer characteristics, 124–27, 158–63

budget allocation decisions, 262

budget requests

    justifying, 3–4

    key issues in results-based budgeting and, 247–48

    steps for examining performance information in, 253–62

budgeting, 229, 305, 307. *See also* results-based budgeting

    based on outcomes vs. outputs, 230

    performance measurement and, 9

"budgeting for outcomes," 249–50

"budgeting-by-objectives," 249–50

C

capital budgeting, 248–49

community impact indicators, 64, 67–69, 70

comparative outcome indicator data, 146–47, 148

comparison period, 140–41

comparison-group design, 171

complaint data, 85–86

compliance outcomes, 258

compliance perspective, 18

comprehensiveness of indicators, 61

condition rating, 104

confidentiality, 85, 93, 97, 98, 114

contractors. *See* performance contracting

control. *See* influence/control, level of

control limits, 165

cost-benefit analysis, 251–52

cost-effectiveness analysis, 251

costs

    assessing, 7

    of data collection, 62, 98–100, 111, 115, 124

    of performance measurement systems, 268, 288–89

credibility, 111, 113

customer complaint data, 85–86

customer feedback, 115, 223. *See also* customer surveys

customer participation, 24–25, 169

customer satisfaction, 25–26, 77, 85, 86, 89, 90

customer surveys, 85–100, 167–69

    administration methods, 92–95

    advantages and disadvantages, 86, 305

    breakout categories and, 124

    content, 87, 168–69

    design and administration, 97–98

    elements to include in contracts for, 98

    examples of questionnaires, 88–92

    explanatory information and, 167–69

    household vs. user surveys, 87–88

    how many people to survey, 95

    information obtainable from, 86

    multiple uses, 90

    seeking information on citizen participation rates, 169

    trained observer procedures, 100–108

    ways to reduce costs, 98–100

    whom to survey, 95–97

customers. *See also* difficulty, workload/ customer/client; focus groups

    breakouts by, 125

    defined, 45n.3

    identifying categories of, 42–44

indicator breakouts. *See* breakouts/disaggregation

indicator data, comparative outcome, 142–44, 146–47, 148

indicator definitions, 59

indicator specification sheet, 279, 290, 291

indicator stability over time, maintaining, 289–90

indicators

    community impact, 64, 67–69, 70

    consistency of data across, 163–64

    constructing, to help identify causes, 77–79

    defined, 15

    examining set of, 164

    identifying overarching, 261–62

    measure vs., 27n.2

    need to be clear about time covered by, 61

    numerical forms, 69–71

    providing for qualitative outcomes, 77–79

    reliability and validity, 273

    results-based budgeting, 247

    selection of

        criteria for, 62

        factors affecting, 72–73

    use of outcome-sequence charts to identify, 64–67

    use of special equipment to collect data for, 111–13

influence/control, level of, 21, 62, 77, 165, 247

information. *See* performance information

infrequent events, 155–56

innovation, type and amount of service used to encourage, 133

input information, 14–15

inputs, 14–15, 48–49

    defined, 14, 15

    linking to expected future results, 236–40

intermediate outcomes, 18–21, 24, 255–57

    customer satisfaction, 25

    defined, 15, 20

    linking end outcomes to, 240

    linking inputs to, 237–38

internal reporting, 178–80

internal support activities and services, 90

    applying results-based budgeting to, 248

Internet

    reporting, 176–78

    surveys, 94

J

Job Training Partnership Act (JTPA), 145–46, 151n.4

L

legislating for results, 11n.1

legislating performance measurement, 229

legislation, 45, 152, 165

legislative priorities, changes in, 289

legislative support, 295–96

legislators, need for training, 308

line graphs, 184

logic models/outcome sequence charts, 26, 51–57

    used to identify outcomes and indicators, 65–67

M

mail surveys, 92

    ways to increase response to, 93

management practices, performance-based, 274

managers

    data quality and, 280–81

    fear and resistance from, 290–92

    flexibility and accountability given to, 207–208

    guidelines for, 284–86

    importance of performance information for, 3–4

managing by results, 11n.1

managing-for-results, 3, 7, 11n.1, 288

manipulability of indicators, 62

maps, 185, 186–87

measure, meaning of, 27n.2

measurement. *See also specific types of measurement*

    taken at different points in time, 72

media, 163, 192, 291, 297, 309

meetings, 48, 49–51

minors, data from, 116n.6

mission/objectives statement, 39–42. *See also* program missions/objectives

    sources of information on, 42

    suggestions for developing, 40–41

motivational programs, interagency, 213–14